THE PRINTER'S KISS

CIVIL WAR IN THE NORTH

Broken Glass: Caleb Cushing and the Shattering of the Union
John M. Belohlavek

Banners South: A Northern Community at War
Edmund J. Raus

"Circumstances are destiny": An Antebellum Woman's Struggle to Define Sphere
Tina Stewart Brakebill

More Than a Contest between Armies: Essays on the Civil War
Edited by James Marten and A. Kristen Foster

August Willich's Gallant Dutchmen:
Civil War Letters from the 32nd Indiana Infantry
Translated and Edited by Joseph R. Reinhart

Meade's Army: The Private Notebooks of Lt. Col. Theodore Lyman
Edited by David W. Lowe

Dispatches from Bermuda:
The Civil War Letters of Charles Maxwell Allen, U.S. Consul at Bermuda,
1861–1888
Edited by Glen N. Wiche

The Antebellum Crisis and America's First Bohemians
Mark A. Lause

Orlando M. Poe: Civil War General and Great Lakes Engineer
Paul Taylor

Northerners at War: Reflections on the Civil War Home Front
J. Matthew Gallman

A German Hurrah!
Civil War Letters of Friedrich Bertsch and Wilhelm Stängel, 9th Ohio Infantry
Translated and Edited by Joseph R. Reinhart

"They Have Left Us Here to Die":
The Civil War Prison Diary of Sgt. Lyle G. Adair, 111th U.S. Colored Infantry
Edited by Glenn Robins

The Story of a Thousand:
Being a History of the Service of the 105th Ohio Volunteer Infantry in the
War for the Union, from August 21, 1862, to June 6, 1865
Albion W. Tourgee, Edited by Peter C. Luebke

The Election of 1860 Reconsidered
Edited by A. James Fuller

"A Punishment on the Nation": An Iowa Soldier Endures the Civil War
Edited by Brian Craig Miller

Yankee Dutchmen under Fire: Civil War Letters from the 82nd Illinois Infantry
Translated and Edited by Joseph R. Reinhart

The Printer's Kiss:
The Life and Letters of a Civil War Newspaperman and His Family
Edited by Patricia A. Donohoe

The Printer's Kiss

The Life and Letters
of a Civil War Newspaperman
and His Family

Edited by
Patricia A. Donohoe

For Judy and Clint –
Hope you enjoy reading
about Eliza Wylie, whose
kinfolk hailed from the
same neck of the woods as
the Peases! Thanks for your
interest and support over
the years! Pat

THE KENT STATE UNIVERSITY PRESS
Kent, Ohio

© 2014 by The Kent State University Press, Kent, Ohio 44242
All rights reserved
Library of Congress Catalog Card Number 2013049038
ISBN 978-1-60635-216-8
Manufactured in the United States of America

Library of Congress Cataloging-in-Publication Data
The printer's kiss : the life and letters of a Civil War newspaperman and his family /
edited by Patricia A. Donohoe.
pages cm. — (Civil War in the North)
Includes bibliographical references and index.
ISBN 978-1-60635-216-8 (hardcover) ∞
1. Tomlinson, Will, 1823-1863.
2. Newspaper editors—United States—Biography.
3. Tomlinson, Will, 1823-1863—Correspondence.
4. Tomlinson, Eliza Wylie, 1815-1885—Correspondence.
5. Tomlinson, William Byers, 1847-1917—Correspondence.
6. Tomlinson, Sarah Isabella, 1853-1925—Correspondence.
I. Donohoe, Patricia A., 1944- editor of compilation.
II. Tomlinson, Will, 1823-1863. Correspondence. Selections.
PN4874.T5955P75 2014
070.4'1092—dc23
[B]

2013049038

18 17 16 15 14   5 4 3 2 1

To the descendants of
Will and Eliza Wylie Tomlinson
and their sisters and brothers in spirit

Contents

Preface   ix

Acknowledgments   xiii

Introduction   xvii

Editing Notes   xxiii

Cast of Historical Characters   xxvii

1. Tomlinson's Origins   1

2. Eliza's Heritage   5

3. Bringing Forth   12

4. Looking for Relief   21

5. Together and Apart   34

6. Collision Courses   54

7. Volunteer Frenzy   70

8. Rushed Waiting   81

9. Into the Hills   94

10. Curse This Idleness   103

11. Mustering Men and Courage   116

12. Mountain Desperadoes   130

13. Disarmed   143

14. Hatching New Hope   154

15. Attacks from Within and Without   173

16. This Sea of Passion   186

17. Nursing the Wounded   200

18. Close to Home   216

19. Partisan Fever   230

20. Freedom's Casket   240

Epilogue: The Journey of the Letters   253

Appendix   259

Notes   261

Selected References   283

Index   293

Preface

IT ALL BEGAN with my sister's curiosity. My sister and I were in Portsmouth, Ohio, for our father's funeral in 1970 and staying at our grandparent's house. My sister, Betsy, asked our Aunt Betsy why an old green and white cracker tin was wedged between some books on a hallway shelf. Our Aunt Betsy, for whom my sister was named, took the tin down, blew some dust off the top, and lifted the lid. Inside, pressed together like fragile pages in an ancient tome, were dozens of old letters from our ancestors. Seeing our excitement about the letters, our aunt passed them on to us. She then took us up to an attic cubbyhole over the front porch and unlocked a Hobbit-sized door to a tiny closet. As we knelt down beneath the eaves, we found boxes of other family documents. Among them was an original copy of the October 10, 1863, edition of the *Loyal Scout,* the last newspaper published by our great-great-grandfather, Will Tomlinson.

Over the years my sister and I took turns being steward of the letters. We yearned to do something with them but never found the time. Occasionally when we were together, we would carefully ease some letters out from the old tin, gently unfold them, and try to decipher their contents. Who were these people? What were their lives like, and what did that mean for us? Yes, they were our ancestors, but how much of our identities sprang from theirs? One question would beget another and another until, overwhelmed with the time and energy it would take to answer them, we would close the tin once more and put it back on the shelf for another day. It was the time of life when we were busy raising families, pursuing careers, acquiring additional educational credentials, and moving back and forth across the country. The letters still beckoned, however, and sometimes we felt guilty that they lay there, waiting for our attention. My sister and I had both taught English and then had successful careers in communications. Surely, we thought, we were equipped to do something with the collection. But exactly what—and when—eluded us.

Eventually, in 1999, when my children were grown and I was between careers, I had time to transcribe all the letters in the tin, about 140 of them, plus assorted documents. In the process, I discovered that my interest in doing something with the collection was becoming a driving passion. My sister's passion, meanwhile, led in another direction, to an accomplished career in education. In September 2000, my career path also led in another direction when I was ordained as a minister in the Presbyterian Church (USA). I was excited about serving as the associate minister of the Presbyterian church in Shepherdstown, West Virginia, but disappointed that my work with the letter collection would have to be put on hold.

In the autumn of 2003, as I was approaching my fifty-ninth birthday and grandchildren were beginning to proliferate in our family, I realized that if I were ever going to do anything with the letter collection, I had to get serious about it. Thanks to my husband, Dave, and his enthusiastic support, I had an opportunity to retire from my ministerial position and spend more time working on the letter collection. I made the heart-wrenching decision to leave a congregation I felt deeply connected to and, with a lot of gratitude and a little trepidation, began devoting my working time to the letter collection.

During the three years I served the church, I continued working on the letter collection whenever I could, and Dave and I visited Ripley, Ohio, to research my family history. On our first trip there we were fortunate to meet the director of Union Township Library, Alison Gibson. She and I stayed in touch, and in January 2006, Alison sent me an email with startling news. Letters from the Tomlinson family were for sale on eBay! I had never been on eBay and would never have looked there for letters written by my ancestors. But there they were! Thanks to Alison and helpful eBay vendors, I was able to purchase at least another 150 letters over the next several years. EBay vendors I contacted said they purchased the letters in New York, where my great-grandfather's sister lived. I was unable to acquire about a half dozen letters posted on eBay, including one that appeared on the site in March 2013. But finally, some 150 years after apparently being divided by my great-grandfather and his sister, most of the letters have come back together. Perhaps even more remarkable is that they came together while I, a direct descendant of Will and Eliza Wylie Tomlinson, was working on a book using the letters that had been passed down to my sister and me.

The Wylie-Tomlinson Letter Collection now includes approximately 300 personal letters, plus assorted documents, written from the 1830s through the 1890s. These letters have never been published before. In *The Printer's Kiss* I have used the heart of the collection, 124 letters written from 1844 to 1864, to tell the story of my great-great-grandparents, Will and Eliza Wylie Tomlinson. I have also included published versions of letters Tomlinson and his wife wrote to newspaper editors, as well as excerpts from letters in other collections, from newspapers Tomlinson edited, and from his short story in *Columbian Magazine*. In addition, I have integrated carefully researched background material to provide a historical backdrop for the letters and flesh out the story they tell. My time with the Wylie-Tomlinson Letter Collection and *The Printer's Kiss* has been full of unexpected discoveries and rewards. My hope is that yours will be, too.

Patricia A. Donohoe
October 2013

Acknowledgments

LITTLE IN LIFE is done solo, least of all a book based on the work of others. So many people have contributed to *The Printer's Kiss* that it would take another book to list them with their contributions and thank them in the manner they deserve. For all of the resources, expertise, and encouragement that so many have so generously shared on my forty-year sojourn with the Wylie-Tomlinson Letter Collection and the fifteen-year book project that emerged from it, I will always be grateful. Without their help, this book would never exist. Indeed, without the instrumental actions of a number of people, the Wylie-Tomlinson Letter Collection itself would not exist. So although I cannot list everyone whose thumbprint has graced this project, I would at least like to acknowledge some who have had a major hand in its production.

I am, of course, fortunate that my ancestors were "people of the word" who not only wrote but also saved their letters. Thank goodness they also passed on their appreciation of the written word to their descendants, including my grandmother, Florence Adele Tomlinson Donohoe, who preserved the portion of the letter collection she received from her father, William Byers Tomlinson, in an old 1924 Edgemont cracker tin. As a DAR Regent, she also preserved the genealogical record, "The Family History," which noted our ancestors' participation in the American Revolution and showed how they were related to each other. Unfortunately, she died when I was a young child, before I ever learned about the letter collection.

Who knows where the letters and documents that our grandmother saved would have ended up if it had not been for my sister Betsy and our Aunt Betsy! As I already noted, it was my sister Betsy (Elizabeth Ross Donohoe) who asked our Aunt Betsy (Elizabeth Ross Donohoe Keller) about an old cracker tin on a hallway shelf in the home where our grandparents and aunt lived. Throughout the years, my sister played a key role in preserving the part of the letter collection given to us by our aunt. She also spurred me on when work on the book seemed interminable and provided helpful suggestions throughout its evolution.

Half of the letter collection would never have been united with the other half had it not been for the perspicacity and altruistic professionalism of Alison Gibson, director of Union Township Library in Ripley, Ohio. It was she who repeatedly alerted me to fact that letters from my ancestors were for sale on eBay! I had never used eBay before Alison emailed me about the letter offerings in January 2006. Thanks to Alison, the letter collection more than doubled in size from what my sister and I inherited. But Alison's contributions did not stop there. She clued me into Tomlinson's letters to the editor and often provided information and resources critical to the development of the book. She was always delighted to help and often went beyond the call of duty. Simply put, in my book, she is Saint Alison.

A number of other Ripley residents have also been gracious in their help over the years. David Gray spent an afternoon giving my husband Dave and me a fascinating tour of the town, including the residence of the last Doc Wylie, replete with a sketch of his eccentric personality. Cynthia Thompson of the Ripley Museum provided files of material on the Wylies at the drop of a hat; Ann Hagedorn, author of *Beyond the River: The Untold Story of Heroes of the Underground Railroad,* shared insights regarding local culture; Betsy and Vic Billingsley, at the Signal House Bed and Breakfast, provided comfortable accommodations on many visits; Thomas and Jane Zachman photographed and sent me images of an old Ripley map; and Melody Kokensparger and Theresa Robinson guided us around a local cemetery and persisted in research that yielded copies of wills, tax records, and other documents pertaining to the Wylies and Tomlinsons.

I am also indebted to a host of other people, including eBay vendor John A. Rerecic for keeping a lookout for other letters from my ancestors; Jo Burgess, former director of the Wylie House Museum at Indiana University, for a personally guided tour that gave me a tangible feel for the Wylie family culture, introduced me to letters and documents from the Andrew Wylie branch of the family, and connected me to Steven St. Martin, who shared his research on Wylie genealogy; Howard Orenstein for tips on genealogical research; genealogical researchers in England and in Ironton, Ohio; and tour guides Gordon Ross and David Frood of Scotland for helping me track down ancestral roots in Ireland and northern England.

Gregory A. Borchard generously shared his expertise in Civil War journalism and politics, and, along with Leonne M. Hudson, provided feedback that significantly improved the manuscript. Daniel Sutherland kindly responded to my questions, and his book, *A Savage Conflict: The Guerrillas in the American Civil War,* helped me locate additional letters dealing with my great-great-grandfather's involvement in guerrilla warfare. Other people who helped me in the development of the book include Ellen Hoffman, whose analytical mind and professional writer's background helped me clarify my ideas in countless discussions; Marie Tyler McGraw, who first introduced me to the complexities of abolitionism; Canadian historian Jim Manson, who acquainted me with the Patriots' Revolution; Terry Reimer, who checked records for me at the National Museum of Civil War Medicine; Brian P. Lawler at the Shakespeare Press Museum in California and volunteers at the Cincinnati History Museum, who all helped me understand how iron hand presses and the typesetting process worked; Michael Horsely, who freely shared his expertise in archival photography; Tom White, who helped me locate resources at the George Tyler Moore Center for the Study of the Civil War in Shepherdstown; interloan librarians at the Martinsburg-Berkeley County Library; and numerous archivists and resource librarians who provided essential materials, especially Catherine Rakowski at the West Virginia and Regional History Center at West Virginia University Libraries and Terry Lowry at the West Virginia Division of Culture and History. A special round of thanks goes to Shirley Boggs Webster, who scoured the countryside for material on Camp Pickens, West Virginia, and, along with her husband, took my husband and me on a guided tour of the camp site.

The quality of the book and my sense of equilibrium benefited greatly from the insight, technical expertise, and sense of humor of a number of people, including Bill Howard, who scanned and transmitted images of letters, photographs, and documents from the Wylie-Tomlinson Letter Collection; Elizabeth Howard, whose careful copyediting made the manuscript presentable; and the outstanding editorial and production staff at Kent State University Press, especially Will Underwood, director; Mary D. Young, managing editor; Christine Brooks, design and production manager; Susan L. Cash, marketing manager; and Rebekah Cotton, whose astute copyediting readied the book for printing. Thanks to their patience and enthusiasm, the production process was an enjoyable adventure. I would also like to acknowledge one person in particular at Kent State University Press for her role in the successful transformation of a rough-hewn manuscript into a publishable book: Joyce Harrison, acquiring editor. She was a true joy to work with, from beginning to end, and her keen insight and kind manner enabled me to take the manuscript to the next level time and again.

I will always treasure the feedback of two early readers of the manuscript: my sister-in-law Carol and my daughter, Lora. Their interest and enthusiasm at critical junctures kept me going. Nobody could have had a more caring family and community than I have over the years. Lora and Carl, Scott and McKenzie, Kim and John, and Eric and Therese, Julie, and all my nieces, nephews, and grandchildren—you all have not only been part of the journey but the reason for the journey.

Last, and most important, I will be eternally grateful to my husband, David C. Borchard. His numerous reviews of the manuscript provided crucial feedback, and thanks to his gentle prodding, I persisted in investigating my great-great-grandfather's role as captain of a company of counterinsurgents in West Virginia. The result was a whole new chapter that deepened and expanded the book's storyline. It is no exaggeration to say that my husband has been a fun and loving companion with every step I have taken in this journey. His unflagging support and confidence in my abilities enabled me to turn a lifelong dream into a reality. Thanks, Dave, for being the best soul mate this writer could ever have.

Introduction

"A Printer's Kiss"
PRINT on my lip another kiss,
The picture of thy glowing passion;
Nay, this won't do—nor this—nor this—
But now—Ay, that's a *proof impression!*
—*Songs of the Press,* C. H. Timperley, 1833

IN THE TURBULENT DECADES from 1843 to 1863, in the treacherous borderlands of southern Ohio, my great-great-grandfather, Will Tomlinson, published newspapers of a controversial nature. His newspapers covered everything from antislavery sentiment to spiritualist fervor to the rabid invective of partisan politics—not surprising, perhaps, for a man considered to be controversial himself. Described by his contemporaries as brilliant and erratic, literary and coarse, he was a man of high ideals and acute shortcomings. Even the circumstances of his death were disputed, raising the question of whether he died a hero or a scoundrel. In short, he was something of an enigma, and in many ways, in his life and work, he illustrated the best and worst of small-town newspaper editors before and during the Civil War.[1]

Like most publishers of country weeklies, Tomlinson was a printer by trade. As such, he shared many traits in common with his colleagues. Despite their various backgrounds, most country printers in the 1800s learned the trade through an apprentice system and, after achieving journeyman's status, often took their skills on the road before setting up their own shops in small towns with promising opportunities. As a rule, country printers worked long hours with little or no help—except for what they found in a bottle. Aided by this constant "companion," they did everything from setting type, backward and upside down, one letter at a time, to printing each page, one side at a time, before pulling it off the bed of a rudimentary hand press. A lot of strength and stamina went into printing a few hundred copies of a newspaper.[2]

The first page off the press with just the right amount of ink and pressure to produce a bright, clear impression was called a "printer's kiss." The printer's kiss was a "proof impression" indicating that a printer had successfully calibrated the art and science of every step of the printing process, from mixing and spreading ink on the type, to dampening and aligning the paper, and, finally, to pulling the platen down with just the right touch. Devoutly to be sought, the "printer's kiss" signaled that it was time to raise the bottle in celebration instead of frustration.[3]

If excessive drinking did not get a printer into trouble, another aspect of the business often did. Most small-town newspapers were subsidized either directly or indirectly by the prevailing political party of the area— usually the Jacksonian wing of the Democratic Party in the vast, rural territory of nineteenth-century America. Editors of all political affiliations, however, prided themselves on producing the most offensive descriptions of their party's opponents that they could print. The contentious language competing editors employed frequently led to brawling, in print and in person, and in an age devoid of electronic media, the baiting and fighting of feisty editors often generated the most colorful entertainment rural readers had. Yet for all of his hard work, political networking, and pugnacious posturing, the typical printer barely eked out a living and seldom lasted anywhere for long.[4]

The trail of ink left by Will Tomlinson showed that, by and large, he was no exception to the rule. From 1844 to 1863, he edited and published ten newspapers, all of them in central and southern Ohio—except for one in Iowa, where he lived from 1854 to 1860. Wherever he landed, he conducted his business in a way that was, for the most part, typical of small-town newspaper editors of that era. As an entrepreneurial Democrat of populist persuasion, he was imaginative and unrepentant in his editorial abuse. As a printer incessantly plagued by a weakness for alcohol, he was impulsive and unpredictable in his behavior. And, as a vociferous editor with a belligerent nature, he had a knack for getting into trouble and was usually in a row with someone.[5]

Generally speaking, Tomlinson was a man of extremes, and his flaws not only reflected but often exceeded those of the typical small-town editor. But the same could also be said of his endowments. His childhood in Lower Canada probably provided him with the kind of solid education that many country printers lacked. And following his immigration to the

United States at the age of fourteen, he was fortunate to be instructed in the trade at the *St. Lawrence Republican,* one of the best country newspapers in the state of New York. Such early training equipped him with advantages seldom experienced by the average farm boy, whose rustic beginnings barely qualified him for apprenticing as a grimy printer's devil. Tomlinson also had a natural talent for writing and analyzing arguments and ideas. Even one of his chief detractors noted his extraordinary abilities, and his writings, both published and unpublished, show an articulate and eloquent use of the English language, especially in the promotion of altruistic goals.[6]

His altruism frequently found expression in his appreciation for the plight of the common man. Yet, at the same time, he was far from being immune to some of the commonly held prejudices of the era. As a result, he was often conflicted about current issues: Whom should he believe in the heated battle between opposing extremists—self-righteous abolitionists on the one hand or incendiary secessionists on the other? Which rights and services should rest with the states and which with the federal government? What would be entailed by the emancipation of slaves and the large numbers of uneducated blacks who would have to be integrated into a social structure dominated by white supremacists and an economic system stressed by the exigencies of war? How could he stay loyal to an administration that curtailed freedom of speech, censored the press, and allowed one inept military leader after another to sacrifice tens of thousands of lives? And what role should African Americans play in the war effort?[7]

Like many Northern Democrats, Tomlinson was pulled in different directions. He despised the poisonous demagoguery of Copperhead politicians like Clement Vallandigham but found it difficult to swallow some of the frightful antidotes of abolitionist zealots in the Lincoln administration. Of course, he was hardly alone in struggling with such issues, but when he took a stance, he did so under pressure of a deadline and had much more at stake than most people. As a newspaper publisher and editor, his views were not just table talk but published in newspapers meant to mold public opinion. What he printed was critical to his professional reputation and financial success.[8]

Regardless of his doubts about the country's leadership, he was unfaltering in his loyalty to the Union and was among the first in April 1861 to enlist in Ohio's Volunteer Infantry. He served as a quartermaster sergeant in the Fifth Ohio in western Virginia until that fall and was then elected captain of a company of counterinsurgents in the West Virginia State Troops. After his official military career came to an end a few months later, he continued to support the Union cause by participating in unofficial scouting expeditions and working as a compositor (typesetter) for the pro-Union *Cincinnati Gazette*. In addition, in 1863 he promoted the Union ticket in Brown County, Ohio, by publishing the *Loyal Scout* and blasting local Copperheads, including one he likened to "a pig following a cow—picking up what others drop." He gladly volunteered to teach "the pot house loafer and liar and dog...the merits of a good thrashing and the world the value of a Congressman's carcass well skined [*sic*]."[9]

The publication of such defamatory language could have spawned dangerous enemies anywhere, but in the volatile border country along the Ohio River, it was potentially lethal. As a major terminal on the Underground Railroad and home to prominent leaders in the antislavery and abolitionist movements, Ripley, Ohio, and the surrounding area were especially prone to violent confrontations between Kentucky slave hunters and Ohio abolitionists. Ongoing conflict frequently erupted into outright battles like one in 1839 when Kentucky kidnappers killed a woman as she tried to stop them from carrying off a neighbor in Brush Creek. In 1841 six Kentuckians attacked the Ripley home of abolitionist leader and Presbyterian minister John Rankin, and in 1844 incensed slave hunters killed two Underground Railroad agents in Red Oak.[10]

That same year Tomlinson launched his first newspaper, *Freedom's Casket*, in Ripley. No doubt, the meaning of the word *casket* referred to a small container for jewels and other valuables, but unfortunately the more common meaning of the word proved prophetic. Tomlinson buried the paper just two months after its inception. He left no record of the reason for its early demise, but it is possible that he overestimated the number of Ripley residents who would welcome having the *Casket*'s slogan of "Principles—Not Prejudice" in plain view on a parlor table. To protect their families and businesses, many area residents involved in the Underground Railroad, antislavery societies, or abolitionist movement often did so surreptitiously, despite the town's reputation among Southern sympathizers as an "abolitionist hellhole."[11]

The town's reputation as a stronghold of abolitionist sentiment may have been the initial reason Tomlinson selected Ripley as the site for his first newspaper. He could also have been attracted to the town for its proximity to the intellectual milieu of various utopian and spiritualist communities in the surrounding countryside. Equally appealing was the town's easy access, via the Ohio River, to the burgeoning publishing industry in Cincinnati, just fifty miles downstream. In addition, the town's large operations in boat building, pork processing, and agricultural production made it a thriving commercial site for an ambitious printer. There were many reasons Tomlinson could have chosen Ripley for the location of his first newspaper. But he could also have chosen other commercially viable communities in the country's vast interior between southwestern Ohio and northeastern New York, where he had worked on the *St. Lawrence Republican*.[12]

Only Ripley, however, was home to Eliza Wylie, the woman who would become his wife in October 1844. As the intelligent and learned daughter of Dr. Adam Wylie, she was not without suitors. There was one, in fact, who would have arrayed himself and her "in all the flattering, glistening trappings which wealth could bestow." But then, she wrote, she would have lacked "a companion who could have entered into [her] feelings and held communion with [her] spirit." How she first met the man she regarded as her soul mate remains in the realm of speculation, but one possibility is that her younger brother William introduced them and, in so doing, presented Tomlinson with another, maybe even primary, reason for choosing Ripley as the place to publish his first newspaper.[13]

Although the Tomlinsons lived in other places during their time together, it was to Ripley that they kept returning. Most of their five children were born there. Most of Eliza's family continued to live and work there. Tomlinson published his first and last newspapers there, and it was there, along the banks of the Ohio, that his final confrontation occurred. His remains were laid to rest just beyond the river's edge, but the cause of his death was not. Exactly what happened in that fatal affray remains uncertain to this day. But tantalizing clues have emerged with regard to what some of the contributing factors may have been, including the exposure of politicians who supported subversive activities. In the end, however, there is no way of knowing whether he died a hero or a scoundrel and whether his final kiss to Eliza left the imprint of truth or treachery.[14]

Outside of being an enigmatic and obscure country newspaper editor who lived and died in middle America in the mid–nineteenth century, just who was Will Tomlinson, and why should anyone care about him today? Ultimately, of course, historians and readers from each new generation will have to decide what kind of legacy he (and Eliza) left. But if, as psychologist Erik Erikson believed, we are what survives us, the Tomlinsons were more fortunate than most. Not only did Tomlinson leave a body of published work that is still accessible through his newspapers and other publications, but he and Eliza left an impressive collection of personal correspondence that gives a compelling portrait of how they dealt with a nation at war with itself and the resulting impact on their family. In today's world of staccato communications that are quickly deleted, the story of a family told through personal letters is increasingly rare. The story of the Tomlinsons is one of ordinary but outspoken people who cared deeply for their family and country. It is also a story of writers who shared what they felt and thought in language that still resonates with power and beauty today.[15]

While Tomlinson's newspapers and publications ring with the voice of a wordsmith, his personal letters often resonate with his most eloquent use of language. His letters written to those back home reveal the man behind the press, the one thrown off key by the love and tension in his marriage, the distance and tenderness he felt with his children, and the desire for alcohol and adventure he could never satiate. Only when writing to Eliza did he vent his frustration in trying to raise a company of Negro troops in racially charged Cincinnati, his pain from standing fourteen hours at a compositor's table, his disgust in shooting enough cattle to feed hundreds of hungry soldiers, and his discomfort in the mud-soaked camps of western Virginia. Only in his private correspondence did he convey the depth of his despair from repeated Union defeats or the extent of his joy over Union victories. Only in writing to those he loved and trusted did he use the language of the heart.

Eliza was much freer in expressing her feelings and was always ready to share her opinions on a wide range of topics. "Patriotism is something more than a name to amuse old women and children," she wrote in a letter to her husband on July 3, 1861. Besides making pronouncements about current events, her letters pulse with the everyday rhythms of a Union family in the borderlands, trying to survive the constant threats of epidemic disease, financial ruin, and marauding Confederates like Morgan's Raiders. But there is also good news: the children's recovery from illness, their progress in school, and the canary's new eggs. And there is always the latest anecdote to relate or another dose of instruction on how Tomlinson should attend to his health and conduct his military affairs.

Perhaps the real meaning of what the Tomlinsons wrote, however, was not in what was said or not said, but in the way their letters created order out of chaos, hope out of loss, and a sense of identity out of confusion. For those who wrote and received them, the letters affirmed that they mattered to someone else. Readers today may be left with an equally important affirmation: the story of ordinary but articulate people who refused to let extraordinary times rob them of the most precious gifts of life.

Editing Notes

THE PUBLICATION of original letters always presents the challenge of whether to stay true to a letter writer's variations in form, spelling, punctuation, syntax, and paragraphing, or to do some careful editing with reader accessibility in mind. For the most part, I have attempted to follow the latter approach. Salutations and closings, spelling, punctuation, syntax, and paragraphing have been standardized to make the letters more reader friendly. By and large, the letters written by Tomlinson are usually written in ink in a clear, legible script and need little editing; they could, in fact, serve as models of good writing. The letters written by Eliza, on the other hand, are often written in pencil in a script that is frequently difficult to read and decipher. They often need extensive editing with respect to the standardization of spelling, punctuation, and paragraphing. However, when variations from standardized usage do not significantly interrupt the flow, I have sometimes retained them, especially in the case of letters written by the Tomlinson children, Byers and Belle.

Another problematic area for editing letters in this collection arose in conjunction with the use of the same name for multiple individuals and multiple names for one person. Child-naming traditions in the Scotch-Irish and English borderer traditions, from which the Wylies and Tomlinsons derived, can be confusing, to say the least. Names were passed down from generation to generation and also reused within the same generation of one nuclear family. Thus the name "William" was given to two of Eliza's younger brothers, one who died in infancy and another who died at the age of thirty-six in 1860. The name "William" was also, of course, the name of Eliza's husband, William Tomlinson, who went by Will, and their son, William Byers Tomlinson, who went by Byers. Besides being the name for Will and Eliza's son, "Byers" was the family of origin name for Eliza's mother, Sarah, and the middle name for Eliza's brother, Thomas Byers Wylie, who also was called "Byers."[1]

To help the reader sort through such convoluted onomastic practices, I have often prefaced individual names with a clarifying identifier. The name "Byers," for example, is frequently accompanied by the appositive of "brother" or "son," if not already specified by the letter writer. I have also tried to simplify another confusing practice of the Wylies and Tomlinsons by using only one first name for each individual, even when multiple names were often used for that particular person. For example, in the original versions of the letters, the Tomlinson's surviving daughter, Sarah Isabella, is referred to by several nicknames, including Sis, Sissy, Lis, Lissy, Lissie, Lizzie, or Belle. To minimize confusion, I have consistently referred to her throughout as Belle, the name she chose for herself in adulthood.

Some additional impediments to the modern reader that I have updated, amended, or minimized include, but are not limited to, changing "&c" to "etc."; slight revisions or corrections to the text to avoid the use of [*sic*] whenever possible; and the addition of apostrophes in contractions. While I have spelled out many abbreviations, I have retained the use of "inst." for "instant" or "instanter," a convention used by letter writers of that time to indicate the current month in conjunction with the date of a previous letter. When the content of a letter would not be compromised, I usually deleted repetitious or distracting material. Finally, although the transcription of the letters has been conducted with care and dedication to accuracy, there is always the possibility for error in such a painstaking process, especially when words or lines have been omitted, torn, or damaged in some way. For any errors in the transcription or editing of the letters in this publication, I assume complete responsibility.

I also assume complete responsibility for any mistakes in the dating and placement of letters that have a partial date or, in a few cases, no date. Most letters in the collection are fully dated, and my lengthy familiarity with the letter collection has been an advantage in dating letters that are not and placing them in their proper sequence. But usually the context of letters lacking complete dates can also be established by allusions to current events, community life (such as friends and neighbors who died), and family news. Ongoing dialogue between letter writers, stylistic traits of letter writers, and postmarked envelopes also help to date letters.

All things considered, it is fortunate that the letters are in such good shape and have finally come together after more than 150 years of being scattered here and there. I will always be grateful to all the people who helped to reconstitute the collection and for the opportunity to serve as a steward of it for this generation. More information about my journey with the letters is available in the Epilogue. For now, the reader is invited to meet the Cast of Historical Characters.

Cast of
Historical Characters

MAIN CHARACTERS

Will Tomlinson (1823–1863): newspaper publisher and editor
Eliza Wylie Tomlinson (1815–1885): Will's wife; writer and homemaker
William Byers Tomlinson (Byers) (1847–1917): Will and Eliza's son
Sarah Isabella Tomlinson (Belle) (1853–1925): Will and Eliza's daughter

OTHER CHARACTERS

Anne Tomlinson Hunter Skinner (1810–n.d.): Will's sister
Sarah Byers Wylie (1788–1880): Eliza's mother
Dr. Adam Wylie II (1785–1839): Eliza's father; medical doctor
Dr. Thomas Byers Wylie (Byers) (1811–1864): Eliza's oldest brother;
    medical doctor
Sarah Ann Elizabeth Cook Wylie (1819–1904): wife of Dr. Thomas
    Byers Wylie
Dr. Adam Newton Wylie (Newt) (1813–1891): Eliza's older brother;
    medical doctor
Elizabeth Pangburn Wylie (Lizzie) (1837–1862): wife of Dr. Adam
    Newton Wylie
William B. Franklin Wylie, Esquire (1824–1860): Eliza's younger
    brother; a lawyer
Margaret Shannon Wylie (Maggie) (1826–1846): Eliza's younger sister

CHAPTER ONE

Tomlinson's Origins

Who that has his God and country near his heart,
will run the fearful risk by cowardly remaining at home?
—*Hickory Sprout*, Piketon, Ohio, October 3, 1844

INFORMATION about the background of Will Tomlinson is sketchy and inconclusive prior to his turning up in Ripley, Ohio, sometime in the early 1840s. According to the genealogy that comprises "The Family History," he was born on August 2, 1823, in northern England. There is some question as to whether he was born in the county of Northumberland or its neighboring county to the west, Cumberland, but records recovered to date seem to point to the latter and to his baptism there in September 1824, by the Church of England in the Parish of Camerton, adjacent to the village of Seaton. It is unclear whether his father, George Tomlinson, was a captain in the Royal Navy, as family records suggest, or a stonemason, as recent research may indicate, or possibly both at one time or another. It is also unclear as to whether his mother, Jane Todhunter, was "Lady Jane," the daughter of Sir William Todhunter, as family accounts maintain, or simply the offspring of a local farmer or auctioneer, according to local records. Tomlinson never mentioned his father in his letters, and he alluded to his mother but once and that only in passing. "The Family History" does not list any siblings for Tomlinson, even though the letter collection includes three letters from Anne T. Hunter Skinner, who identifies herself as his sister and Tomlinson as her only brother.[1]

Regardless of his parents' background or which county his birthplace was, Tomlinson would have been born into a culture with some distinctive characteristics. Because of their proximity to Scotland, the northern reaches of Cumberland and Northumberland were generally known as border country, and residents referred to themselves as "borderers." Derived from the same ethnic stock that settled Northern Ireland, the clans of northern England had been entangled in border disputes between Scotland and England for more than seven centuries. Constantly at war with outsiders and with each other as control of their homeland shifted, borderers developed a distinctive warrior culture that not only strongly differentiated them from other English-speaking immigrants but also came to dominate the American backcountry, where they settled in large numbers. Their child-rearing practices were geared to mold their offspring into strong, wily survivors. Male children were taught to be fiercely independent, proud, and courageous. Unfortunately, such programming could also lead to minimal impulse control and quick, explosive reaction to opposition. The cultural expectation that women should be long-suffering workers who knew their place often led to a sense of alienation and pent-up emotions that sometimes resulted in polarized and violent relationships.[2]

These cultural tendencies appear to be reflected in Tomlinson's values and behavior—with one important exception. There is no indication of violence in the relationship between him and Eliza. But in many other respects, Tomlinson was definitely a product of his culture. He obviously loved a good fight with other men—in print or in person. He was also proud of his family and his work, and the choices he made as an editor and a soldier could be seen as demonstrating courageous leadership. It is also interesting that he chose to spend most of his adult life in southern Ohio, where the Appalachian culture of the Scotch-Irish and English border people tended to be dominant in the early 1800s. It was in Brown County, Ohio, in fact, that Tomlinson swore allegiance to his adopted country. In his naturalization record, dated November 6, 1845, he stated that he left his native Cumberland and arrived in Quebec in Lower Canada in 1828, when he was four years old. According to own testimony, he came to the United States through Fort Covington, Franklin County, New York, in 1838 when he was fourteen years old and lived in the United States from then on, including the requisite two-year residency in the state of Ohio preceding his petition for naturalization.[3]

The dates of his arrival in Canada and later in the United States are particularly interesting from a historical perspective. The early nineteenth century brought rapid growth in manufacturing and mining in northern England. Coal mines and iron works shredded the landscape, while small landowners, who had been an important part of a rural economy, quickly found themselves displaced by laws that favored land barons. By 1828, the date that Tomlinson emigrated from Cumberland to Quebec, so many immigrants had already left the northern regions of Great Britain for North America that serious concerns arose as to how the dwindling labor pool could supply the region's industry. To make matters worse, some of the workers left behind tended to be less skilled and motivated than those who could afford the costs of transatlantic relocation. As a four-year-old, Tomlinson was, of course, too young to be part of the labor pool when he came to North America, but he was obviously part of a large migration from northern England during that time. There is no indication whether he traveled to Canada with his parents or with other relatives or acquaintances. The absence of any references or details about his parents in his letters, however, could suggest that he was separated from them at an early age and immigrated with other adults who acted as his guardians.[4]

Tomlinson's immigration to the United States in 1838 and the fact that he lived a while in Ogdensburg, New York, could also be linked to a historical event, the Canadian Patriot Movement, otherwise known as the Rebellions of 1837 and 1838. The British government's dismissal of the patriots' demand for self-government led to armed rebellion against a privileged oligarchy. British forces quickly captured many rebels and summarily executed or imprisoned them. But some escaped across the border into northern New York, where they regrouped and recruited sympathetic Americans. In November 1838 they launched an unsuccessful attack against the British from Ogdensburg. Many of the captured rebels were executed or sent to a brutal penal colony in Tasmania, then known as Van Dieman's Land. Few prisoners, political or criminal, ever returned from this devil's island at end of the earth. Of seventy-two Canadians imprisoned under cruel conditions there, thirteen died and forty apparently never returned home.[5]

No evidence has emerged to directly link Tomlinson or a relative to the Canadian rebels, but in June 1844, in the fourth issue of *Freedom's Casket*, Tomlinson chose to feature a *New York Tribune* review of a pamphlet detailing the inhuman ordeal of a prisoner sent to Van Dieman's Land for participating in the attack that originated from Ogdensburg. The fact that Tomlinson chose that one article to feature from hundreds at his disposal and placed it in a prominent position on the front page of his first news-paper, some six years and seven hundred miles distant from the scene of the "ill-fated" expedition, raises questions about his involvement in the revolt or association with the patriots. It is possible that he left Canada at that particular time because he or those close to him were at least in sympathy with the rebels, if not in league with them.[6]

At any rate, when Tomlinson arrived in Ripley in the early 1840s, the youthful twenty-year-old brought with him an age-old heritage grounded in the fight for independence, a passion for eradicating tyranny, and a degree of journalistic acumen and life experience that already imbued his voice with an air of authority. In the June 8, 1844, issue of *Freedom's Casket,* he printed his response to the following question submitted to him the previous week: "Can the members of the Methodist Episcopal Conference, after the late action of that body, and other denominations which have either taken similar ground, or gone a step further in rebuke of slavery, with christian [*sic*] *consistency,* lend their suffrages to elevate men to important civil offices known to be wedded to slavery, in its actual practice, and pledged for its perpetuation?" Tomlinson's answer: "decid-edly in the negative."[7]

CHAPTER TWO

Eliza's Heritage

Resistance to Tyrants is Obedience to God!
—Whig petition, June 10, 1848, Brown County, Ohio

THE SCOTCH-IRISH ORIGINS of Eliza Wylie Tomlinson would, for the most part, have drawn upon the same ethnic stock as her husband's ancestors in northern England. Like her husband, Eliza placed high a value on independence and identified with those who rebelled against tyranny at home and abroad. In fact, one of her Wylie ancestors left County Antrim in Ireland in 1797 because of his participation in the struggle for Irish independence, and both sets of her grandparents settled in an area of southwestern Pennsylvania that became known as a nursery of Scotch Presbyterian rebels. In addition, both of Eliza's grandfathers served in the American War for Independence.[1]

Given the nonconformist origins of Scottish Presbyterians, it is likely that as an infant Eliza was rocked to the tune of *"Nooo* bishops!" As a "cradle Presbyterian," she, like her parents before her, would probably have learned at an early age never to swear allegiance to any civil or religious authority that interfered with a person's direct access to God through Jesus Christ as revealed in scripture. Her faith would have been grounded in such basic tenets of the Reformed Tradition as the doctrines of grace and gratitude and the declaration that "God alone is Lord of the conscience." No doubt her theological bias would have led her to abhor the hierarchy of the Roman Catholic Church, distrust the Quaker emphasis on experience and inner light, and disdain anyone or anything she saw as ostentatious or excessive. For Eliza, the good life would have been one lived in moderation, with the freedom to choose one's religion and the right to representative government—in church and state.[2]

In addition to stories about resistance, rebellion, and the right to self-government, which Eliza probably heard growing up, she would also have heard accounts of life on the frontier. When her ancestral clans hopscotched westward across Pennsylvania and settled on the edge of the frontier in the Allegheny Mountains in the mid- to late 1700s, there were still uprisings from Native Americans in the area. In 1789, Indians killed a family living near Eliza's maternal grandfather, Thomas Byers, who had settled just three years before on Stonecoal, a 400-acre tract in West Finley Township of Washington County. In 1784 her paternal grandfather, Adam Wylie, had acquired 339 acres in Canton Township but took his family to safer ground for a number of years. Several years later, a son of Adam Wylie, Dr. Adam Wylie, purchased 140 acres from his father, and it was on that tract that Eliza and her two older brothers were born. But life for Eliza in southwestern Pennsylvania among her kith and kin was not to be.[3]

In 1817, Dr. Adam Wylie, his wife, Sarah, and their three children, Thomas Byers, Adam Newton, and Eliza—ages six, four, and two—made the short journey from their home in Washington County to the Ohio River. There they probably boarded a flatboat, the most common mode of river transportation for families moving west at that time. Between 1810 and 1820 an average of three thousand flatboats floated down the Ohio every year. They varied greatly in size and construction, but the more substantial ones looked like a barge with a wooden shoebox on top. A comfortably sized flatboat, about fifteen feet wide and thirty-five to one hundred feet long, could carry an extended family with everything from household goods to livestock. Although a vessel outfitted in such a manner might look more like an ancient ark or American pigsty than a riverworthy vessel, flatboats were especially useful to pioneers. Upon reaching their destination, they could easily dismantle the boat and sell the wood for cash or use it for building a house or barn.[4]

The trip downriver to Ripley, Ohio, probably took Eliza's family about six days. To make themselves less vulnerable to attacks from Indians and river pirates, they probably traveled in the spring, when the river was high and fast, and as part of a flatboat flotilla of other families, including some from Washington County. In Ripley, the Wylies joined several families from Virginia who wanted to remove themselves from the slaveholding practices of that region. A number of these families had much in common with the Wylies; besides their Scotch-Irish heritage and Presbyterian faith, they shared an abhorrence of any encroachment on their individual freedoms. Hardworking, resilient, and thrifty, they just wanted to be left alone to develop their little plats on the frontier into prosperous enterprises.[5]

Eliza's parents, married just twenty years after the American Revolution, quickly adapted to life in the new state of Ohio. They soon made inroads into the wild, but growing, little river town of Ripley and joined twenty-two other residents to form the Presbyterian Church there. The church included many of the town's leading families, and in 1822 the congregation called the Reverend John Rankin, an avowed abolitionist, to be its installed pastor. Meanwhile, the name Wylie became well known in Ripley. A local newspaper listed Dr. Adam Wylie as one of three physicians among 120 residents in 1827. He became one of the town's first officers, serving as a trustee for at least six terms from 1826 to 1831. In 1831 he was one of fourteen physicians in Brown County reported as being taxed on their income, and his was apparently enough to invest in real estate and pay taxes on six town lots.[6]

As Eliza grew into a young woman, life in Ripley became more complicated. Increasing numbers of slaves escaping across the Ohio River brought more parties of slave catchers in hot pursuit. Slave hunters with mercenary motives became an increasing menace, especially to townspeople suspected of aiding fugitives. In 1820 it became legal for slaveholders to return a slave to Kentucky from any state. Meanwhile, on the national scene, the Missouri Compromise and slave revolts in the South kindled fears that the emancipation of slaves would threaten the prevailing social order in the North as well as the South. But the Reverend Rankin was undaunted. He agreed to have the *Castigator*, a Ripley newspaper, publish letters he had written to his brother on the evils of slavery. By the mid- to late 1820s, Ripley's reputation had taken a bold step in the direction of earning its eventual epithet as an "abolitionist hellhole."[7]

In the 1830s, when Eliza would have been rounding out her second decade and surveying the prospects for a husband and home of her own, she found herself tied to her parents' hearth more than ever. Eliza's mother, Sarah, had never been physically strong and was frequently bedridden with sickness. No doubt Sarah's frailty meant that Eliza became the primary caretaker not only of her mother but also of her younger brother

View of Ripley, Ohio, in the 1840s, from the Kentucky side of the Ohio River. The house at the top of the hill may be the home of the Rev. John Rankin and his family, active in the Underground Railroad. (Courtesy of the Ohio Historical Society, AL02872.tif)

and sister, William B. F. and Margaret Shannon. The huge flood of 1832, when much of Ripley was underwater, also presented serious challenges. Even though the Wylie house was on high ground above the flood plain, Dr. Wylie would have been at the forefront in dealing with flood-induced cholera. Then, a few years later, on the heels of President Jackson's requirement in 1836 that only gold and silver currency could be used for the purchase of federal lands, the Panic of 1837 plunged the economy into the country's first great depression. It lasted six years. Banks called in loans but were unable to cover withdrawals by alarmed customers. At the same time, British funds for land speculation dried up. So many Ohioans lost their savings that some started printing their own money.[8]

To make matters worse, the Wylie family lost their primary source of income when Dr. Adam Wylie died in 1839, after a long and intensely painful illness that his medical colleagues were unable to diagnose or treat effectively. Eliza's mother became so inconsolable and fatigued that the family feared she would not weather the shock. Once again, Eliza must have borne the burden of caring for her mother and younger siblings. On top of those responsibilities, she also apparently took over the management of the family's finances. Her two older brothers were no longer at home, and at least one of them needed help himself. In 1840 her brother Newt wrote to her with a request for fifty dollars to continue his medical studies at Transylvania University in Lexington, Kentucky. His explanation that he would need nothing more since the semester was already half over may have been written in deference to the family's shrinking financial resources.[9]

Dr. Wylie had left the six lots on which he had paid taxes to his wife, but in 1844 she and Newt, administrators of his estate, made their first petition to the Court of Common Pleas in Brown County to sell four of the lots at public auction in order to pay off debts. An inventory of Dr. Wylie's "goods and chattels" at the time of his death listed nothing of unusual value; his surgical instruments, medical supplies, household furniture and goods, and livestock all together were worth only about $200. Also included, however, were ninety-two books—a rather substantial number for a small-town doctor in that time and place. But Dr. Wylie's bookish orientation should not be surprising, given the proclivities of the Wylie clan. Two of his brothers, William and Andrew, were Presbyterian ministers, and one of them, Andrew, became the first president of Indiana University. Described as "very intellectual" and "thoroughly conversant with all the metaphysical theories that had agitated the world," Andrew was also fluent in five languages and known as an outstanding scholar of belles lettres. In addition to his siblings, Dr. Wylie's family tree also included Presbyterian ministers Theophilus Adam Wylie, a professor and collector of rare books at Indiana University, and Theophilus's father, Samuel Brown Wylie, a professor of ancient languages at the University of Pennsylvania and senior pastor of the First Reformed Presbyterian Church in Philadelphia.[10]

With such a predisposition to matters of the mind in her family background, Eliza appears to have come naturally to her own "wonderful mental power" and questioning intellect. Her letters show that she was a voracious reader of newspapers and journals, a knowledgeable commentator on public affairs, and had more than a passing familiarity with many medical practices of the day. If something interesting was going on in town, there was a good chance that Eliza was involved in it or at least knew about it. In fact, in 1840, her brother Newt expressed concern about her being exposed to the cold "by attending night meetings through the disagreeable part of the winter." The subject of those meetings is left unspecified, but one possibility is that she was participating in

Methodist discussion groups studying the memoirs of John Wesley's family and their experiences with poltergeists and unexplained phenomena. *Memoirs of the Wesley Family* had been reissued many times since its first publication in 1823, and a new edition issued by Margaret Fuller in 1840 quickly became a popular subject of Methodist study groups. At any rate, something about Methodism clearly appealed to Eliza, for at some point during her early life she and her mother left the Presbyterian church and became Methodists. Perhaps they found communion with the Methodists to be more comforting, especially in light of Reverend Rankin's radical views on abolition. If that were the case, their involvement in Ripley's most historically significant "industry," the Underground Railroad, would probably have been unlikely, at least after the death of Dr. Wylie.[11]

It is hard to talk about Ripley and a family like Eliza's, one that was actively involved in town life and with families known to be connected to the Railroad, without wondering whether the Wylies also participated in it, and, if so, to what extent. Eliza's brother Newt was married to Lizzie Pangburn, who came from a family known to be involved, and Newt may also have provided assistance to the operation. In addition, Eliza and her husband were friends with another family known to be involved, the Evans family. Although the Wylie-Tomlinson letters do not contain any explicit references to the Railroad, there are two allusions that suggest that the writers—Eliza in one case and her son, Byers, in the other—both had positive associations with the Railroad.[12]

Without any clear-cut evidence, however, it is impossible to determine what role the Wylies did or did not play in the Railroad. But lack of evidence does not rule out their participation. Many participants destroyed anything that could connect them to such an illegal, dangerous enterprise, especially after the Fugitive Slave Law of 1850, which decreed heavy penalties for those assisting escaped slaves. One historian estimates that the Ripley area had as many as 150 to 200 known participants as well as a much larger clandestine community that contributed to the success of the underground operation, which helped more than two thousand people slip the bonds of slavery without being caught. The medical services that Eliza's father and two brothers could have supplied would certainly have been vital to the health and well-being of all involved. But many kinds of help—food, clothing, shelter, transportation, money, documentation, directions, and information about safe places and people who could be trusted—were all crucial in the journey of those on their way to freedom. There is a strong possibility that Eliza's family was involved to some ex-

Dr. Thomas Byers Wylie, the oldest brother of Eliza Wylie Tomlinson, was in the second of four generations of doctors from the Wylie family in Ripley. (From the Collection of Union Township Library, Ripley, Ohio)

tent, especially while her father was alive, but after his death the remaining family members were probably unable to continue their support since the household would then have consisted of only one elderly and ailing widow, one young woman, one sixteen-year-old son, and one fourteen-year-old daughter. Such a household, in conjunction with the fact that they were dealing with some survival issues themselves, would hardly be a dependable resource for the Railroad.[13]

Whatever the extent of the Wylies' involvement in the Railroad, their intellectual orientation, Scotch-Irish Presbyterian heritage, active participation in rebellion in Ireland and America, and pioneering spirit in forging westward into sparsely settled lands would all have played a role in the kind of person Eliza became. In 1843 she would have been twenty-eight years old. Her upbringing and ever-expanding responsibilities at home would have shaped her into a person of substance and strength. Combined with her insatiable curiosity and exceptional intelligence, she would have been a force to be reckoned with by any enterprising bachelor daring enough to court her.

CHAPTER THREE

~_

Bringing Forth

SOLEMN FACT: It requires five times more talent, more tact and more
capital to start a successful paper now than it did five years ago. We pity
anyone who is smitten with the newspaper publishing mania.
—*Hickory Sprout*, August 29, 1844

IN THE SPRING of 1844 Eliza would have been twenty-nine and still living at home. The fact that she had not gone "the way of the world" and
gotten married gave one of her cousins some cause for concern.

* * * * *

George McMillan (Cousin) to Eliza
Hibernia, Pennsylvania, March 27, 1844

Cousin Eliza,

By the politeness of Mr. Tweed, I drop to you a few lines, I had almost
said as an excuse for not calling with you in person, but perhaps that
would savor too much of the provocative. Be assured, that it is not for
want of good will, that I do not now, yea, and have not long since called
upon you. I have two companions with me, whom I cannot conveniently
leave; I have been five months from home, and am anxious to arrive there
as quickly as possible; and lastly my funds are so nearly exhausted, as not
to warrant me in making any further delay. I hope however, that I shall
be able to stop as I pass next fall. But enough of such nonsense—

Thank you for your compliments to me, sent last summer by cousin Jas. W. Miller; but am sorry to be compelled to give you ground for the same again. I believe that I told you in my last that I had commenced a course at Canonsburg Theol. Sem. I am still pursuing that course. Our friends in the vicinity of Canonsburg are well. I know not whether or not you have received any intelligence from Indiana since last summer. But lest you have not I will inform you that Sis. Jane went the way of the world last November, i.e. by leaving her father's hearth and board for those of a certain John Gillespie, of Madison, Ind. And I know not how many more may be going or gone by this time. I received a letter from home some three weeks since, which informed me that our folks had nearly all had measles, but were then nearly recovered. A few cases of small pox had been in that vicinity during the winter, but were then also nearly recovered. There was an attempt made last winter to remove Hanover College to Madison, which I fear may result not only in a failure there; but in the total overthrow of the whole concern.

It is so long since I have been at home, especially to remain any considerable time, that I am utterly devoid of news which would be interesting to you. And moreover, not feeling very well this evening, and consequently not in a very propitious mood for writing, I hope that you will excuse both the scrawl and the dryness of the style of this short epistle.

Please give my best respects to your mother, your sister, and to the rest of the family, and please write to me as soon as convenient, if not sooner, to S. Hanover, and tell me all about how you all flourish. I was once informed that you were perhaps both married, i.e. you and your sister, but was sorry to find afterward that I had been misinformed. Now I hope soon to have such information founded on truth. Come now, cous Eliza, I think that it is pretty nearly time that you, at least, were deciding for yourself and casting your bark upon the waters. But perhaps it has been out long enough, yet perhaps not with the requisite rigging; for I cannot indulge the thought that it has never met a favorable gale.

But I remain your affectionate Cousin,
George McMillan

* * * * *

Little did Eliza's cousin know that she not only had the requisite rigging but had met with some favorable gales. As her following letter explains, she had already declined one proposal of marriage before marrying Will

Tomlinson on October 12, 1844. A few weeks later the newlyweds moved fifty miles east of Ripley to Piketon, on the Scioto River, where Tomlinson had already started his second newspaper, the *Hickory Sprout*. The six-columned tabloid supported Democratic candidates James K. Polk for president, George M. Dallas for vice president, and David Tod for governor of Ohio. Its slogan was "As little government as possible; that little emanating from and controlled by the People, and uniform in its application to all." In the issue for October 3, a Democrat was defined as one "who is politically on the side of those who live upon the profits of their own labor," while a Whig was depicted as being "politically on the side of those who live upon the profits of other men's labor." An earlier issue raised the question of whether or not anything should be done to extend slavery. The answer: "We think not." Henry Clay, the Whig candidate for president, was quoted as saying that he would "continue to oppose any scheme whatever of Emancipation gradual or immediate."[1]

Despite Tomlinson's denunciation of the Whig platform, his inquiry about his "Whig mother" in the following letter was probably an attempt to engage his new mother-in-law, Sarah Wylie, in some humorous banter. His other "legal mother," of course, would have been his birth mother, who is not mentioned anywhere else in his letters. Wherever she was at that time, she was evidently not a Whig, since Tomlinson reserved that designation specifically for Eliza's mother. Unlike Tomlinson, who was clearly a Democrat, the Wylies—with the possible exception of Eliza and maybe her brother Newt—were probably Whigs. A Whig protest dated June 10, 1848, shows the name of Eliza's younger brother William at the top of thirty-six signatures of local men. It is likely that Eliza's brother Byers was also sympathetic to Whig policies since his eldest son was named Henry Clay. In general, Whigs tended to be from the more educated, prosperous, and urban classes. They drew heavily from white Protestants promoting socioeconomic reform and the Gospel of Success. They usually opposed the laissez-faire policies of President Andrew Jackson and favored federal infrastructures supporting public education, road construction, stiffer tariff protection, and a national banking system.[2]

Political differences apparently did not keep Eliza's husband and younger brother from enjoying a friendly relationship. They were, after all, close in age. Tomlinson, eight years younger than Eliza, was just a year or so older than William, who was almost twenty at the time and had a reputation for profligate living. The two young men may have been drinking buddies, and it may have been through William that Tomlinson

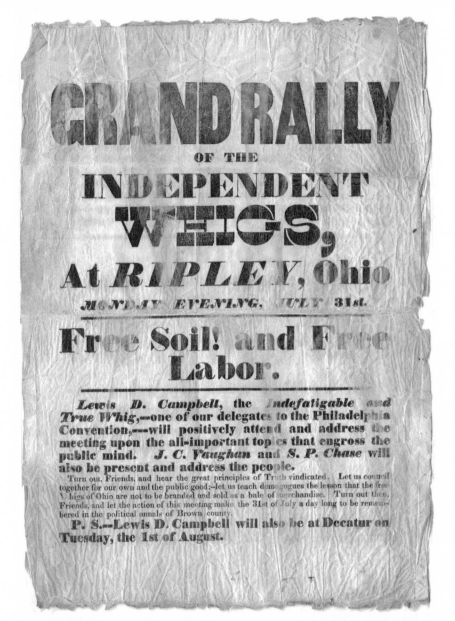

Probably dating from the 1840s, this poster shows the kind of political platform some of Eliza Wylie Tomlinson's kinfolk supported. It was found in the attic of the home of the author's grandparents. (Wylie-Tomlinson Letter Collection)

was introduced to the spirited woman who would become his wife. In berating his new brother-in-law for not writing, Tomlinson sarcastically alluded to the "Gospel Plow," an old American folk song also known as "Hold On, Hold On." The lyrics are derived from Luke 9:62, where Jesus tells a would-be follower, "No one who puts a hand to the plow and looks back is fit for the kingdom of God." But Tomlinson's sarcasm also targeted a widely publicized prophecy that was supposed to have taken place on October 22, just ten days after his marriage to Eliza. That was the date when Christ's second coming would supposedly have heralded the end of the world, at least according to William Miller. A self-educated farmer from New York who had thousands of followers in Ohio, Miller had been proselytizing in Cincinnati in August. When the world did not end on his first predicted date in October, or on his revised date the following spring, thousands of disappointed followers in Ohio were destitute after contributing all their worldly goods to the movement. In November 1844, however, when Tomlinson and Eliza were writing to her mother and sister back in Ripley, the movement was regrouping for their prophesied millennium in the spring, which Tomlinson also glibly dismissed.[3]

He was busy setting up shop again. Eliza was confident he would succeed in his new business venture and turned her attention to answering questions about her choice of husband. She was also planning her strategies for making new friends in Piketon. Meanwhile, she wanted to know what was happening with her friends and relatives back home, especially her two older brothers, Newt and Byers. As graduates of Transylvania University in Lexington, Kentucky, both were practicing physicians, and Byers, who had lived in the South for several years, had recently moved back to Ohio and settled his family in Decatur, about fifteen miles northeast of Ripley. By and large, it was a time of guarded optimism for the Wylie clan.[4]

On the national scene, new elections, revolutionizing inventions, and idealistic fervor were quickly dispelling lingering gloom left from the Panic of 1837. The recovery had been slow, but by 1842 the country was beginning to feel the effects of prosperity, both positive and negative. The burgeoning railroad network helped businesses like the printing trade and resort development flourish, and everything seemed to be growing by leaps and bounds. The 1840 census revealed that the United States population of seventeen million was close to catching up with that of Great Britain. Even though American manufacturing still lagged behind English industry, America's rapid industrial expansion enabled some entrepreneurs to accumulate so much wealth that the term "millionaire" entered the lexicon. A burgeoning middle class made books like Catharine Beecher's *Treatise on Domestic Economy* popular, while utopian communities in the hills around Cincinnati disavowed the rise of materialism. Urban tenements in the Queen City became increasingly unhealthy from pollutants in the air and water as sprawling industrial empires raced to produce everything from billiard tables to textbooks to yeasty German beer and refined soaps. New telegraph lines and railroad tracks linked the Midwest closer to eastern markets, and even small villages like Piketon, tucked away in Ohio's rolling interior, were brought closer to the outside world.[5]

* * * * *

Tomlinson to Sarah (Mother-in-Law) and Margaret (Sister-in-Law) Piketon, Ohio, November 5, 1844

Dear Mother and sister,

Presuming that you would be expecting a letter from us about this time, we have concluded that is it best to write even if we cannot give as satisfactory information as we wish. Our health has been good as we trust yours is also—We got on a boat about 8 o'clock on the evening of Tuesday and arrived safe and sound at Portsmouth about half past 2 in the morning. We sat up at the tavern till daylight. At nine o'clock we got on the stage for Piketon. It was a cold raw morning and continued so all day. We arrived at Piketon about 3 o'clock, where we hope we will not have to leave for some time. We have not yet got a house, but will soon be settled somewhere. I expect to have another press here in two or three weeks. Till then times will be rather dull. Election is now over, and I hope much of old enmity with it. Our preacher, who is one of the cleverest little fellows in existence, gave us a sermon or moral lecture on Sunday last, which will make busy times among delinquents here, if strictly attended to.

Is there any news in Ripley? Have you heard from brother Byers? When will you start for Pennsylvania? What theme engages the sage brains and yard-long tongues of the renowned citizens of Ripley? Wonder what sized glasses I drink whisky out of, or whether I don't drink it out of a pocket flask, as they are so handy? How is my "Whig Mother?" What a favored child of fortune I must be to have so many legal mothers! How is William, and when is he going to Decatur? Tell him from me that if he don't write, woe and disappointment will be his companions, destruction will victimize him, the "Gospel Plow" will never get finished, and the inevitable result will be a grand, general, Millerite bustification of the solar system. I especially charge sis or Margaret to be particular in pointing out the consequence of a neglect of this duty. Not having much information to impart and feeling at this time rather lazy and unmusical, I will leave the remainder of this sheet to Eliza. I want you to write as soon as convenient. If I have any friend in Ripley who thinks me worth inquiring after, tell them if they're in debt I hope they'll soon get out, and if not, they will prosper better minding their own business than troubling themselves about me. I remain, in the bonds of affection,

Your son and brother,

W. Tomlinson

Eliza to Sarah (Mother) and Margaret (Sister)
Piketon, Ohio, November 5, 1844

Dear Mother and Sister,

I am happy in having the pleasure of informing you that I am well and well pleased with this place and the people so far as I have seen and become acquainted with the one and the other. We are boarding with a family by the name of Murphey. He is Auditor and I think a very fine man; his wife is a very pleasant, agreeable woman. She is an Aunt to Shelby Campbell's wife so that I have almost got among kin folks.

Now sis with regard to the promise which you exacted of me I can honestly, candidly and truly say that I have had no cause to repent of the step which I have taken, but on the contrary the object of my choice daily rises to a higher standard in my esteem and regard. In fact I think myself most happy in the selection which I have made. You are aware that I might have married a rich fool, one who would have arrayed himself and me in all the flattering, glistening trappings which wealth could bestow, but then I should have lacked a companion who could have entered into my feelings and held communion with my spirit. Oh who would barter the heart's best treasure for sordid gold? Not I. Although poor I have found a treasure in a spirit which I would not part with for all the wealth of the Indies. I hope that what I have said on this will be satisfactory—I do not know when we shall get to housekeeping, perhaps next week. As yet I have not taken a promenade around the city but I can see the principal part of it from the porch of the house in which we board. It is not so large as Ripley but presents a more inviting appearance. A few evenings ago I had the pleasure of an invitation to the village Poetess who is quite an intelligent, intellectual Lady. I do not desire to form many acquaintances; I intend that my friends shall be few and well chosen.

I did not go to church on last Sabbath as the weather was very bad. I have not written to Sarah Stewart yet but intend doing so in a day or two. Please write soon and tell me all the news, what your prospects are, etc., etc. Are you going to Pa.? If so, how soon will you be off? Please tell me all that is going on, as you know that any thing relative to Ripley would be interesting to me. Please give my love to Harriet, Ellen and all others who may inquire for me. Has brother Byers got back? How do the folks get along in Decatur? Has Newton got over his cold? So far as I have examined, our things are all safe and sound, nothing broken or lost. As I had no pen convenient I have written this with a pencil. You will therefore excuse me. I hope that you will be able to read it. If not, you will not be much of a loser by it. Mr. Tomlinson has a good prospect of being again soon established in business if he succeeds in getting a press. I have no doubt but that he will do well here. Write soon. I ever remain your affectional Daughter and Sister, etc.

Eliza Wylie Tomlinson

* * * * *

Eliza's confidence in her husband's success in Piketon was premature. Tomlinson had started publishing the *Hickory Sprout* there on July 24, but after eleven issues, the equipment used to print it was burned. How or why it was burned remains a mystery, but the provenance of the equipment raises questions about possible motives for its destruction. Tomlinson had used the same equipment to print *Freedom's Casket,* which made his antislavery views explicit. But perhaps even more significant was the fact that David Ammen had used the same press twenty years earlier to print the *Castigator,* the Ripley newspaper that first published John Rankin's antislavery letters. William Lloyd Garrison later serialized the letters in the *Liberator,* and they were subsequently collected and published in various book editions from 1833 to 1850, giving them an even wider audience. Equipment used to publish arguments for the abolition of slavery may not have been welcome in the Piketon area. Waverly, just five miles from Piketon, had a history of harassing Negroes, and gangs of rampaging whites eventually drove every African American from the town limits. If the racist elements of Pike County heard about Tomlinson's antislavery views, the history of his press, and his and Eliza's associations with "abolition-ized" Ripley, they may have made short work of his printing operation.[6]

As 1844 drew to a close, the Tomlinsons had no home and no news-paper to publish. They were, however, with child. There was also another new development for the young couple: the debut of Tomlinson's literary career. His short story, "The Poison Cup," was published in the October 1844 issue of the *Columbian Magazine*. The same issue included "The Angel of the Odd—An Extravaganza," by Edgar A. Poe. Tomlinson's story, a satire of the gothic literary genre, featured a villainous count jealous of his cousin's passion for the village beauty. Tomlinson made it clear at the beginning of the story that his tale employed a number of elements typi-cal of gothic literature, including a profligate noble, a betrayed damsel, and a defeated rival. As the story progressed, the count discovered that he had mistakenly drunk the poison intended for his cousin. He pleaded for absolution for his "long catalogue of sins." But thanks to drugs that could "make a gentleman feel very ill without killing him," the count re-covered and lived a long, productive life with the village beauty.[7]

Despite its auspicious beginnings, Tomlinson's literary career was ap-parently even more short-lived than his first two newspapers. The father-to-be barely skipped a beat, however, before donning another printer's apron. Early in 1845 he and Eliza moved back to Brown County, to the county seat in Georgetown, twelve miles northwest of Ripley. In July of that year Eliza gave birth to their first child, George Wylie, and her husband began publishing the *Western Wreath* a few months later. Tomlinson also took over the publishing of the *Democratic Standard*, which ran until 1850, except for a year's hiatus in the late 1840s, when he apparently served in the Mexican War. He may have been recruited by Gen. Thomas L. Hamer, the U.S. congressman from Georgetown who had appointed Ulysses S. Grant to West Point in 1839. With her husband in Mexico, Eliza returned to Ripley, where a second son, William Byers, was born in March 1847. After the war effectively ended in September of that year, Tomlinson re-turned home. The following July he and Eliza greeted their first daughter, Margaret Eliza, also born in Ripley. She was named partly in memory of Eliza's younger sister Margaret, who had died two years before, in 1846. Another son, Adam Newton, was born in December 1850. By the end of that year, the Tomlinsons had been married six years. During that time, they had given birth to four children and four newspapers.[8]

CHAPTER FOUR

~

Looking for Relief

Should you see afar off that worth winning,
Set out on the journey with trust,
And ne'er heed if your path beginning,
Should be among brambles and dust . . .
And hardships may hinder and stay,
Keep a heart, and be sure you'll get through it,
For "Where there's a will there's a way."
—Eliza Cook, "Where There's a Will There's a Way,"
Democratic Standard, July 16, 1850

AFTER HIS RETURN from Mexico, Tomlinson took his family back to Georgetown. Their oldest child, five-year-old George, and his baby sister, Margaret, went with them. For some reason, they left two-year-old Byers in Ripley, perhaps because he was ill and not up to traveling. The road from the river up through the hills to Georgetown on the northern plateau of Brown County was long and winding, especially when the trip involved traveling by wagon in bitter winter weather.

* * * * *

Tomlinson to Sarah (Mother-in-Law)
Georgetown, Ohio, February 25, 1849

Dear Mother:

We reached here about two o'clock on Friday. We had a very tough time of it. One of the traces broke twice. We stopped at Mr. Shepherd's, and got some milk for little Margaret, and bread and butter for George, and apples for all, and after warming and feeling refreshed, we pushed on through the mud here. We have a comfortable and handy room to stay in, but the wood we have to burn in the fireplace is wet and disagreeable to deal with. Yesterday we succeeded in renting a house to live in—it is a frame building on the corner opposite the jail, built by David Crawford, and will make a very comfortable home. The rent is 42 dollars a year. We have also got a room for an office—the frame on the corner opposite where we used to live, where Sallie now lives—rent 24 dollars.

We cannot now say when a wagon will be down, but in a few days anyhow. As to the furniture and materials we shall want, I cannot now speak. We shall probably make a trade with DeWitt Johnston for his furniture, as he has broken up house-keeping and wants to sell off his goods. George often wants pap to take him Home. We don't like the idea of this being home.

We will get moved into our own house before this day week, when we hope to feel a little more at home ourselves.

W. Tomlinson

Eliza to Sarah (Mother)
Georgetown, Ohio, February 25, 1849

Dear Mother,

We are all as well as what we were when we left. I have nothing more to add at present.

Yours etc.,

Oh poor little Byers. Kiss him for me.

Adieu,

Eliza W. Tomlinson

* * * * *

In Georgetown, Tomlinson resumed publication of the *Democratic Standard*, which he soon merged with another local weekly, the *Democrat and Journal*, to form the *Democratic Union*. Meanwhile, at home, heartbreak and sorrow began to intrude upon the young family. The Tomlinson's infant son, Adam Newton, died of lung fever on January 2, 1851, before he was even a month old. Spring must have seemed especially slow in coming that year. Eliza, at home alone with two-year-old Margaret or "Sis," was anxious to hear from her mother, Sarah, and cousin, Sarah McMillan.[1]

* * * * *

Eliza to Sarah (Mother)
Georgetown, Ohio, May 7, 1851

Dear Mother,

I was sadly disappointed in not hearing from you on last Saturday. I understood Cousin Sarah to say that she would write me at that time. Her failing to do so has caused me much anxiety. I hope you will let me know how you are by the first opportunity. George has had a very bad cough and high fever almost ever since I came home. He was a little better this morning and I sent him and Byers both to school. Mr. Pearce from Decatur called here today. He says that brother Byers and family are all well. I suppose that we will have Dick with us again as Tomlinson sent him the money he requested of him. It is now supper time. I must therefore be brief.

Yours etc.,
Eliza Tomlinson

Now confirm Sarah. I wish you to write to me as soon as you receive this. If you have only time to write three words (all is well), or if otherwise, just say so. Have you heard any thing from Uncle and Aunt since they left or from home? If all is well, I shall expect you out soon without fail. There are a great many people in town since court was in session, but what is going on I know not. Please give my love and respects to any of my friends that you may happen to see, Mr. Benington, especially.

Adieu Dear Cuz, do write,
Eliza W. Tomlinson

Tuesday morning: As I failed to get this in the mail on last evening, I open it to tell you that I am alone today. Tomlinson has gone to Higginsport. George and Byers are at school so that I have no company except Sis. I hope that I shall hear from you today: If well, write immediately.
E W T

* * * * *

Little George's cough was apparently the beginning of a serious illness. Seven weeks after writing her mother at the beginning of May, Eliza was back in Ripley with George, perhaps to put him under the care of her brother Newt. But his illness took a turn for the worse, and on June 28,

Eliza's firstborn died of inflammation of the brain. He would have been six years old on July 23. Of the four children Eliza and her husband had given birth to, two were left: William Byers, now age four; and Margaret Eliza, who would be three on July 26. The loss of two children in six months must have been quite a blow to the young couple. But with two small children still needing constant care and newspaper deadlines to meet, the Tomlinsons must have had little time time for grieving. A year passed, and an unexpected request resulted in another reconfiguration of their family.[2]

* * * * *

Anne (Sister) to Tomlinson
Dubuque, Iowa, July 21, 1852

My Dear Brother,

You will be surprised at hearing from me so soon, especially as I have not yet received an answer to the letter which I wrote you last. My reason for writing so soon is this. I find that my boy's time is worse than running to waste. He is so much from home necessarily and unnecessarily, and when from home he is so surrounded by wicked companions that I scarcely know what to do with him. However, I have thought of advising with you about it and ascertaining whether my plan meets with your and Eliza's approbation or not. It is this: if you can take him under your care, so as to see that he is placed under proper discipline and learns something useful, I will sell or mortgage the vacant lot which we still own in order to fit him out, and pay his way, and pay for his schooling for as long a time as you might judge actually necessary.

You may be led to suppose from my writing thus that he is a very bad boy, but it is not so. He is quite a good boy for this place, for I think the boys of Dubuque exceed any thing I ever knew for wickedness. But I see that he requires a master. His time is too much at his own disposal, and he is just forming his habits for life. If he falls into good hands, he may be made a blessing and an honor to his country and his kindred. But should he be allowed to spend his time as he pleases and in what company he pleases, he will be fit for the penitentiary by the time he is twenty-one. He prefers printing to any other business, but he prefers fishing and sailing on the river in a shift to printing.

The night before last I heard him say in his sleep, God damn you. I did not know that he was in the habit of using profane language until then, and it gives me a heavy, painful feeling at my heart to think of it. I know not what he may do or say when away from home. Swearing is the order of the day here. Little boys who cannot speak plain will manage to utter an oath when it suits them. If you think it is best to take him under your care, and can do it, let me know immediately. Also, how it will answer to send him alone, and the best way to send some money. I want to send thirty or forty dollars, if I send him, and sell the lot, and I am afraid that he might be careless enough to let it be stolen. I would like to have Eliza's opinion about it because I would not have him go unwelcome on any conditions, and I think she can see a little farther into a millstone than you can. Should you think it advisable to have him down, please give me all necessary directions. I hope you are all in good health, and prospering in soul and body. We are all well just now, thank the giver of every blessing for it.

Give my love to Eliza and her Mother and the children and accept the same yourself.

Yours truly,

Anne T. Hunter

P.S. I do not know what a telegraphic dispatch would cost, but if it would fall on me, I would willingly pay it. If you think of having him go to you, the word, come, would answer every purpose. If you think he had better stay at home, do not telegraph. I shall not take any further steps in the matter until I hear from you.

Your Affectionate Sister Anne

Anne to Tomlinson
Dubuque, August 2, 1852

My Dear Brother,

I think my boy will get off today, and I solemnly commend him to the care of the orphan's God. I feel confident that He will preserve him (in the slippery paths of youth, from evil and willful sins).

Now let me give him up to you. I know that you will be a kind and judicious Father, to my Fatherless boy. Treat him as you would your own, correct him when he requires it, and see that he obeys your commands punctually, know how he spends his sabbaths, do not let him loiter about on that day, and never let him stay out after early candlelighting. These rules I have strictly adhered to myself, since his Father's death, so you will not think me presuming to name them to you. I am well convinced that you know better than I can tell you, how to bring him up, and that you will do it for my sake, if for no other reason. The task is an onerous one I know, but God will reward you if I cannot. I have not yet succeeded in selling the lot, and I fear it will go for less than half it is worth, but I feel I am doing my duty and God will take care of the rest.

The coat and pants which you will find in the trunk, you can do what you please with. I thought they might possibly be of some use to you. I would have sent a fuller wardrobe with Willey, but I was afraid that he would have too great a load! How are you all? We are all well, thank God for it. Please write so soon as Willey arrives, for you know that I shall be anxious to hear from him. You will find my likeness in the trunk.

Give my love to all and kiss the dear little children for me. The children send their love to Uncle, and Aunt, and little cousins.

Yours Affectionately,

Anne T. Hunter

* * * * *

Willey may have provided a welcome diversion from the heartbreak and loss the Tomlinson family had suffered. No doubt Tomlinson also took some delight in training a nephew in the printing trade, especially when there were additional newspapers to publish. Besides publishing the *Democratic Union* in Georgetown, in 1852 he also began publishing the *Ripley Herald* and *The Granite Rock*. The latter was a short-term Democratic campaign sheet for presidential candidate Franklin A. Pierce, who was a relatively unknown Yankee until Nathaniel Hawthorne repackaged him into a national icon. As the only candidate Northern and Southern Democrats could agree upon, he was elected by a landslide, becoming the fourteenth president of the United States.[3]

With a president from their own party occupying the White House again, the ruling Democratic majority in Congress resumed pretending that they had, for the most part, taken care of the slavery issue when they passed the Compromise of 1850. It had prohibited slave trade in the District of Columbia, admitted California as a Free State, permitted no retrictions on slavery in the territories of Utah and New Mexico, and paid the State of Texas to settle its border dispute with New Mexico. But its most significant impact for people living in the borderlands was a stricter interpretation of fugitive slave laws. Kentucky slave catchers were only too happy to have stronger legal sanctions for their mercenary raids on suspected fugitives and Underground Railroad participants. Yet the number of slaves escaping across the river to Ripley continued to increase, thanks to the courageous acts of conductors like John Parker, a freed African American who owned a successful foundry at the end of Front Street, and the continued efforts of the Rankins and other Ripley families.[4]

Members of the white community in Ripley were also trying to improve the living conditions of African Americans in other ways. In the May 27, 1852, edition of the *Ripley Herald,* an article titled "Western Fair" sought support for an event aimed at raising funds for the completion of a church where "the colored population" of the area could worship. The article stated that everyone would benefit from "the elevation of the moral and intellectual capacity" of Negroes. Although such sentiment would be recognized as racist today, in the Ohio River borderlands of the 1850s, the majority of whites—including those opposed to slavery—would have seen such efforts on behalf of their African American brethren as socially progressive. Such an agenda may have been a strong enticement for Tomlinson to take on editing yet another newspaper, but it was probably the *Ripley Herald*'s association with a company of spiritualists that had the strongest appeal.[5]

In proclaiming the free communication of thought as an invaluable right, the newspaper not only questioned the political and social status quo, it also critiqued religious doctrines and promoted alternative beliefs. The edition for May 27 included lengthy excerpts describing the ghostly apparitions experienced by the family of John Wesley, the eighteenth-century English clergyman credited as the founder of Methodism. As the editor of the *Ripley Herald,* Tomlinson may have personally selected the excerpts from the *Memoirs of the Wesley Family* to lend credence to the existence of supernatural phenomena. But he also probably had fun noting that the excerpts came from a book belonging to the town's Methodist Episcopal Sabbath School Library. He may even have learned about the memoirs from his wife, who could have participated in a Methodist discussion group that studied the book earlier. Regardless of how the Wesley memoirs found their way into the *Ripley Herald,* the spiritualists in Ripley were hardly alone in their interest in the occult.[6]

By the early 1850s, the spiritualist movement had swept the country, thanks to Kate and Maggie Fox, two young sisters from Hydesville, New York. Their claim to have talked with the dead attracted a large following in Cincinnati, where they visited in 1850 and 1851. There were also other psychics who found favor with the city's intellectual elite. Another New

York medium, Mrs. G. B. Bushnell, drew a substantial number of devotees to her drawing room seances, including William T. Coggeshall, who in 1851 published *The Signs of the Times: A History of the Spirit-Rappings, in Cincinnati and Other Places.* Spiritualism became so popular, in fact, that the *Ripley Herald* quoted the *Cincinnati Sun* in reporting that city authorities in Louisville were charging spirit rappers five dollars a day for the privilege of rapping.[7]

The Tomlinsons must have found it refreshing to be involved in the kind of intellectual fervor that challenged the norms of traditional religion and called for reform of social institutions. They would have felt at home with people interested in the impact of new scientific theories, such as evolution, and the emergence of new technologies, such as the telegraph. After all, Tomlinson's livelihood increasingly depended on telegraphic transmission of the latest information. It would have taken only a small leap of the imagination for them to apply the new technology to spiritual realms and surmise that another kind of telegraphic communication could contact those who had departed earthly habitations.[8]

Such a possibility would have been a healing solace for the Tomlinsons after the deaths of two children. As one correspondent wrote in the *Ripley Herald* issue for May 27, 1852: "It is a very consoling thought to me, that my dear loved ones who have gone before me to the Spirit World *can* and *do* come and communicate with me, and encourage me to persevere in well-doing." The article signed by "A Lady" could easily have been written by Eliza, especially given her own recent loss of "dear loved ones," the fact that she usually used *noms de plumes* for her published writings, and her immediate access to the editor. She may also have been the anonymous author of another aticle in the same issue. "Progressive Wonder" reported direct communication with spirits in Ripley "without the use of the organs of a medium." The wonders of spiritualism, however, must have eventually lost their attraction for Eliza and her husband. After nineteen issues of the *Ripley Herald,* Tomlinson sold his interest in the newspaper.[9]

Soon after, he tried his hand at a venture farther afield in terms of distance. From April 9, 1853, to August 24, 1954, he published *The Nor'wester* in the small farming community of Kenton in northwestern Ohio. The twenty-four columned Democratic newspaper was described as having a "commendable appearance," but Tomlinson may have been more interested in the paper for its location. He and Eliza may have been looking for a new place to live. If so, their plans were tragically disrupted. On August 2, 1853—Tomlinson's thirtieth birthday—his and Eliza's daughter

Margaret passed away. She was just five years old when scarlet fever took her life. She was the third young child that the Tomlinsons had lost in three years. Byers, the one surviving son, was six years old at the time. Sarah Isabella, the new baby in the family, was barely five months old. Like her older brother, Byers, and unlike the three siblings who predeceased her, Belle—as she would eventually be called—had been born in the month of March, in Ripley. Whether or not that would turn out to be a good omen remained to be seen.[10]

Meanwhile, Ripley must have become a vale of sorrow for the grieving family. There was so much there to remind them of all that they had lost. The healing process was surely slow and painful, and yet, once again, Eliza and her husband somehow managed to find the strength needed to move forward and create a new vision for their family. They may have needed a new vista, however—someplace away from the cloying vapors of the Ohio River valley, someplace with a healthier environment for Byers and Belle, and someplace with fresh opportunities for themselves. Like many Americans of that period, they turned west. Tomlinson already had a relative living in Iowa—his sister, Anne, whom they had recently helped by providing a home in Ohio for her son Willey. Maybe now she could help them get settled in Iowa. At any rate, they soon joined the 70,000 Ohioans who moved to Iowa between 1850 and 1870. The new state had many attractions, including ample mineral deposits, rich soil, and land that sold for no more than $1.25 per acre.[11]

By the spring of 1854, Tomlinson had sold his interests in the *Ripley Herald, Nor'wester,* and *Democratic Union,* and relocated to Dubuque, where his sister lived. He probably went alone to scout things out and find suitable living accommodations for Eliza and the children. He soon found work at the *Dubuque Express and Herald,* a Democratic newspaper edited by Dennis A. Mahony. Mahony's tactics as an Irish firebrand and leading Copperhead mouthpiece would land him in a federal prison in 1862. But in 1854, the Democrats were still calling the shots in the eight-year-old state, and Mahony had the lucrative contract for being the official state printer. His contentious temperament, however, kept him at odds with nearly everyone, including his own managing editor—a more moderately tempered man who later volunteered for the Union Army and died in a Confederate prison. Despite the pitfalls of party politics and personalities, as well as his own temperamental challenges, Tomlinson quickly made inroads into the Dubuque community and somehow managed to dance around Mahony's relentless feuding, perhaps by moving farther west to Des Moines in the fall of 1855.[12]

After losing the Ramage press he used to print his first two newspapers, Tomlinson probably used a Washington press like this one to publish his subsequent newspapers in the 1840s and 1850s. (Brian P. Lawler, Shakespeare Press Museum, California Polytechnic State University)

The small frontier town presented ample opportunity for enterprising printers and aspiring politicians. An ambitious group of politicians and businessmen were working to have it designated as the state's new capital. They apparently welcomed Tomlinson into their ranks, and, having also been admitted into the practice of law there, he soon began enjoying the "spoils" of the political system. The town also probably appealed to Tomlinson and Eliza as a good place to rear their two surviving children. It was touted as being in the best possible latitude for mental and physical development, although getting there was no easy task. Railroads were just beginning to penetrate the state, so the likely mode of transportation from Ripley to Des Moines would have entailed traveling by steamboat down the Ohio, up the Mississippi, and then possibly up the Des Moines River. But the latter was often too shallow for steamboat traffic, so they probably traveled overland by wagon or stagecoach from Davenport or Dubuque to Des Moines. The journey from Ohio would have taken them several days, perhaps weeks, depending on the modes of transportation used and delays encountered. There is no indication of whether Tomlinson went back to bring Eliza and the two children out West, or whether Eliza and the children made the trip on their own. What happened to Tomlinson's nephew Willey, who would have been about sixteen years of age at the time, also remains unclear. A reference to him in a letter his mother wrote years later indicates that in 1864 he was in the South, but she had not seen him in seven years, which would have been in 1857. That was during the time the Tomlinsons were living in Iowa, so it may be that he made the trip with them but did not stay.[13]

In the fast-changing Iowa landscape, newspapers sprouted and died before a crop of corn could be planted and harvested. Political factions blossomed and withered almost as fast. Turmoil in neighboring Kansas aroused anxieties in Iowa voters, and in 1856 James W. Grimes became Iowa's first Republican governor, signaling the end of the Democratic Party's heyday in state politics as well as a growing antipathy to slavery. But Tomlinson seemed to thrive on change and the risks it involved. He continued publishing the *Iowa Statesman,* a Democratic newspaper, and held various civil offices, including justice of the peace, alderman, and street commissioner. He also served as a clerk for the Iowa House of Representatives. In 1857, he became a charter member and an officer of Capital Lodge No. 106 of the Independent Order of Odd Fellows, a popular service fraternity. And he joined a pack of shrewd, aggressive developers who made lax use of state funds to finance building the state capitol east of the river in Des Moines.[14]

Yet all of his hard work and political savvy amounted to nothing when the Panic of 1857 struck and leveled the Midwest like a pack of tornadoes. America's rapid increase in exports, rampant land speculation, and inflated stock and bond prices all crashed when British and French investors redirected their capital to ailing economies at home. Although the panic was only two years in length, unlike the one twenty years before, the recovery came too late for Tomlinson and many of his Democratic cronies. They became easy targets for prowling political opponents and angry voters reeling from financial ruin at the hands of manipulative profiteers. Tomlinson had to sell the *Statesman* and found himself scrambling to find work. Pushed to his limits, he apparently allowed his explosive temper to get the best of him. A former colleague described him as "an individual of no refinement of character or expression, and largely endowed with the rhetoric of Billingsgate." In other words, his behavior and language reeked of London's most offensive fish market.[15]

The Democratic Party in Iowa was also scrambling. It had splintered into factions that spent more time and energy fighting each other than the rising Republican Party. Extremists from both parties invoked the wrath of God on those who strayed from their particular paths of righteousness. The bloody raids of John Brown rained death and destruction on Kansas in 1856 and Harpers Ferry, Virginia, in 1859. Law-abiding citizens feared insurrection and retribution at every turn, especially in the Border States. Meanwhile, Tomlinson, who was no stranger to the magnetic pull of strong convictions, suddenly found himself without a political compass. He could not embrace Republicanism but found it increasingly difficult to see where—or if—he belonged in any Democratic fold, especially in Iowa, where some of his colleagues were sounding more and more like southern-sympathizing Copperheads. Like most small-town newspaper editors and printers, he depended on contacts from a strong party affiliation to steer business his way. But most of his resources had dried up. Yet he somehow managed to parlay the dregs of a diminishing reputation into a position as associate editor of the *Iowa State Journal*. He also joined the campaign for Gen. A. C. Dodge as Democratic candidate for governor in 1859.[16]

Dodge had been elected as one of the state's first U.S. senators in 1848 but lost the race seven years later to a Free-Soil candidate. After serving as minister to Spain, he returned to Iowa in 1859, only to be beaten in the gubernatorial election by a Republican candidate. Whatever chances of success he may have had were not helped by the small retinue of men who stumped for him. Apparently one of his most offensive campaigners was Tomlinson. According to Republican newspapers in the state, Tomlinson not only spread "wild stories" and inaccurate information about Republican candidates, he was so drunk most of the time that on at least one occasion he had to be carried to bed. Even after he finally returned to Ohio, his reputation as a "drunken loafer" was still making the rounds. In May 1860 the Davenport *Daily Gazette* quipped that his return to the East would surely make the price of whisky go down there.[17]

CHAPTER FIVE

Together and Apart

The *Gazette* has been regularly issued, at Cincinnati, for upward of sixty
years, and during all that time, has maintained a high character, and
leading position among Western journals. . . . The chief Editor . . . is a
decided opponent of the extension of Slavery, but not a hot-headed, violent
partisan. . . . The *Gazette* is regarded as the best paper, for traders and
merchants, to be had in the Mississippi Valley.
—*Ripley Bee*, April 18, 1857

EARLY IN 1860 the Tomlinsons apparently made a hasty retreat to Ohio,
leaving pets, property holdings, and household goods in Des Moines.
They trusted a few friends to take care of everything they left behind—including unresolved business and property issues. The fluctuating conditions of their financial affairs in Iowa became a recurring annoyance that
strained the relationship between Tomlinson and Eliza, especially since
their own communications were primarily carried on at a distance. He
was in Cincinnati and often seemed to drag his feet in dealing with all the
niggling details his wife asked him to attend to. She was in Ripley with
the children and had to forward correspondence to her husband, remind
him of her unanswered questions, and then wait for a reply or his next
visit before she could respond to questions from friends in Des Moines.

F. P. (Frank) Yokauer, the author of the letter below, was apparently a
friend who was supposed to be looking after their affairs in Iowa. He and
Tomlinson were fellow lodge members in the Independent Order of the
Odd Fellows, and Yokauer was sending Tomlinson some official communications from the lodge's ruling Noble Grand. Two other friends mentioned
in the letter, William Lowry and Gen. James A. Williamson, were both involved with Tomlinson in building the state capitol east of the river in Des
Moines. The other three men mentioned in the letter were apparently not on

the best of terms with Tomlinson. John Teesdale, editor of the Republican newspaper, *Tri-Weekly Citizen*, had lucrative state printing contracts. Jonathan Cattell was a Republican abolitionist elected to the Iowa State Senate in 1856, during the period that Tomlinson clerked for the legislature.[1]

Will Porter, another name mentioned in the letter, apparently owed money to Tomlinson and Yokauer and had an interesting history with Tomlinson, who may have known him in Ohio. Porter was born in 1833, a few counties upriver from Ripley, and began his printing career at the *Ripley Bee*. After studying law and working in other places, he moved to Des Moines in 1855 at the encouragement of an uncle there. He then worked for Tomlinson at the office of the *Iowa Statesman*. In 1857 he bought the paper from Tomlinson and changed its name to the *State Journal*. At some point, the two must have fallen out. In his book on the history of Des Moines, published in 1898, Porter described his former boss as being impulsive, hot headed, abusive of his opponents, and usually in a fight with someone. But, as Eliza's letter of November 3, 1860, would reveal, Porter was not above resorting to scurrilous means himself.[2]

Given Yokauer's fluency with terms from the printing trade, it may be that he was also a printer who worked with Tomlinson. One of the terms that Yokauer mentioned, a *quire*, refers to one-twentieth of a ream of paper and consists of twenty-four or twenty-five sheets of the same size. The "yeas & nays" alluded to by Yokauer were probably legislative ballots procured or printed by Tomlinson. They both had access to legislative supplies since each wrote letters using letterhead from the Iowa Senate Chamber. Yokauer's letter below, however, was written on plain paper, folded in half like a booklet.[3]

* * * * *

Frank Yokauer to Tomlinson
East Des Moines, Iowa, April 6, 1860
8½ o'clock P. M.

Dear friend Will,

This moment I came home from the Lodge. A card has been granted, as, also, a request to the N.G.—to give you the T.P.W. You will find both enclosed.

The house as yet stands on the same place. Lowry fixed up the fence, in front, today. It is not yet finished but will be I suppose tomorrow. He is fixing up bars in the corner next to Williamson's so that it will be unnecessary to tear down the whole fence for the purpose of driving the yard. Williamson got very sick the night after you left, but is getting better. I feel very lonesome, less so today than yesterday—for Lowry was here all day and so I had hale company and could help him once in a while a little. But the day after you left I hardly knew how to dispose of my time; I could not even read—certainly a bad sign.

I have not yet heard of Mrs. Tomlinson's muff. I put advertisements in the Journal and the Commonwealth. The one will appear tomorrow, the other on Thursday next. Porter, when I dunned him today, denied owing us anything. He said his recollection was he had settled all square up. I suppose I must sue him.

Eddy is well and singing all day.

Tell Byers that Ring is well, but it seems to me he is mourning for him.

Kitty Clyde is running all over the house in search of the "old folks (not) at home;" but the accompanying tune is not quite as melodious as the one to which the namesake is set.

After all an old Batchelorlife is not so bad. I have Lowry for my guest today and served up so well that he resolved to leave the "American" and board with me next week. I know Mrs. T. is anxious to learn how I gained his favor. I therefore annex the bill of fare—fried eggs, pancakes, boiled veal with an extra good article of catsup, toasted bread and tea. Isn't that a pretty good bill of fare for a Batchelor of my size?

I have not received a paper since you left. I spoke to some of the Aldermen about the office of Recorder and find that W. D. Wylie tries to get it—Well, we'll see.

Yesterday afternoon I got Cattell in a tight place about those yeas & nays. he I was up in his office and while speaking about Teesdale's vouchers, he showed me that y. & n. are counted and charged as blanks, and i.e., $.1.46 for the first & 40 cents for subsequent quires. I showed him then a couple of charges: 150 y. & n.—$9.00. I wanted him to figure that out, but he isn't sure yet.

I trust that Mrs. T.'s brother is better and that you all arrived there well and none the worse for wear. I long to hear from you soon.

In the meantime I am

Yours Fraternally,

Frank

Give my best respects to Mrs. Tomlinson and tell Byers and Belle that I want them to learn right smart.

F.

Sunday—1 P.M.

"Jimmy" was here just now. He said that you promised to let him have that piece of ground east of town to put in a crop. But as the fence is burned, he cannot do everything. He said that if you find the lumber and get it on the ground, he will put up a tip-top fence for the crop. He is anxious to get an answer.

I had to keep your card to get your Degree put in according to the resolution that the G.L. passed at the last session and which Whitney had forgotten.

* * * * *

While Yokauer was seeing to the family's unsettled affairs in Iowa, Tomlinson was in Cincinnati. It was the closest city to Ripley and one of the largest publishing centers in the Midwest. So many newspapers and literary periodicals were published in the Queen City that it was known as the "Literary Emporium of the West." William T. Coggeshall, who published his own book on spiritualism in 1851, was a leading publisher of literary works in the city. But dabbling in spiritualism or literary pursuits must have been far from Tomlinson's mind; he needed solid work that would feed a family.[4]

His experience as an editor, a wordsmith, and a printer more than qualified him to work as a compositor, with a fairly dependable income. Compositors were highly skilled typesetters who "composed" the pages of a publication by manually inserting the type for each letter, punctuation mark, rule, and space, line by line, column by column, page by page. It was tedious work and required deftness of hand, eye, and mind. Each letter and space for a line of copy had to be inserted backward and upside down, from left to right, in a composing stick held in the left hand. If a line of copy needed justifying, miniscule spaces were added, and strips of leading had to be inserted between the lines of copy.[5]

Since typewriters were not in common usage then, the copy or "matter" that was original or "live" came in handwritten format. "Dead matter," type that had already been set and published, could be reused, but there also had to be plenty of fresh copy to interest readers. Regardless of where the matter originated—from another publication or previously unpublished material—good compositors needed to have a lot of stamina for standing fourteen to sixteen hours a day at a compositor's table. They also needed a comprehensive knowledge of the English language, with all its quirky practices in spelling, punctuation, syntax, and grammar. Sometimes the copy to be set was poorly written and needed quite a bit of correcting by compositors, who also had to work fast, especially for a daily publication like the *Cincinnati Gazette*. Tomlinson would probably have preferred the slower pace, greater prestige, and variety of work that came with publishing a country weekly, but he had little choice in the matter.[6]

He may also have disliked being separated from his family. Since his income as a substitute compositor fluctuated, however, it would have been impractical for Eliza and the children to live in Cincinnati, where a housing shortage resulted in a high cost of living. Urban living also brought other challenges, including rampant crime and multiple health hazards from factory pollution, inadequate sanitation, and crowded conditions. So Eliza and the children were back in Ripley living with her mother, Sarah. But life in Ripley had a dark side, too. The Wylie household was once again shrouded in mourning. Eliza's younger brother, William B. F., died on April 5, 1860, at the age of thirty-six. He had just been reelected as prosecuting attorney for Brown County.[7]

Both of Eliza's two older brothers, Byers and Newt, were also living in Ripley. But Byers, who had a large family of his own, had been ill for some time. A notice the year before in the *Ripley Bee* requested immediate settlement of accounts for his and Newt's professional services. The notice may have been prompted by Byers's weakened condition—probably exacerbated over the years by the deaths of six of his ten children. Newt also had good reasons for consolidating his resources. In 1856, while Eliza was still in Iowa, he had married Lizzie Pangburn, and the time must have come for them to have their own home, especially after Eliza and the children moved back into Sarah's house. In 1859 Newt bought the shares Eliza and their brother William owned on Lot 61, which bordered the river on one side and backed up to Sarah's residence on Second Street on the other. But before Newt could build on the lot, his beloved Lizzie died, just six years after their wedding, and Newt sold the lot to Milo Chase, who later founded a piano factory in Ripley. The Wylies had their share of grief, but for better or for worse, Eliza and the children were back in the bosom of the family, and Tomlinson was only a half day away by steamboat. Perhaps at some point they could be together again. In the meantime, their letters kept them in touch.[8]

* * * * *

Dearest Eliza,

I thought that this, being the holy Sabbath, would be just as suitable a day as could be selected to write you a few lines. Yours, in response to my first, was received yesterday. I had sent word to Byers the day before as to what I was doing, and where to be found. Of course he duly informed you, as I requested him. Well, this being understood, let me tell you that I obtained a sub situation in the Gazette office at noon of the day after leaving you, mainly through "Dick's" influence.

You wonder, no doubt, what sort of situation is called "sub." For your enlightenment let me explain. The Gazette office has 21 regular compositors on the daily paper. These are known as regular, permanent hands. But they must, from not only necessity but inclination, have occasional relaxation and relief from labor. Besides, sometimes sickness of self or friends, or social visits to distant relatives, require absence. To supply these various contingencies, a system of "subbing" is adopted. A number of printers are enrolled as substitutes for each particular office, who are chosen by the temporary absentees to take their cases. Each regular hand has, in the Gazette office, cases of minion and nonpareil. In the G. office there are nine "subs." I am the ninth on the list. Whenever a vacancy occurs in the "regular" office force, it is filled from the list of "subs." Outsiders (those not on either the "regular" or "sub" roll) cannot get any work in the office. So you see I stand a chance for a regular berth after a while.

But a "sub" in this office gets about as much work as he can do. The regular hands only work five days, if they can possibly get a "sub" for the other two. I have been at work nearly ever since my name was enrolled. I expect to make from nine to twelve dollars per week when I get fairly established, and my hand in. The regular hours for work are: At 10 a.m., the matter is given out, to distribute. We distribute as much as we can, or all the dead matter, before dinner, which is at ½ past 12. At ½ past one we commence on copy, and work till from one to three in the morning. At that hour we get off, go to bed, and sleep till woke up at nine, a.m. Notwithstanding that I work till two o'clock in the night, I cannot sleep after 7. The first night work was very severe. My ankle swelled up till my boot was full. Since then it has not affected me near so much. I bought a pair of 75 cent slippers, which are easier than the boots. How I did wish that those Kellogg slippers had been in my carpet sack.

I am boarding a square and a half from the office with a widow White-side. The house is No. 107 west 5th street, near the Market house, west end. The office is on the corner of Fourth & Walnut. I have a bed to myself, but two others are in the room. It is one of the best in this large house. Board $3.00 per week. Every other weekday the huckster and market vapors are spread along this street from squares.

"Dick" is a candidate for the office of Recorder of Brown county, subject to the Democratic nomination, which will be made early in August. He wants me to go up a few weeks before that time and electioneer for him, he paying expenses and wages. But my sheet is full before I have said half, so I had better "dry up."

Yesterday a poor woman fell backwards from a window just opposite where I was working, and was badly hurt. It made me sick at the stomach for several hours.

I have bought me a new cane, which cost $1.50. It is handsome and serviceable.

* * * * *

As Tomlinson settled into a new situation, a new election year widened the divide over issues dealing with state's rights and slavery. At the Republican Party Convention in Chicago that May, the nomination of Abraham Lincoln for president received a crescendo of cheers from thousands in attendance. A month before in April the Democratic Party formalized its split into Northern and Southern factions when fifty-one Southern delegates to its convention in Charleston, South Carolina, walked out in protest over a platform that did not promote proslavery interests. Stephen A. Douglas attempted to bridge the chasm dividing Northern and Southern factions, but John Brown's raids still smoldered in Southern camps. In June, when a second Democratic convention met in Baltimore and nominated Douglas for president, Southern "fire-eaters" pushing for secession staged an even larger walkout and reconvened in Richmond, Virginia, to nominate their own candidate, John C. Breckinridge of Kentucky.[9]

Tomlinson knew some of the Iowa delegates to the Democratic conventions, including Daniel O. Finch, a successful attorney in Des Moines and one of the state's leading Democrats. Finch had also edited one of Des Moines's early newspapers, the *Star*, before Tomlinson bought it in 1854 and changed its name to the *Iowa Statesman*. Since then Tomlinson's political loyalties had become as fragmented as the party he had formerly promoted. Like many Northern Democrats, he found himself facing an increasingly difficult choice: he could stay on board with the party that had helped to keep him afloat for many years but was now listing more and more toward Southern interests, or he could follow his conscience and jump ship, hoping he could find a vessel that reflected his evolving political values. Perhaps his circumstances presented him with an opportunity for exploring political affiliations more in line with his changing priorities. He was not an enthusiastic fan of Abraham Lincoln, and he refused to join the Republican Party, even though he worked for the *Cincinnati Gazette,* a newspaper that was decidedly Republican.[10]

Most of southern Ohio was still steeped in the culture of upland Southern settlers with Democratic loyalties. Though not of Southern origins, the Tomlinsons, like many of their neighbors, probably had mixed feelings about each of the presidential candidates as the November election approached. Republicans had gained support throughout the Midwest by recruiting former Whigs and disillusioned Democrats, but some disaffected Democrats were still loath to call themselves Republicans or join the Constitutional Unionists. The Tomlinsons, who were probably among the disaffected Democrats, may have supported Douglas more out of default than decisiveness. But Eliza and Tomlinson also had more immediate concerns. Their unresolved business dealings continued to plague them, and problems with tenants became even more complicated when one of their tenants turned out to be Will Wylie, a distant relative of Eliza's.[11]

* * * * *

Frank Yokauer to Eliza
Des Moines, Iowa, June 24, 1860

Mrs. E. W. Tomlinson:

Your kind letter was received in due time, but I could not get time to answer any sooner, Mr. Williamson having left for Baltimore and New York last Tuesday a week ago and being kept therefore pretty busy all the time. Mr. Williamson, Emma and the children went down to Mrs. Inegary's at the same time, although I heard since that Mrs. W. went along to Baltimore.

I have not heard from Mr. Lambis ever since he wrote from Ripley. A letter from him to Mr. Williamson arrived here some time ago, which I opened. He wants Mr. W. to rent out his two houses. So I suppose you do not intend returning to Des Moines very soon.

Wylie's folks moved last week. Your house (on Walnut) ought to be inhabited. The rats make bad work there. I air it so often as I can, as also the feather beds. Lowry wrote to me from Omaha and from Ft. Kearney. The Co. are getting along very well. Mary is still in town. Des Moines is as dull as any town of its size can be.

The excitement about the Charleston Convention here is intense. To-day the news of the secession of some of the Delegations reached us. You can see politicians, in groups of three and more, stand on the corners of the streets, discussing the probable result of the Convention. We are anxiously waiting for a letter from D. O. Finch but have not heard since he left. I never saw the people as much excited as they are about Douglas.

The Masons celebrated the 24th yesterday, and the Iowa Templars had a picnic about 10 miles from town. Five lodges participated; and I learn they had a fine time.

You heard doubtlessly before this time of the ravages of the late tornado in this State.

Byers seems to be improving in his studies. His letters are well written and the spelling better than it used to be. I will soon answer his letter.

Please tell both Byers and Belle that I think very often of them. Praying you to write as soon as convenient.

Respectfully,

F. P. Yokauer

Eliza to Tomlinson
Ripley, Ohio, July 3, 1860

Dear Husband,

I received yours of the 1st inst.—last night, am happy to learn that your health continues good, hope that you will take every precaution to preserve it.

Our family are all about as well as usual. Tomorrow the different Sunday schools have a picnic above town in a grove, some place near where the Odd Fellows had theirs. The children are anxious to attend, so I suppose I shall have to fix them up a basket, and let them go. The weather is very hot! We have the coolest place in town; therefore suffer less from heat than most folks.

As to that Hyde matter, I think with you that it is best to put our property beyond the possibility of being taken for so unjust a thing! I therefore think that you had better make out a deed to Newt for any nominal sum, say fifteen hundred or two thousand dollars, and sign your name to it. I can sign mine here and obtain witness to it, but you understand better than I can tell you how such matters should be arranged.

On Saturday night I received this letter from Frank, so as you had not heard anything, I thought best to send it to you. I suppose, from what Frank says, that the rats are about to take the house. I wish Frank would give them some poison. Should you write to him, tell him that there is a vial of poison in a cup on a shelf under the stairs. He can mix it in cornmeal and put it in different places about the house. The children and mother join me in love to you.

Ever yours etc.,

Eliza W. Tomlinson

* * * * *

While day-to-day concerns about finances, parenting, and household management continued to occupy most of Eliza's attention, political pundits were waiting to see what would happen in October in Ohio's state and local elections. The early timing of the state's elections and the composition of its population made it a key bellwether state. It ranked third in the nation in terms of wealth and population, and its population, with the northern half comprised of many New Englanders with antislavery views and the southern half consisting of many upland Southerners more sympathetic to Southern issues, tended to reflect the great national divide between North and South. In addition, the state counted large numbers of immigrants among its residents; in the 1860 census, it ranked second in the number of German immigrants, third in English, and fifth in Irish and Scottish. But first things first—Eliza apparently wanted her teeth back.[12]

* * * * *

Eliza to Tomlinson

Ripley, Ohio, August 7, 1860

Dear Husband,

As Mr. Shaw tells me he is going down to the city today, I embrace the opportunity to let you know that we are all in the enjoyment of our usual health.

Newt and Lizzy talk of going down in a day or two. Their object is to purchase a Parlons carpet, etc.! Tom Collins' wife died on last Monday and was buried yesterday. I have settled up that insurance matter with Baird. It amounted to $18.48.

If you have attended to having those teeth fixed, you can send them up by Mr. Shaw. Should your health be not better than when you wrote, you had better come up and recruit. Mother and the children join me in love to you, etc.!

Eliza W. Tomlinson

Tomlinson to Eliza
Cincinnati, Ohio, October 5, 1860

Dearest Eliza,

I had no time after discovering the boat, to sit down and bid you good-bye. We got here about 9 o'clock in the evening. Found things about as usual. Dick has got a regular sit, and so have I, probably. The weather is warm. I cut off my mustaches, and have taken off my undershirt.

I called on Dr. Hamlin about those teeth. He says he wants you down to fit them to the mouth. So you can make me a visit if you feel like it. Let me know beforehand, so that I can meet you at boat.

No special news

Yours ever and in a hurry,

Will Tomlinson

Eliza to Tomlinson
Ripley, Ohio, October 15, 1860

Dear Husband,

I arrived safely at home at about eight o' clock the same day on which I left you. The folks were all well. I found Uncle and Aunt Gates here from Va. They came the same night I left for Cin., and left about twelve o'clock, the same night that I got home, so I did not have the pleasure of seeing much of them. Aunt is nine years younger than mother and looks as if she was at least 18 or 20 younger. It is about two months since they left home. They have been visiting round at Bucyras, Bellefountaine, Sidney, and various other places.

The day before I got home the folks all dined at Newt's. Belle is fond of experiments you know, so she and Jess got hold of some bottles of medicine out in the smoke house and rubbed the contents of one of them on their faces. Next morning they were all over in blisters and Jess's eyes were so badly swollen that she could scarcely see. Belle's face was not quite so bad, but the skin is all coming off. Upon examination we found that it was Croton oil which they had rubbed over their faces.

Only see what a mistake I have made as to keeping to the paper lines. I will try and do better next time. Please give my best respects to Mrs. Olcroft and Mrs. Shaw. I know of no news that would be of interest to you.

Ever yours etc.,
Eliza W. Tomlinson

Belle is at school today. She was much pleased with her dishes. Byers was also pleased with his puzzle; he mastered it in a very short time. It is no longer a puzzle to either him or Belle.

* * * * *

Small amounts of croton oil, a highly toxic substance from a tropical plant, are found in some purgatives and external liniments. Newt must have stored chemicals and medicines for his medical practice in the smoke-house, where he probably thought they were safely kept out of harm's way. But for a curious seven-year-old like Belle, the temptation to play doctor and experiment with various remedies must have been irresistible. Fortunately, no permanent damage resulted. The same could not be said about the national scene. One irritation after another festered in the body politic, spreading contagion throughout and creating open wounds impossible to heal. Especially irritating for Tomlinson was William Yancey, a Southern defender of slavery and agitator for secession. When Yancey came to Cincinnati to make a pitch for Breckinridge, Tomlinson could find nothing positive to say about him. But then he was no fan of the Republicans, either.[13]

* * * * *

Tomlinson to Eliza
Cincinnati, October 22, 1860

Dearest Eliza,

Yours last week ought to have been answered more promptly, but I had nothing to write about. My health is good. Dick will move his family down this week. He has rented two rooms. There was another man found about midnight last night, on corner Broadway and Columbia, badly stabbed, probably fatally.

Byers' composition was very acceptable, and I took great interest in examining it and see tokens of intellectual vigor and originality of a high order, and I trust my noble boy will not fail to cultivate to the fullest extent those rare gifts of mind with which God has endowed him, and always with a view to honor his Creator and benefit his age and country. I would like him to write more and frequently, sending me copies. I will write him a long letter some of these days.

And that freak of Belle's with the medicine—has it disfigured her? I hope she will leave all suspicious cosmetics and vials alone after this. I feel thankful things were not worse.

Yancey, the great southern fire-eater, spoke here Saturday evening. I did not go to hear him, as I have no love for traitors and disunionists. Lincoln I have no doubt will be elected. Defeat to the Democracy, however, is not death. As in times past that old party will arise, unified and strong, unless Providence has given over our country to confusion and an ultimate resort to a monarchy and titled aristocracy, which is the aim of those who seek to blight our prosperity and crush the hopes of the oppressed of the world.

But I must close, take this to boat and go to work. God bless you.
Will Tomlinson

* * * * *

In 1860 Byers would have been thirteen years old. Only two essays from his youth survived, one about an event that would take place a few years later, and the one below, which may have been the one referred to by his father in the previous letter. If so, his father's praise was both generous and ironic, given the essay's topic and Tomlinson's susceptibility to alcoholism. Perhaps his father's praise was what prompted Byers to save it.

Answer to the composition of Miss E. Denison on
Temperance and Intemperance

Miss Denison: you said in your last composition that when an Irish or Duchman got a five dollar bill he would spend it for whiskey and set up a place called a dogery. I noticed something in your composition which is very common among the republicans when they speak of the faults of others. It is that they never speak of themselves or their dear little Negroes. So it was with you. You never said any thing about the Americans or the Negroes, but laid all the blame on the duch and Irish.

Now my little girl you should remember in your youth that you and others too should allways tell the truth, so in the future day no more about the Duchman's Whisky Shop or Store.

The Bible says first cast the beam out of thine own eye, and then shalt thou see clearly to cast the moat out of thy brother's eye. First clear the Americans, your own countrymen, of the sin of owning dogeries, and then it is time to cast the moat out of the eyes of your friends the duch and Irish, although it must be said that the eyes of some of them are clearer than your own.

My dear little miss, mind what you say about the Duch and be very carefull that you don't say to much. Those eyes now so bright and sparkling with delight might in future be dimed with tears of woe by marrying one of those Duchmen. You know for sure he would be hard on whisky and wine and would be too intemperate for a husband of thine.

I hope ere you go home a lesson you will have learned is Dutchmen and Irish men are not always to be spurned.[14]

Byers had a vested interest in defending the Irish and the "Dutch" (German), since his lineage included both. But he also may have felt compelled to offer an indirect defense of his father's politics and inclinations. Regardless of his motives, he chose a topic that was highly controversial at that time, especially in southern Ohio, where many Irish and German immigrants thought the temperance movement reflected a bias against their cultures. They placed great importance on social gatherings in public places that served alcoholic beverages. They were not the only consumers of alcohol, however. The production of alcoholic beverages, in the forms of wine, beer, and pure grain alcohol, played an important role in the state's economy, and "Ohio Whisky" had a national reputation. Cincinnati was proud of its breweries and beer gardens; in 1860 it had more than two thousand businesses that sold liquor. Temperance workers in the Queen City were not particularly welcome, and ordinances for closing beer gardens and pubs on Sundays were simply ignored.[15]

Tomlinson was certainly no stranger to the city's drinking establishments, and Eliza probably had good cause to be concerned about her husband's alcoholic consumption. Yet even she knew how to make a potent blackberry cordial. She jotted down her recipe for it on the back of the last page of a letter. Unfortunately, only the last page of the letter survived, but the front of the page listed details regarding property she owned south of the Grant House in Georgetown and urged the recipient (probably her husband) to attend to the matter "as soon as possible." Regardless of what happened to the property, her recipe was saved and, in her own words, appears below:

Blackberry Cordial

Good ripe fruit, simmer them over a moderate fire till they break to pieces. I then strain them through a flannel cloth. To each pint of liquor add a pint of sugar, half an ounce of powdered cinnamon, a quarter of an ounce of powdered mace, two teaspoons full of powdered cloves. Boil all fifteen minutes, strain it, and when cool, add to each pint of syrup, a wine glass of good, French Brandy. Bottle, cork, and seal it. I keep it cool.[16]

* * * * *

As the 1860 election drew near, political parades proliferated, even in the village of Ripley, where young men known as Wide Awakes marched in militia formations down the street at night. Their enameled black capes reflected the light of hoisted torches, which also gave an eerie glow to the eyeball painted on each raised banner. The use of such tactics to signal their unblinking loyalty to the Republican Party sent chills down the spines of Southerners, who called them "Black Republicans." But Northerners also had reservations about the faction's paramilitary pageantry and aggressive display of youthful power. Mounting tension on the national scene seemed to be reflected in the Tomlinson household. As one challenge after another piled up, friction between Eliza and her husband increased. Besides their ongoing financial struggles, the children were ill, and Tomlinson had apparently injured his knee in an accident. On top of everything else, he became lackadaiscal and disinclined to write or visit.[17]

Although not as grand as this procession in New York in 1860, a parade of Wide Awakes in Ripley was noted by Eliza Wylie Tomlinson in her letter of November 6, 1860. (Library of Congress Prints and Photographs Division)

* * * * *

Eliza to Tomlinson
Ripley, Ohio, November 3, 1860

Dear Husband,

Yours of the 29th by an unknown hand came safely to hand on yesterday. I am happy to learn that your health continues good.

We are all as well as usual. The children started to school this morning; I am glad to have them in school once more.

I was very much surprised at the liberty which Porter has taken in breaking open our house, etc. Few circumstances would justify such an act. If he wanted to get hold of your newspaper file, he certainly could have got the papers some place else; if he wanted to get hold of some of your private papers, he took a very unlawful way to get what he had no business with whatever. As to taking our wood, he can offer no excuse in my opinion for such a larceny. Frank says that the Register notices the sale of 18 feet off our lot to Newt; this is somewhat strange. What object can any one have in making such a notice? What do you think about it? Is it possible that lost deed has gotten into the hands of some one who will give us trouble about it?

Frank also asks in behalf of Williamson where that deed is which you was to leave him for Withrow. Of one thing I am certain—that you put it in your packet saying that you was going to give it to Williamson, and I am pretty certain that you afterward told me that you had done so. Williamson has probably either lost or mislaid it.

I have not yet written to Frank, shall probably do so in a day or two. I shall send this by Will Shaw, who is, I understand, going down tonight. As to getting that cost, I thought that I would not do so until I heard from you again.

I understand that the widow Penn has taken unto herself a young husband by the name of Hannows. Her sons threaten to kill him, so he had better look out for daggers, pistols, poison, etc.! Pleasant, ain't it?

Nothing of interest that I know of going on here at present. Adieu! Adieu!
Eliza W. Tomlinson

P.S. The enclosed bill was all right, Thank you! O, do you think that I had best go out to Des Moines this fall, or what do you think about it. Would the cost overrun the profit? Do you think of going back to Des Moines to live?

E. W. T.

The children have just come in from school. Byers says that he takes about the highest stand of any in his school. Belle is in a third Reader class: both are much pleased.

Eliza to Tomlinson
Ripley, Ohio, November 6, 1860

Dear Husband,

I fear that there is something more the matter with you beside your knee. We have been looking for you up ever since you wrote of your accident. I fear that you are sick or you would surely have written. How you are getting along? If able, you had better come up and stay until you are able to resume work. If it is necessary, let me know and I will come down at any time. I hope that you do not want for attention.

I have not heard anything more from Des Moines although I wrote Frank three weeks ago directing him to do as you told me with any funds of ours which he might have in his hands. If able now, when you cannot work, I wish you would write to him and Williamson relative to our affairs. Williamson would pay no attention to anything that I would say.

Well today determines the presidential contest. I for my part will be glad when it is over. I suppose that there is no chance for Douglas.

Last night the Democrats and wide awakes were both out in procession. The Democrats did not come down this far, so I did not see them. Byers was up a little while; he says that they made a fine appearance. They carried square lanterns with banners, they had forty or more oxen in the procession, a man on the back of every one. They were addressed by some gent on Market St. Please let us know how you are getting along as soon as possible.

Ever yours,

E. W. Tomlinson

Eliza to Tomlinson
Ripley, November 27, 1860

Dear Husband,

We have heard nothing from you since you left. I confidently expected one by yesterday's mail, but was disappointed. From what cause you have failed to write, I cannot imagine, but hope that it was not caused by sickness or any thing of that sort.

The health of this family is only tolerably good. Mother and the children have had colds. Byers's and Belle's throats have been worse and hurting them considerably for the last week. They do not get any worse, but since the weather has been so bad, I have kept them at home from school. Enclosed I send you a letter which I received from Frank this morning. You had better write to him and tell him if possible to get the balance which is wanting to pay the taxes out of Will Wylie, and if that is impossible, to get it from Williamson. Please write to me and let me know how your knee is getting. I am afraid that you have been using it too much. You will write to Frank, won't you? I think that the sooner that tax matter is attended to, the better. It appears a large sum, but it has been running on for so many years, is the trouble. Will Wylie is a mean rascal and ought by all means be made to pay up. He has treated us from the very first meanly. But I must conclude or I shall not get this in today's mail.

Ever yours,

Eliza W. Tomlinson

Tomlinson to Eliza
Cincinnati, December 3, 1860

Dearest Eliza,

Yours was duly received last Friday, and I should have replied earlier but I have been so tired. On coming back I found the new type on, and three regular cases vacated on account of the new type being larger than the old. So that I was again a sub. Week before last I had no work—last week I worked all week. My health is generally good. My heart bothers me occasionally.

I have not written to Frank—I have been pestered so much about it that I don't know that I shall do so at all.

What time does the school vacation take place, and are you going to send Byers down at that time?

I know nothing of interest. My leg is nearly well.

I send this by the boat in hopes that it may reach you early.

Ever yours,

Will Tomlinson

Tomlinson to Eliza
Cincinnati, December 10, 1860

Dearest Eliza,

I cannot account for it why letter-writing has become so irksome a task to me. I love to receive letters, but the aversion to writing is increasing. Your last requested an immediate answer; but I suppose that about the time I got yours you received mine. My health is about as usual. My heart threatens me frequently. Last week I had a sore throat, seeming to be an enlargement about the "apple." It is nearly well again. My knee is so that I can walk on the leg about as well as ever on a level or going down stairs; but going up stairs is more difficult. I hope that you are all better. I wish you would inquire of Byers or Newt whether the disease in the children's throats is incurable. I am getting much alarmed about it, and hope that no remedy will be spared.

The weather is miserably changeable, last night and this morning being too warm for an overcoat, and now (noon) it is blowing quite cold. We had a heavy rain this morning.

Politically the skies are gloomy. The President's message has only made matters worse, and I can see no light through the gloom. The abolitionists have finally done their work, and instead of the Union strong, great and respected, we are to become a divided, quarrelling, and unhappy people—a mere collection of petty states, without power of resistance to a foreign enemy, and without character to command the respect of the world. And all this for what? Merely to indulge the fratricidal ambition for place and power of a few leading sectional demagogues. On their leader and fomenter, the perjured and dishonored James Buchanan, be the tenfold curses of our children's children, heaped up until his memory shall utterly rot out, or live only to brighten the name of Arnold by its darker contrast.

Supper Time—I got along so far while waiting for dinner, and now I propose to fill out the page anyhow while waiting for supper. (There—just as I finished that last word the candle gave out.) So I'll just wind up for this time by the flicker of the wick.

Ever yours,
Will Tomlinson

* * * * *

Abraham Lincoln was elected the sixteenth president of the United States on November 6, 1860, with 40 percent of the popular vote and 180 of the 303 electoral votes. Southern Ohio, for all its ties to Southern interests, became a Republican stronghold that helped send him to the White House. Voters in Union Township in Brown County cast 628 votes for Lincoln; 343 for Douglas; and 45 for John Bell, the Constitutional Union Party candidate. Apparently none were tallied for John C. Breckinridge, the candidate from the Southern contingency of the Democratic Party. Meanwhile, James Buchanan was still the sitting president and would be until Lincoln's inauguration the following March. On December 4, Buchanan delivered his State of the Union address to Congress. In it he deplored the current state of affairs but offered no effective resolutions. Both sides, the North and the South, felt insulted by his remarks, but many Northerners felt particularly aggrieved since he placed most of the blame for the country's bitter divisiveness on Northern abolitionists who insisted on eliminating slavery. For the South, the election of Lincoln was the final breaking point, triggering a rapid secession of Southern states. On December 20, the state of South Carolina withdrew from the Union. Six days later, in the harbor at Charleston, U.S. Maj. Robert Anderson moved his men into battle-ready positions at Fort Sumter.[18]

CHAPTER SIX

Collision Courses

To embitter domestic life—maintain your opinion on
small matters at the point of the bayonet.
—*Freedom's Casket*, June 15, 1844

THE FIRST LIGHT of 1861 cast long, dark shadows on a country on the brink of civil war. As President-elect Lincoln, at home in Springfield, Illinois, navigated the choppy waters of assembling an administrative cabinet, preparations for war were already underway. Although war would not be officially declared until mid-April, on January 5, the merchant vessel *Star of the West* sailed from New York with fresh troops and supplies for the Union soldiers stationed at Fort Sumter, South Carolina. Meanwhile, the South had already begun seizing federal arsenals, and within a month's time six more states would follow South Carolina in seceding from the Union. In southern Ohio, Tomlinson and Eliza were dealing with a serious disagreement in their own relationship as a result of some remarks made by Eliza's mother. Their correspondence over the next few months would require thoughtful responses from each of them as they tried to repair the rift and also deal Tomlinson's proposal to relocate the family. In addition, there were still outstanding property issues requiring their attention, and the family had its share of health challenges.[1]

* * * * *

Dear Father,

We are all well except our throats, bad colds. During the vacation my throat was very sore and I spat blood and Uncles Byers and Newt told me to take care of myself or it might settle on my lungs and turn to the consumption—for that reason I did not go to Cincinnati. School had commenced again. We had only the time between Christmas and New Year for a vacation. I study the same books as last session. Uncle Byers said that smoking would do me no good. Mr. Hindman died last week. Alfred Belchambers has started a wholesale and retail grocery across the road. I received those two papers that you sent me. I have been too fast when I told you about our health, for Grandmother has been very unwell for the last week or two.

W. B. Tomlinson

Eliza to Tomlinson
Ripley, Ohio, January 6, 1861

Dear Husband,

As Byers has left so much blank paper, I thought that I would add a few lines. As I wrote you every week, I was surprised that when informed of the state of Byers' health, aside from pecuniary considerations, that you should expect one to send him to the city. It is absolutely necessary that he should be very careful of himself. I started him to school last week as usual, but have discontinued the Dutch [German] lessons owing to his having to attend them so late in the evening.

Sometime since I wrote to Mrs. Wylie telling her that I had repeatedly written to Will asking him for money, but as he paid no attention to my requests, I thought it useless to write to him again and in fact I did not know which to look to—him or her—for the rent. I told her that there had been nothing paid excepting what they had expended in fixing up the house, etc. I wished them to pay it over to Frank [Yokauer] to pay the taxes. In reply Nellie says he rented the property from you and will settle with you. Does he tell me the truth when he says that upon inquiring of you that I shall find that there is something paid?

I was thinking that probably he would bring in something in reference to that buggy business. I know one thing—that it was an unfortunate investment for us. He traded off our buggy and we lost by the operation $120 or $125, which you paid upon it besides other expenses. My opinion is that Will is a very great scoundrel and intends living in our house as long as he can without paying anything. You may write to him and tell him that the house is mine, that it was by my permission that you rented to him and that you have no more to do with it than he has with property for which he is agent. One thing—Will was a minor when he rented the property; therefore, I suppose he could not be held responsible, but I suppose that his mother could.

I have deferred writing to them until I should hear from you, but I would rather you would write to Will yourself. I have not heard anything from Frank for a long time. I wrote to him some 6 or 8 weeks ago and told him that I wanted him to get the money from Will Wylie and pay off those taxes, or if he could not, get it out of Will to get it from Williamson. I suppose that Frank thinks that he has sufficient to do to attend to his own business without troubling with mine. Well, I suppose that I was not only in a more gloomy mood than usual, but had the horrors badly when I wrote you last, but of one thing certain, my bad feelings were not caused by my being with mother.

On the contrary, I am thankful that I am with her; poor Mother has not only bad health and the infirmities of age to contend with but many other troubles, and I am very sorry that any one connected with her should entertain anything but kind feelings toward her, for surely there does not exist a human being who takes a warmer interest in the welfare of others than what she does in that of ours and all other branches of our family, not only in the things pertaining to this life but that which is to come. When she sees any of us violate the laws of nature and of God, she is sorely grieved! And if she remonstrates with us, 'tis only for our own good! We all ought to look into our own hearts and see if all is right there, and if not, strive to make so.

Ever yours, etc.,
Eliza W. Tomlinson

Dearest Eliza,

Yours and Byers of the 5th was received Thursday. I supposed Byers had dated it wrongly, but I find it postmarked on the 7th. I was very glad indeed to find some little explanation of your former letter, though it is not fully cleared up yet. Something has happened which I don't understand. As to mother, I can say that I have not an unkind feeling toward her, but her expression of ridicule and unbelief in my desire to promote her comfort and happiness, on that memorable night, will never be forgotten, and like the costly vase once broken, can never be repaired to its original soundness. A thing of that kind sinks deeply within me—more so than those who only know my rough exterior might suppose possible. My health is not quite as good as I could wish, as I have caught cold, and it is settled in my right breast as a painful pleurisy. Whether or no it will wear off without medical remedies, I can't say. I suffer a good deal with it, and an accompanying cough. I have not yet got a case, and depend on chance jobs of "subbing" for meeting current expenses. I have hopes that things will shortly mend in this respect.

Well, the war is upon us—blood will shortly flow—the strong arms of the North and hot heads of the South will probably meet in collision in a few days. Where it will end God only knows. I look ahead a few weeks and see the cities of the South smoking in ruins—their inhabitants seeking shelter in negro cabins—their people starving and terror-stricken—their four millions of slaves rebelling, rising rampant and spreading flames and massacre—business stopped and ruin everywhere. Here men will be called upon to arm—to march—to fight their fellow-countrymen. And all for why? Because of the success of a miserable faction of false philanthropists and banded political renegades and public plunderers. Already our country has suffered the loss of millions upon millions—the poor are starving—the rich trembling. And this, too, in the midst of bountiful harvests, peace with all foreign nations, and all the teachings and facilities of the gospel of good will.

Will it come directly home to us—to our own families and firesides? I fear it will. If Kentucky goes, as it seems probable she will be driven to do by Black Republican policy—if Missouri, Virginia, and Maryland join the ultra southern confederacy, as the same cause seems to be forcing them to do—then right here on the Ohio River—in Ripley and Cincinnati—will bloody work ensue more terrible ten thousand fold than were ever known in the romantic days of the Boones, Kentons, etc. I may be called upon by my government, and even my boy may yet be subject to draft in the same war. I now see no hope. War is declared. Four states have declared their independence—the others of the fifteen will probably follow. The State of Mississippi has ordered and planted cannon at Vicksburg to intercept free navigation.

Enclosed find $2.00.

Ever yours,

Will Tomlinson

P.S.—I never received any money or anything else from Will. Wylie on rent. He or Mrs. Wylie owes you for the whole time they have been there at the rate of $5.00 per month. I will write to Will, as you request, and insist on payment. I did not agree to ever allow for painting the house and will not now.

Eliza to Tomlinson
Ripley, Ohio, January 21, 1861

Dear Husband,

From your letter of last week I am sorry to learn that you were not very well. I hope that you have recovered entirely ere this. You should take every precaution to preserve your health, or to restore it when not good. We also have had bad colds, are some better at present. There are some expressions in your letter which I do not understand. You were glad to find some explanation of my former letter, though it is not fully cleared up yet. Something, you say, has happened which you do not understand. What a strange fancy you have taken. I can assure you that any thing you wish to know of which I have any knowledge, you only have just mention the fact and I will give you all the satisfaction in my power. I have ever tried to perform my duties in all relations of life and have no concealments to make. I am truly sorry that your feelings are not altogether what I could desire towards mother. She, you should remember, is not now either mentally or physically what she once was. Would you retain resentment towards a child for any expression it might make to you! I know that you would not because of the undeveloped state of its intellect. Then why should we not much more overlook the imperfections of age, this not being the period when the mind is daily gaining vigor, but on the contrary losing the power to reason. But I wish now forever to bid adieu to this subject!

Sarah Ann had a young daughter on last Thursday. I am told that it is a very large child; both mother and child are doing well. Our friends in this section are all well so far as I have any knowledge. The weather is fine for this season of the year. The river is quite high, and yet rising I am told, so no fear of its freezing over this winter.

If you have not got well, you had better come up and stay until you can recruit your health.

You draw a deplorable picture of the future prospects of our country! Should all the southern states secede, then truly we shall be crippled in our energies, but I trust that they have wisdom enough to perceive that their own safety and wellbeing depends upon their connection with this federal government. The seceding states deserve a good drubbing. They are <u>traitors</u> every one of them, but I hope that affairs will be satisfactorily adjusted without bloodshed.

There is no news of interest that I know of. The children join me in love to Pap. I ever remain yours affectionately,

Eliza W. Tomlinson

Tomlinson to Eliza
Cincinnati, February 4, 1861

Dearest Eliza,

It is now two o'clock Monday morning so I must be very brief. I intended writing Sunday afternoon, but went to sleep. I received a letter from Will Wylie. He wants to settle, but says he has no money. He is going to open a Dry goods store in the tannery block. Enclosed $.

Eliza to Tomlinson
Ripley, Ohio, February 12, 1861

Dear Husband,

I presume you have quite exciting times in the city today, as I understand that Lincoln is to pass through on his way to Washington City. Lyons Pangburn and Mag went down last night, I suppose to get a sight of the great man. Doubtless there were others went—I know not. Mother and I have both been so unwell that we have not been out any place to hear what is going on. As I wrote you before, I have had a severe cold for some time. It still troubles me considerably, but I think that I do not feel quite so bad this morning as what I did. The children are both as well as usual. Br. Newt is not very well; he has a very bad cough and looks badly.

Thank you for the enclosed bill in your last. I expected a letter from you by last night's mail, but it did not come, probably it may tonight. I know of nothing of interest going on here just now aside from the general anxiety felt by all in the deplorable state of disorganization in which our country is at present. The weather is fine, almost too fine I fear for health, or the future interest of fruit growers. O, I had almost forgotten to tell you that Belle has been promoted to the first class. She is very much pleased, but I am somewhat afraid that the studies will be too hard for her, and she will not be able to keep up. The scholars in the class are all so much older than what she is. But I must bid you adieu for the present.

Ever yours etc.,
Eliza W. Tomlinson

* * * * *

Eliza's news was accurate. February 12 was indeed an exciting day in Cincinnati. On the day of his fifty-second birthday, President-elect Lincoln stopped there on his way to the nation's capital. Crowds jammed the streets from the train depot to the Burnett House, the grand hotel where he stayed and delivered two addresses. In an address to a crowd of German immigrants, Lincoln declared his commitment to the greatest good for the greatest number and affirmed working men as the basis of all governments. On the burning issues of the day, however, he offered no enlightenment or indication of what was to come. But that did not stop the press from mythologizing the giant but humble man. According to one *New York Times* correspondent, the applause and cheers at Lincoln's speeches were loud enough to bring the walls of Jericho down; and his boots, resting outside his hotel room that night, were as long as a sheet of foolscap—a piece of paper thirteen to sixteen inches in length. On the same day that the lanky giant left his footprints in the Queen City, another president-elect, Jefferson Davis, was on the way to his own inauguration in the Confederate capital, Montgomery, Alabama. Meanwhile, along the Ohio River, the trials and triumphs of everyday life still took center stage for those who labored out of the limelight.[2]

William Lowry (Friend) to Eliza
Des Moines, Iowa, February 17, 1861

Dear Friend,

Your letter of January 18th reached us in due time. Mary was up home at the time, so I forwarded it to her. We were pleased to hear from you. Mary is still at home and I presume by this time has answered your letter. I have spoken to Frank about renting your house; I have rented it for $50 per year from the 1st of March. For the times the rent is rather high, but I will always try to meet it. The Wileys are still in the house. Frank was to notify them yesterday. My respects to Mr. Tomlinson.

Yours truly,

William Lowry

Eliza to Tomlinson
Note on back of Lowry's letter

In thinking over matters, I think that you had probably best write to him and tell him where to ship the goods to. I have just written to him requesting him to make sale of what things remain unsold, and to box up our beds, bedding, wearing apparel, books, paper, etc., and have them ready for shipment when ordered. You would understand better what directions to give than what I do. But write immediately what you do and what you wish one to do.

* * * * *

While Lincoln stole into Washington undercover to thwart an assassination plot, Tomlinson was evidently on a secret mission of his own. Without telling Eliza, he had slipped across the state to Athens, a college town tucked in the hills along the Hocking River. Perhaps he was looking for a safer place than Ripley where the family could be together again and ride out the coming war. He may also have heard about the town's reputation as a center of learning. Ohio University, founded there in 1804 as the state's first public institution of higher education, would offer excellent educational opportunities for Byers and Belle and provide an intellectual milieu that was missing in Ripley. In writing to Eliza, Tomlinson pointed out that Athens also had a new high school to challenge Byers and a seminary, or upper-level school for girls, where Belle could continue her education.[3]

* * * * *

Tomlinson to Eliza
Athens, Ohio, March 3, 1861

Dearest Eliza,

I suppose Dick passed through Ripley and let you know about my coming up here, as he promised me he would. Therefore I deferred writing until I should know exactly what I had to write about.

My health is excellent, and I feel already more "settled down" than I ever did. I have full charge of the mechanical department of the "Messenger," a copy of which I sent you on Thursday. I arrived here on Tuesday afternoon and went to work on Wednesday. My wages are $10 per week, payable every Saturday, or whenever I want it. The office is well supplied with material, all the type being new. The proprietor is not a printer—is married but has no children yet. I am boarding at the hotel.

Athens is a very fine town, built in and all around a hill, with hills around in every course. It is about the size of Ripley. The Marietta and Cincinnati Railroad passes through here. There is also a branch striking off about 20 miles below here for Portsmouth. So that to get here from Ripley the route would be to take the Portsmouth packet, and then the railroad for Athens. The exact fare I cannot say, but it is $4.75 from Cincinnati.

Here are the best facilities for a thorough education of any town in Ohio. The Union School House is a fine large building, about 75 feet square, three stories high. The upper story is all one hall. There is also a seminary, but the particulars about it I have not ascertained. Then to complete those primary institutions is the University, which is celebrated for turning out thorough scholars and prudent, practical men.

I have been inquiring some about a house to rent, but it will be difficult. However, the gentleman whose place I take in the office has a house which would suit, with about half an acre of ground attached. He moves out on the 20th of this month, into the jail building, he having been appointed Sheriff to fill a vacancy by resignation. There is an encumbrance on the property to the amount of about $500. He asks $800 altogether for the property, and thinks he could make arrangements to release the encumbrances for Iowa property at a fair rate. But I will inquire further about matters and things, there being plenty of time, and my contract runs by the year.

I should judge from what little I have seen, that living here would be cheaper than in Ripley.

The excitement hereabouts on the subject of Petroleum or Coil Oil wells is something like the Pike's Peak fever at Des Moines. This is in the region of oil wells, and yesterday I printed a lot of blank leases for "Oil Diggings."

Since I have been able to get my regular sleep again, I feel a great deal better. It certainly must have been the want of sleep which for the last few months has made me feel so unnaturally cross, careless and wicked. I feel as if I was just coming to myself again, and I have once more some hopes for the future, especially for the welfare of you and our beloved children. The great drawback in all this is, that it seems cruel to separate you and mother, but I see no other way unless she would come with you, which would be to me the most desirable and happy arrangement.

If I buy property, there will be room enough for us all. But I have just hinted at a number of things, of which I want you to write me fully and freely. As to going back to Iowa, and comparing the winter they have had there with the one here, I have now no notion. After the education of the children has been properly attended to, I shall feel satisfied with anything. But I do not want you to live here or in any other place (because I do) unless you can be satisfied, and enjoy yourself, as to know you were discontented and miserable would be wretchedness itself to me.

Last night I met with a very esteemed old friend—Lot Smith—who studied law with Hamer. He was formerly Senator from this District and is one of the principal men of the county. He is a lawyer. I shall consult him fully as to any property before I touch it.

The robins, and other sweet warblers of the spring, awaken me early, so that I have had breakfast, and finish this by 8 o'clock.

Ever yours,
Will Tomlinson
Enclosed find $2.
Mary's letter is all safe.

* * * * *

The Hamer that Tomlinson mentioned was probably Thomas Lyon Hamer, mentioned in Chapter 3, in connection with Tomlinson's service in the Mexican War. Hamer had died in 1846 but probably knew Tomlinson in Georgetown even before the war. Tomlinson, it seems, had a knack for running into people he knew or had some association with. Although he did not specify who led him to the *Messenger* in Athens, it is interesting to note that, once again, he was seeking employment with a newspaper that was Republican. Of course, it was a propitious time for finding work with newspapers supporting the new administration. On March 4, the day after Tomlinson wrote to Eliza of his arrival in Athens, Lincoln was sworn in as president of the United States. Eliza, meanwhile, had made a big decision. But she was still unsure of the logistics involved, including what to do with their pet bird Eddy.[4]

* * * * *

Eliza to Tomlinson
Ripley, Ohio, March 6, 1861

Dear Husband,

I have just received yours of the 3rd inst., from which I am most happy to learn that your health is good. You took me very much by surprise by leaving the city, but I presume it was the best thing you could have done. I do not think that you get very liberal wages, but probably considering the expenses of the place, $10 would amount to as much as $15 in some other places. Athens is a town that I know but little about, but presume that it is a desirable location to any person having children to educate. This with me is an object that I would be willing to make almost any sacrifice to accomplish. My only objection as you anticipate is that of leaving Mother now when she is so feeble, and life's remaining sands appear to be so few! Having been tried so recently in the furnace of affliction, I feel reluctant to cause her one additional pang, but I am sensible that I owe a duty to my children that is paramount to all duties, and I think that I can probably best fulfill that obligation by joining you in Athens. That is, as soon as we can make our arrangement to suit. This of course cannot be for some weeks to come.

I shall write to Frank to ship our goods for this point. I do not know but that it would be better to have them shipped directly for Athens, but as it takes up so much time to consult you, I think that I will have them shipped here in the first place, but upon second thought, I think that I shall await your answer to this, so you will please answer immediately and let me know what you wish me to do.

Lowry has rented our house, but I shall enclose his letter. As to trading for property in Athens, you had probably best not be in a hurry. Possibly you can do better; our house in Des Moines is valuable, and if not at present, will in the future command a high price. Probably that gentleman would trade for that land of mine; it ought to be worth something considerable being located in the best section of the state. By the way, I have forgotten our agent's name in Marshal County, and I presume that it is about time that the tax was paid. His card and letter was deposited in the packet of your trunk. Will you write to him or direct me what to do. I do not know the No. of the land or the necessary items pertaining to the case. I instructed Newt to get his agent to attend to our Walnut St. house (S.E.) renting and collecting the rent, etc. In your letter you did not say what you was going to do with regard to that Brooks property. I think that it would probably be as well just to let it go. If it is ever worth the money, you can probably make some arrangement to take up the mortgage.

My health is only tolerably good. I have had a very bad cold and pain in my side for some time. I am some better of that just now, but have had diarrhea. The children are as well as usual; they are both at school. I believe that they are making pretty good progress in their studies. O, what shall I tell Frank to do with Eddy?

I think it rather strange that Will Wylie is going to open a dry-goods store and yet has no money to pay us. The truth is he never intends doing so. He is a scoundrel and I never intend to give him an opportunity to defraud me again. I did not direct any one to warn Will out of our house but am glad that it has been done. Two years' rent is too much to lose without having the amount increased. I do not know of any news that would be of interest to you. Brothers Byers' and Newt's folks are all as well as usual. Please write immediately.

Ever yours etc.,

Eliza Tomlinson

Please describe the property you mentioned in your letter.

Dear Husband,

Last night I received yours of the 12th inst., from which I am happy to learn that your health continues good. Why my letter should have been so long delayed upon the road I cannot imagine. The health of our family is about as usual—Belle has a bad cold, the pain in my side discommodes one considerably, some times 'tis imposable for me to sew as I used to do. The pain is so intolerable that I cannot work or sit still, but still I manage to keep the children's wardrobe in passable order. I should like very much to know whether you wish to move us up to Athens this spring or summer. As I said before, my principal objection to going is leaving Mother, old, feeble, and infirm as she now is; it does appear almost cruel for me to do so, but Newt's folks will, I am confident, do all in their power to make her comfortable and happy. Lizzie is good and kind.

In my last I informed you that I had written to Frank requesting him to pack up our goods and have them ready to order. Have you written him relative to the matter? Where do you wish them shipped for?

There is nothing of interest going on here that I know of excepting I am informed that Ad Murphy is to be married this week to Fulton's clerk. Her parents were very much opposed to the match for a long time but have finally given their consent.

O what do you think of the President's policy in withdrawing the troops from Fort Sumter? It does appear to me one of the very last measures that I would have adopted to bring traitors back to their allegiance. I would have hung every mother's son of them, high as Hamor first. Such a measure argues imbecility in the present incumbent and want of power upon the part of government. I may be wrong, there may be wisdom in Lincoln's policy, but I must confess 'tis too deep for me to fathom.

Please write at your earliest convenience and let me know what you desire doing regarding your prospects, etc. I wish you would write to Frank; possibly he could do something with your old account books. I am glad that you enjoy your self, are becoming more hopeful, attend church, etc. The performance of our moral and natural duties generally results in a pleasant state of feeling, whereas a violation of the known laws of our being cause anguish. Unhappiness is caused by the misconduct of others; under such circumstances we have nothing to reproach ourselves with. But 'tis time this was in the mail.

Good bye, ever yours, etc.,

Eliza W. Tomlinson

Eliza must have been misinformed about Lincoln's plans for Fort Sumter. For weeks the president had been conferring with his cabinet and military advisers about the precarious situation there. Should more supplies and reinforcements be sent to the Union troops? Should Union troops remain passive in the face of growing Confederate deployments? Although Lincoln never ordered the withdrawal of Union troops from Charleston Harbor, there were those who thought he should, including Gen. Winfield Scott, who made such a recommendation on March 28. Regardless of who proposed such a strategy, Eliza thought that person should be hung as high as Hamor, the Hivite ruler of Shechem and father of Shechem. In the story from Genesis 34, Hamor's son, Shechem, raped Dinah, the daughter of Jacob and Leah. In revenge, her brothers killed Hamor, Shechem, and all the males of the city of Shechem. A violent allusion, to be sure, and one that would, lamentably, become prophetic in the years ahead.[5]

* * * * *

Tomlinson to Eliza
Athens, Ohio, March 14, 1861

Dearest Eliza,

I commenced this letter before breakfast, but whether it will be finished before that meal I cannot now say. My health continues as good as it ever was in my life. I board at Brown's Hotel, get excellent fare, have a nice room, and pay $2.50 per week. I send you the paper every week, from which you can see the prices in the market. Particularly notice beef, which is 4 cents for fore-quarters and 5 cents for hindqr. I think I can save a good snug little sum on $10.00 per week. Besides I get my full rest, and feel content. The town is ancient, and I hear every body speak highly of the goodness, sociability, etc., of the people. As to the educational facilities, they are perhaps the most desirable in the State.

As to mothers' coming up with you, as I suggested, you say nothing. There would be no change of climate, and I think coming here would be a pleasure and benefit to her. There need be no fatigue coming: 6 or 7 o'clock, sleep all night comfortably on the boat; next morning take the cars, and reach here at 5 o'clock in the afternoon, all in daylight. As to our goods, let them be shipped to your address at Ripley. This will be the best. Write so to Frank. I am glad that Lowry is in our house. He is a good tenant and will take good care of everything. I shall write to him and Frank both either this or next week. It is that land of yours that I propose trading in part payment for a house here, if I can do so to any good advantage.

The name of your agent in Marshall Co., Iowa, is Thomas Mercer, Marietta, Marshal Co., Iowa. The numbers of your land are:

S. E. 1/4 N. W. 1/4}

N. E. 1/4 S. W. 1/4}

By writing to him he will let you know the amount of taxes which can be forwarded afterward in Ohio or Eastern paper.

As to that Brooks property, I think the best way is to give it back and raise the mortgage—otherwise it will be a debt hanging over me, swallowing up double or treble the original sum. I shall send to Williamson for a proper form of deed and description.

I am sorry that your health is not good, but of course you take all proper care of yourself. I think this country will just agree with you.

About "Eddy," would it not be best to make Frank a present of him? We can purchase birds at far less cost than it would be to get him here and the rough usage on the road would probably kill poor Eddy. Frank is his friend, and let them not be parted. As to Will Wylie—I have not yet answered his letter. When I do, I shall get all the information possible about the prospect of two years' rent being paid.

Mr. Kason of Des Moines has been appointed by Lincoln to First Assistant Postmaster General of the United States.

You ask me to describe the property I spoke of. To give only an outline, I will say—It contains 6 rooms, is a story-and-a-half frame, back porch, kitchen and corn room attached, well fenced, 55/100ths of an acre of ground, which is over the size of two ordinary town lots. In this lot is a spring of as pure water as there is in the State. It will probably be some two weeks before I know whether I can make a satisfactory trade.

There—I have answered your letter in detail. This is the morning of Belle's birthday anniversary. O, how I would delight to see her on this occasion, but better luck next time. I kiss [a] picture of her instead of her. And Byers, I know he is a good boy, and attentive to his lessons. I would like to have him write me.

The oil excitement is up pretty high here. Some will make fortunes out of it.

My love to mother and Lizzie, etc. Respects to all old friends. By the way, suppose you see Frank Straw and ascertain what it would cost to frame those pictures. I don't believe we can get it done as well here. I want heavy frames, plain rosewood or dark color, with an edging of gilt next the glass-frame to measure at least 3 inches.

But my breakfast bell is ringing, and I think I have done well for one morning.

Ever yours,
Will Tomlinson

* * * * *

Moving from place to place never seemed to bother Tomlinson. In the spring of 1861, he was thirty-seven years old and had already lived in three countries, three states, and a dozen or more towns and cities. Eliza and her family, the Wylies, were deeply rooted in Ripley, however. Extracting her mother from the area where her two remaining sons lived and where her husband, three of her children, and several of her grandchildren were buried would have been a daunting challenge. But regardless of Sarah's ties to Ripley, the next two months would bring momentous change to the Tomlinsons—and the rest of the country as well.[6]

~

CHAPTER SEVEN

Volunteer Frenzy

War is the greatest curse that can
befall a nation, except dishonor or slavery.
—*Freedom's Casket,* June 15, 1844

THE TOMLINSONS never made it to Athens. The war changed everything—
their plans, their lives, their world. On Friday, April 12, 1861, when Confederate forces fired upon Fort Sumter, the news reached Cincinnati
within hours of the attack. On Monday, April 15, when President Lincoln
issued a call for 75,000, ninety-day volunteers from the Northern states,
Ohio was ready. On that same day, Governor William Dennison issued a
call for troops and urged the Ohio legislature to appropriate one million
dollars for the defense of the state and country. On Thursday, April 18,
an item in the *Ripley Bee* stated that "Will Tomlinson acted as Secretary
of a meeting of printers, held at Cincinnati, on Tuesday, to form a volunteer company."[1]

Ohio alone put up more than 12,000 volunteers. Tomlinson was among
the thousands who rallied at Camp Harrison, on the old Trotting Park
at the fairgrounds just outside Cincinnati. Crowds of men jostled and
jousted with each other, excited about doing their part to put down the
traitors across the river. The atmosphere was more like a rowdy picnic
than an orderly enlistment of soldiers. Tomlinson's company of printers
was probably only too glad to join in the euphoria, but the printers were
also regarded as good soldier material. The education, skills, and disci-

pline that their trade required—working with language, numbers, rules, forms, and columns of tightly marshaled files—may have given them an edge over the throngs of more rudimentary tradesmen eager to enlist for three months of service. In becoming Company I of the Fifth Regiment of the Ohio Volunteer Infantry, the men from the Typographical Union were among the first ten companies to be mustered in. When an election was held for regimental officers, Samuel H. Dunning was elected colonel, John H. Patrick as lieutenant colonel, and Charles L. Long as major. Also elected were Caleb C. Whitson as regimental quartermaster and Will Tomlinson as quartermaster sergeant.[2]

The information in the Regimental Descriptive Book for April 20 lists Tomlinson as being five feet eight, with a dark complexion, brown hair, and blue eyes. He is also listed as having been born in Seaton, England, and as being thirty-four years old—three years younger than his real age. It is possible that Tomlinson's age was erroneously recorded, but, given his eagerness to enlist, it is not unlikely that he lied about his age. Perhaps he thought that being younger would increase his chances of being promoted or sent to the battlefront. The average age for Union soldiers when they enlisted was 25.8 years, with only 30 percent being married. Tomlinson, at thirty-seven, was not only older than most enlisted men but was married and had two children at home. He was also among the minority of Union soldiers (24 percent) not born in the United States. An additional note in the Descriptive Book for Company I lists a scar on his left arm near the elbow, caused by a dog bite. He would carry many more scars—most of them inside—before his war service ended. In the spring of 1861, however, he had high hopes for his country and what it stood for—liberty, enlightentment, and justice.[3]

No explicit statement regarding his motives for enlistment has survived, but in his letters Tomlinson wrote that the Union army was God's instrument for crushing "terrorism and despotism" and that its mission was "the same as that wherefore Christ came hither and was crucified." His ideological stance and religious convictions were obviously intertwined, and, like most soldiers in the Civil War, he believed that God and was on his side. It was better, he stated, "to be remembered among the noble army of martyrs than basely live a coward slave, yielding all of manhood, right, and truth and God." His use of the word *manhood* may also suggest the presence of other motives often cited by those who enlisted early in the war: courage, honor, and duty. In addition, given his personal history of always being on the move, his constant involvement in risk-taking situations, and his ambitious desire for public acknowledgment, he probably welcomed the opportunity for adventure and advancement. In letters written during the summer and fall of 1861, he frequently alluded to his persistent campaign for being engaged in battle and obtaining a commission.[4]

Eliza was even more vocal in her support of the Union cause—especially during her husband's period of enlistment in 1861. Her letters emphasize the Union's just and righteous cause in vanquishing traitors and enemies of the best government the sun ever set on. As a granddaughter of two patriots of the American Revolution, she freely invoked the nation's forefathers. Her pride was bursting when her husband enlisted, and she wanted the world to know about it. The April 25 edition of the *Ripley Bee* reprinted the following letter from the *Cincinnati Gazette*:

RIPLEY, O., March 20, 1861

DEAR HUSBAND:—I have just received yours of the 18th, which contains a confirmation of what I saw stated in the papers. You need not entertain any fears of my censuring you for what you have done. However much I deplore the necessity of such a proceeding on your part I cannot the act. On the contrary, I must say that I glory in the patriotic ardor and love of country you display. I would not give a copper for a man who would not volunteer to the rescue of his country, when her institutions, her property, and lives of her citizens were assailed by traitors. Go! I say go! and assist in the redemption of our name, as a nation, from the insult, from the obloquy, cast upon us by a band of unprincipled miscreants who are capable of any crime however dark its hue.

My prayers shall be with you for the prosperity and success of your just and righteous cause. A God of justice—a God of power will not suffer the destruction of this noble fabric, purchased by the toil and privations and sacrifices of our forefathers. No! no! It cannot be that God will forsake us in this hour of need. He will give strength, energy and wisdom to our leaders, and lead our army to victory! The cause of the just shall prosper.

Should your company be called into active service, I should be very glad to have you come up before you leave, if possible; but if you cannot do so conveniently, we will have to be reconciled to separate without saying "good bye" in person * * * My warmest love and best wishes shall go with you, for your happiness and prosperity in time; but when you and I shall throw off "this mortal coil," may we meet in a happier sphere, where whatever our merit, we shall receive our just reward.[5]

ELIZA W. TOMLINSON

* * * * *

One month later, in a personal note written to her husband, Eliza expressed her concerns about the practical aspects of going to war. From the first, Ohio, like most Northern states and the federal government, was hard pressed to supply troops with adequate provisions. Even worse, existing provisions were sometimes constructed of poor material. Such was the case with uniforms distributed to some Ohio regiments. In his June 6, 1861, dispatch to the *Cincinnati Gazette,* war correspondent Whitelaw Reid exposed the shoddy nature of uniforms made from factory sweepings that wore out as fast as wrapping paper. Tomlinson, as a quartermaster sergeant, would have been on the front line for receiving constant complaints from poorly outfitted troops. By October, the need for warm, sturdy clothing and good blankets was so critical that Governor Dennison issued an urgent plea to Ohio's civilians to donate as many serviceable items as they could to the quartermaster general in Columbus. Eliza was doing all she could to provide her husband and his men with comforts from home. But she was also dealing with inadequate provisions, thanks to delinquent renters, so-called friends, and other scoundrels who were playing loose and free with the Tomlinson's property in Iowa.[6]

* * * * *

Eliza to Tomlinson
Ripley, Ohio, April 25, 1861

Dear Husband,

I write this to let you know that I will send you down a couple of blankets on the packet tomorrow. Mr. Fox brought in a couple of nice blankets yesterday; he said that I had better keep them and send you some that had been in use as you would give them rough usage, so I thought that as we had a couple here I would send them instead. One of them is nearly new, having been used very little, and is as good as the new ones. The other one has been more worn but is yet a good blanket and will stand a good deal of usage. You will also find a couple of your old shirts and a pair of drawers in the package. I wish that I had a dozen of good shirts to send you, but as it is not in my power to do so, you will have to empty that lack as best you can.

I hope that you do not fare badly and keep your spirits up! We can doubtless whip the traitors if it comes to a trial of strength! Our men taken in mass are far superior to those of the southern states, not only physically and mentally, but in acquired knowledge far excel them, not only so but they have the energy and all the necessary facilities requisite for carrying on and maintaining war if it should last ten years. I fancy that it will not require ten months, to conquer a peace honorable to our government, and hope it will be done in as many weeks. We have got to choose between a dilemma of two things, either to acknowledge the independence of the southern confederacy or whip them as they do their rebellious slaves until they shall gladly submit to our just requisitions and acknowledge their own folly. I hope that you will take every necessary precaution to preserve your health, and if called into battle never expose your person unnecessarily. Prudence is said to be the better part of valor.

Our family are as well as usual. Newt is quite unwell; he has taken a violent cold and coughs almost incessantly. He does not take anything to relieve it; we feel very uneasy about him. I believe that brother Byers' folks are well; I think if there was anything the matter I would hear it. The excitement continues unabated, there is little talked of excepting war. There is no news here that I know of, of special importance. Good bye, and may the God of justice, love, and mercy ever be with you to shield and to protect you from the evil machinations of wicked and treacherous men and bring our hosts off victorious in every battle in which they may engage is my most ardent desire. Adieu! Adieu! May you be blessed with all that is kind and true.

Ever yours in the bonds of love,
Eliza W. Tomlinson

F. Yokauer to Eliza
Des Moines, Iowa, May 3, 1861

My Dear Friend,

But a few minutes ago W. Lowry told me that you had written him to know whether I was sick or had left town. Neither is the case. Your goods are all packed up with the exception of the picture and the clocks. The large picture I could not pack so as to ensure a safe arrival in Ohio. The same is I am afraid with the clocks. If I had not had my bedding packed a long time ago, I might have put the clock in that. Mr. Tomlinson wrote to me some time ago requesting me to send his hickory cane, the same that was prescribed to him by the locating commissioners; but it is nowhere to be found. I never knew what value T. attached to it and so took no special care of it, and when I went to have it up, I could not find it. So I am afraid that I am to blame for the loss of it. The axe, hoe, rake, and spade, which I left in the shed, were stolen by somebody who wanted to make garden I suppose. I have sold your brown dish for $1.00, one of the two bedsteads and mattress for $3.00 to Lowry. I have not yet packed up the books but will do so at an early day, and if I can not do so in time, I will send you the other goods, 3 boxes in advance. I am just now very busy, getting up a large pamphlet for a lady in Winterset who thinks women ought to preach as well as men, and tries to prove it. On the 15th our Legislature will convene, when I think to get a place as reporter. Every body is excited. M. M. Crocker and D. U. Frick have raised companies. T. W. Jones is captain of a squadron of cavalry. Almost everybody thinks of going to war. Party differences are forgotten and all are now only Union men. T. A. Williamson is capt. of the "Home Guard."

Give Belle my heart and thanks for her presents. Eddy shall have good times provided, green apples, sugar, cabbage, etc.; I can secure them for him.

I spoke to Mr. Williamson repeatedly about that tax business, and he promised as often to attend to it, but I don't think he has done much about it. The property has been sold for taxes and has to be redeemed ere three years. The longer you postpone paying your taxes inside of three years, the less percentage you have to pay, proportionally. Now the percentage will be about 30%, in three years only about 11 or 12%. I understand Mr. B. T. Allen is agent for the house on Walnut Street. A Dr. Beach lives in it since Mrs. Scott left there.

How is your health and the children's? I learn Mr. T. joined a company. Much luck shown to him. When you write to him, tell him that as yet I have not succeeded in settling certain accounts in the encampments owing to the absence of J. W. Jones and afterward of L. Kinsey. You may also tell him that H. Hosie is U.S. Marshal and has not been in town since I received his letter. Until this is satisfactorily settled, I shall not apply for a clearance card.

Hoping to hear soon that all are well and prospering
I am as ever your friend,
F. P. Yokauer

Eliza to Tomlinson
Ripley, Ohio, May 10, 1861

Dear Husband,

Yours of the 5th inst. came to hand yesterday. Am happy to learn that your health continues good and that you are looking forward to a bright future. I have been very uneasy about you since this protracted spell of wet weather. I hope that you are better housed, and more likely furnished with the necessary requisites to render you comfortable than what you were when I was down. I wrote you a letter but Saturday and sent it together with a package containing five very nice silk pockets fancifully turned, which I was at some pains to make as nice as I possibly could. I also in the packet sent you sufficient of that patent soap to last you during the campaign. The packets each of them had the name of one of the officers of your company written on a card and pinned upon it. Sam Pangburn gave the package to Oscar Shaw and requested him to leave it at the Gazette Office, which he promised to do. I am afraid that you have not got it. I should be sorry that it should have fallen into any other hands than yours! Please write and let me know whether you received it or not.

I wrote on yesterday evening by Mrs. Ammen; but as I forgot to enclose that note of C. Baird's, I shall send it this morning. I have been quite sick for the past week, am better now but very weak. The children are as well as usual. Mother's health does not improve any that I can perceive. The rest of the folks are in their usual health so far as I know.

On yesterday I received a couple of letters from Des Moines, which I enclose for your perusal. What do you think of the manner in which Frank has attended to our business or rather failed to attend to it! I for my part do not like it, and immediately wrote back, to Mary, that I wished Lowry to take the business in hand and see to it that the property was redeemed as soon as possible. I told her to get my money from Frank, and if that was not sufficient, to use all available means to that effect. I suppose that Frank will be angry, but I do not care. He has shamefully neglected the business we entrusted to his care! And I fear betrayed our trust! If he has not used our money, why is it that he has not long since paid the taxes and sent me the receipts. I am confident that I have written him one dozen times to do so without further delay. And now when I have written upon three different occasions to him to forward our goods, after waiting more than ample time for them to have arrived, I write to Lowry for information and I find that he has not yet sent them. I am out of all patience with him; however, I do not know that I shall write to him. All join me in warmest expressions of regard to you, etc.!

Ever yours affectionately,

Eliza W. Tomlinson

The names of the officers to whom I sent those pockets were Maj. Long, Capt. Armstrong, Lieut. Rudolph, Lieut. Collins, Lieut. Tomlinson. The package was addressed to you in the usual manner. The letter was glued to the back of the package. Possibly it is yet at the Gazette Office.

* * * * *

If Tomlinson ever received the package of items his wife had so painstakingly prepared, there is no record of it. Caught up in the chaotic rush of preparing troops for war, he probably had little time to write. On May 13, Maj. Gen. George B. McClellan became commander of the Department of the Ohio, with headquarters in Cincinnati. Ten days later, thousands of recruits at Camp Harrison marched across the city to a new staging arena, sixteen miles east of the city. Camp Dennison was bordered by the Little Miami River and a line from the Little Miami Railroad. Federal uniforms had still not arrived, but the distinctive garb of each regiment made for a colorful parade as the troops marched by the crowds lining Sycamore Street. There was the Ninth Ohio, with its German immigrants in white linen jackets; the Sixth Ohio, in the dress of the Guthrie Grays; and the Fifth Ohio, in red flannel shirts. Three days following the transfer to Camp Dennison, McClellan ordered federal troops into western Virginia to secure the Baltimore and Ohio Railroad and protect Union sympathizers in the area. But the Fifth Ohio, Tomlinson's regiment, was not among them. Their job was to wait and drill, in the stifling heat, back and forth, across the stubble of cornfields recently cleared for military maneuvers. When it rained, everything dissolved into a sea of mud. Even when the rain and marching stopped, however, Tomlinson's job was never done. As a quartermaster sergeant, he was always scrambling to get necessary provisions to disillusioned recruits wearing their own clothes and using wooden guns and wooden swords in the seemingly pointless repetition of one drill after another. Back home Eliza was also scrambling to keep an optimistic outlook, especially since she had not heard from her husband for at least three weeks.[7]

Eliza to Tomlinson
Ripley, Ohio, May 28, 1861

Dear Husband,

I was quite sick last night and am better today. Byers came home from school sick this morning. He is not seriously ill. This is a most beautiful morning. Should this weather continue, the soldiers can have nothing to complain of on that score. I see from last night's Gazette, Philander has made a lamentable complaint about the amount of provisions received by the men, etc.! 'Tis hard to please everybody, I suppose. The change from home comforts to the exposure, and privations of camp life, are particularly trying to many who have been nurtured in the lap of luxury, but after volunteering it is too late to complain. The patriot will endure hardship without complaint lest by so doing he might injure the cause which he has sacrificed so much to promote! I hope that all complaints in future will be made to the proper officers who, if competent to the fulfillment of the duties which they have taken upon them, will see to it that justice is done to all.

I hope that you have got fixed up in a comfortable manner in your new quarters ere this. I have not heard from you since Bob Easton got back. I hope that you will write as often as you conveniently can. I feel very anxious to know how you are getting along. Your prospects, etc.! I understand that there is some one coming up almost every day, so you will be at no loss for opportunities for sending news.

Your friends are all well here so far as I know. All join me in the warmest expressions of love to you: May you be prospered in the defense of the good cause in which you have enlisted, be brought off victorious and when all is settled to our satisfaction, may you again return to the bosom of your family to enjoy the merited reward of a faithful and zealous soldier is my most ardent prayer!

Ever yours indefinitely,

Eliza W. Tomlinson

Eliza to Tomlinson
Ripley, Ohio, May 31, 1861

Dear Husband,

Why is it I have not received a line from you since you left? I feel very anxious to hear something special from you, how you have your health, how you like camp life, your prospects, etc. I presume that you have been kept pretty busy since your change of quarters, fixing up, together with official duties, so I excuse your not writing, but I suppose that you must be pretty well fixed up by this time.

I do not feel very well myself and have not for sometime past. Anxiety of mind relative to the unsettled state of our country has considerable influence upon my feelings, not that I have any fears as to the final result (it cannot but be favorable to the north), but the thought that victory will have to be purchased at the expense of so many valuable lives, possibly some of them my own near and dear friends, is a thought painful in the extreme. I try to cast such dark forebodings behind me, but they will intrude again and again. Hope whispers better things, the future smiles with gladness, war is over, we are once more united in hands more enduring than ever, all is peace, prosperity, and happiness. My confidence is in the justice of our cause. A just God will be with us and give us the victory, notwithstanding the subtlety with which the traitors have laid their plans. The pit into which they shall fall is their own digging.

Brother Byers and Sarah Ann Elizabeth Cook Wylie went down to the city yesterday. I presume that Byers will be out at camp. I do not know how long they will remain.

Capt. Cary is up here raising recruits; several of the boys have enlisted. Cary wishes to raise some 25 or 30 men. I suppose that he will get them. All are about as when I wrote you last. I understand that you are going to have a new election of officers in Camp Dennison. How is it with you? Will you continue in Qr. M. Department? I am informed that there is a company of 25 or 30 Germans going down tonight. I do not know whether they enlisted under Cary or not. It is now near the time the boat comes down, so I must close. Mother and the children join me in the warmest expressions of regard to you!

Ever yours,
E. W. Tomlinson

* * * * *

Tomlinson had not written to Eliza since May 5. More than a month would pass before new letters from Tomlinson would turn up, and Eliza, like so many women back home, would have to make do without any support or news from her husband.

CHAPTER EIGHT

~

Rushed Waiting

To keep yourself in a state of discontent—
set your heart on having everything exactly to your mind.
—*Freedom's Casket*, June 15, 1844

As TOMLINSON DEALT with the noxious duties of a quartermaster sergeant, Eliza worried about their son's visits to his father at Camp Dennison, where disease lurked and unregulated elections for officers resulted in unruly behavior among thousands of enlisted men. They acted more like "an armed mob than a body of disciplined soliders," Tomlinson wrote. Like other enlisted men, he was impatient to fight the Rebels, especially as he watched thousands of soldiers leaving camp "with the speed of the locomotive and the power of an avalanche." At last General McClellan was sending Ohio troops into western Virginia. Tomlinson was so busy organizing supplies for the deployment that he feared there would be no time for a visit home to see his wife and children.

* * * * *

Eliza to Tomlinson
Ripley, Ohio, June 1, 1861

Dear Husband,

I am sorry that I am not able to go down according to your request, but as Byers is anxious to go, I thought that I would send him down and let him stay for a day or two. The school will be out in three weeks and it is important that he should attend regularly so as to be able to undergo an examination that he may be promoted to a higher room, so you will please send him home in two or three days—at farthest. I understand that the measles are in camp. Do not let Byers go in that neighborhood! I hardly know that it was prudent for me to let him go on this account.

I believe that there are some receipts in the packet of your trunk which you had best send up by Byers. Or there may be other things that you do not wish to be cumbered with; if so send them up with him.

I have received no word from Iowa yet. What do you say about that insurance matter? I wish we had our money back; it might go for anything I care! Goodby. God bless and protect you from harm, and if called into active service, may you gain a glorious victory and return home in triumph!

Ever yours, etc.!

Eliza W. Tomlinson

Please do not let Byers be exposed at night most especially.

Eliza to Tomlinson
Ripley, Ohio, June 8, 1861

Dear Husband,

This is to inform you that our son Byers on last night about twelve o'clock came safe to hand without accident or mishap, lest you should be uneasy. I thought it best to inform you of the fact. The Capt. of the Bostona charged him full price (I.E.) $1.25. Byers took a bad cold last night being out on the guard watching for Ripley, as he did not come on the Magnolia. I had given him out until she would come up again, and as I feel considerably better, had about concluded to go down today and stay until Monday, but as he has come and says that you intend coming up next week, I shall not go. Such trips are hard on me and almost always make me sick, and another thing, it is necessary that I should husband my resources in pecuniary matters as much as possible. Brother Byers says that camp is no place for ladies. I hope that you will not think hard of me for not coming down! As I have been very much troubled with diarrhea, therefore it was altogether impracticable for me to do so. Mr. Ammen (his present title I do not remember) and Lady came up last night on the Bostona. I have not seen either of them yet, so do not know how long he intends remaining.

The *Bostona* was one of the steamboats the Tomlinsons used for traveling and sending mail between Cincinnati and Ripley, Ohio. (From the Collection of the Public Library of Cincinnati and Hamilton County)

Byers says that he does not know whether you will retain your present position longer than the three months. He says that you are kept very busy. From what he informs me I think your situation is a very onerous one. You know what suits you best, and I suppose that there are so many applicants for office that a man has to be satisfied with what offers, even if it does not suit him as well as what he could wish.

Belle's teacher has taken her scholars out to some grove nearby on a picnic expedition, so I fixed Belle up some dinner and she has gone out with them to spend the day. May victory, prosperity, and happiness ever attend you. All join me in love to you.

Ever yours,
Eliza W. Tomlinson

No news yet from the west. Br. Newt talks of going down with Lizzie and may next Tuesday; if he does he will be out at camp. Your friends are all well.

* * * * *

Eliza's confusion over the current title of Jacob Ammen is understandable. In April he was elected as captain of Ripley's Company H of the Twelfth Ohio and promoted to lieutenant colonel in May. In June he became colonel of the Twenty-Fourth Ohio Volunteer Infantry. After leading a regiment at Cheat Mountain and Greenbrier in western Virginia and a brigade at Shiloh, he was promoted to brigadier general. Ammen and his family had a long history with many Ripleyites, including the Tomlinsons. Jacob's father, David, first published the Reverend John Rankin's antislavery letters in the Ripley newspaper, the *Castigator*, in the 1820s. In the 1840s Tomlinson purchased the press used to print the *Castigator* and printed *Freedom's Casket* and the *Hickory Sprout* on it before it was burned. Jacob and Daniel Ammen were also friends of Ulysses S. Grant, who grew up in neighboring Georgetown and attended school in Ripley. Each of the Ammen brothers had, at different times, saved the life of the man who would become general in chief of the U.S. Armies a year later.[1]

In the spring of 1861, however, Grant was far from the heroic stature he would attain, and, meanwhile, the North was beginning to realize that not all war stories would end in shining glory for the Union. On June 10 at Great Bethel, Virginia, 1,200 Confederate soldiers routed 2,500 Federal troops, forcing them to retreat and causing the North considerable embarrassment. But this was a minor setback compared to what would come, and Tomlinson, much to his chagrin, was still stuck at Camp Dennison, where the major battle he fought was in fending off his repulsion to killing enough cattle to feed a regiment.[2]

* * * * *

CAMP DENNISON,

Will Tomlinson spent most the summer of 1861 at Camp Dennison, east of Cincinnati. (Library of Congress Geography and Map Division)

Tomlinson to Eliza
Camp Dennison, Cincinnati, Ohio, June 12, 1861

Dearest Eliza,

Yesterday I received a short letter from you, explanatory of why it was that you did not come to see me, and of the safe arrival of our beloved boy. I should have answered it by the mail of yesterday, but on account of pressing business I deferred the duty. I would have abundant time and should pen you a very interesting epistle, but what with getting up at 4 o'clock and going after my fresh beef—also the news of that most disgraceful and disastrous affair at Great Bethel, Va.—all have thrown me so off my equilibrium that I thought it barely possible I might write you a few lines, when in comes a whole warehouse full of uniforms—blouses, drawers, pants, etc. We have just got through delivering them, and by writing with lightning speed I may be enabled to get off by private conveyance, once this page of loosely-jointed correspondence. My breath is, considering my morning exposure to the then nauseous vapors around the slaughter-house, very good. I do not weigh, by fourteen pounds, what I did in Iowa, but am fat enough for all practical purposes for this hot weather, and considering the southern trip we expect to be ordered on shortly, I now imagine that my first impressions written to you during the bombardment of Sumter, viz: that the Ohio troops would be ordered to Cairo, Memphis, and New Orleans, will be verified.

As to my position of Q. M. Serg't., I know not whether I shall be continued or not, but I have determined not to come down to the ranks, unless in case of absolute necessity. The government of the State and Nation have so managed things as to bring on a state of insubordination among the troops, men encamped—12,000 men—which causes us to resemble more an armed mob than a body of disciplined soldiers. The reason of this is, that, after the soldiers had served about half the period of their enlistment, the order came for a new election of officers for the three years. The 3 months volunteers were all recognized as having the same right to vote for 3 years officers as the actual recruits for that period, and so electioneering appliances, such as provinces of place, drinks of whisky, barrels of beer, exemption from punishment, etcetera, have been the rule, and honor and sobriety the exception. Hence last night the regiment known as the Guthrie Greys turned out, under arms, to resent an affront to one of their drunken comrades, received while traipsing through our regiment. We were stopped by the Irish Regiment, which lay between us, so that no blood was shed, but if a collision had happened, hundreds would probably have been left dead and dying on the parade ground. The fact is, I begin seriously to doubt the patriotism and integrity of the administration. The enemy could have invented no surer plan of demoralizing this army than that pursued by those whose orders called us from homes, families, business, and civilization.

I will not visit Ripley at present. It may be weeks—perhaps months— before I again see you then. There is some prospect of Col. Rankin being court martialled for lying and other conduct unbecoming an officer. My warmest love to you all, and be assured that I will be among the last to surrender to treason, whether Southern or Northern.

* * * * *

On June 20, the Fifth Ohio was asked to reenlist for three years instead of the three months the men had agreed to in April. Many volunteers, who still had not been paid for the time they had already served, were unhappy about a long-term commitment and refused to sign up. Tomlinson was not among them. He signed on for three years and retained his post as regimental quartermaster sergeant.[3]

* * * * *

Tomlinson to Eliza
Camp Dennison, Cincinnati, Ohio, June 22, 1861

Dearest Eliza,

It is now about ½ past two in the morning as I commence this letter. Having retired very early last night because of the storm, I woke up an hour earlier than usual. The main thing you want to know, of course, is concerning my health, which I am happy to say is excellent. A slight bilious diarrhea is all that has ailed me, of which I am now nearly recovered. Yesterday Mr. Whitson, Q. M., was quite sick, and this threw double duty on me. The day was also extremely hot. Occasionally a man would drop from the ranks, fainting. When Lizzie was down here, I rather intimated that I would be up to see you in a few days. I should be glad to be able to renew that prospect now, but cannot. When I will see you again depends upon the length of the war, and my luck in ever on earth looking back upon this fearful cloud which now covers all the earth before us. Yesterday two regiments left camp, the 3rd and 4th. Today the 10th (Irish) will leave, and we have orders to move as soon as we can get ready, which will probably be about the middle of next week. In a few days this camp will be deserted, and its present occupants on or under the field of battle.

It is a grand sight—this of soldiers moving by thousands with the speed of the locomotive and the power of an avalanche—with the shouting enthusiasm of boys and the faith of the prophets, all glorying in the work laid out before them of being a part of the means used by the Almighty Power reigning in all nations to crush terrorism and despotism, to overthrow the dreams and schemes of mad ambition and treason less justifiable and more devilish than that of Absalom, and more blasphemous against the light and advancement of the 19th century than the making and worshipping of the Golden Calf in the Wilderness by the misguided Israelites.

But as we shall soon be in the midst of the bustle and hurry of the packing up and preparing to leave, I may have no other opportunity of writing at as great length as I have already done. If I fall in this struggle, which is sure to come off in a few days, be kind in the memory of my faults, which have been, O, how many! Remember that I have at least been a loving husband and a fond father, through all exterior roughness. You may put up a prayer to God, the Father of us all, that my sins may be forgiven, and that the manner of my death may cover them in multitudes, for is not the cause the same as that wherefore Christ came hither and was crucified? Be cheerful and brave of soul, for were it not better to be remembered among the noble army of martyrs than basely live a coward slave, yielding all of manhood, right, and truth and God.

It is now daybreak, and I must hasten to the duties of the day. If I have time I shall add some more to this before the mail closes. If not, then in all love to you, and trust and hope for our children, and the bitterness all wiped out of my heart toward my enemies, except those who strike at the flag of the free, I close.

Long and ever your loving husband,
Will Tomlinson

Dearest Eliza—It is now noon—the mail closes in a few minutes. I have to go nearly a half mile to put this in Post Office—orders are to be ready to march next Tuesday. I will be in a great hurry all time—

Excuse haste—20 people are around me—

Good Bye—God bless you,
Will Tomlinson
Will write again tomorrow—

Dear Pap,

I am well and hope you are also well. I heard that you were going to leave the camp for western Virginia. I hope that if you meet the rebels, you will conquer them and make them afraid to show their faces again. Tell Mister Cother that I have not forgotten him and he must not forget me. Goodbye Pap. I hope that you will meet with no accident. If you should happen to see Jeff Davis just send a bullet through his traitor heart, and all posterity will bless you.

Goodbye Pap till we meet again,

W. B. Tomlinson

Eliza to Tomlinson
Ripley, Ohio, June 26, 1861

Dear Husband,

On last evening I received yours of the 24th inst., from which and the papers I learn that your regiment is soon to take up the line of march for Va. I had confidently expected to have seen you once more before you left, but should you leave as soon as what you anticipate, I shall be denied that pleasure. I suppose that it is all hustle and commotion preparatory to leaving, so that even had I the time to go down, there would be but little satisfaction in a visit at this time. The parting would be sorrowful for both you and I, so it is probably best as it is. My prayers shall ever go with you and the hosts of Union loving men who make up our army, and who are now periling all of life which they possess for their country: God bless you and them with health and prosperity, and grant you victory over all enemies who are, or may attempt the overthrow, of the best government the Sun ever shone upon.

The health of our family is about as good as usual. I know of no news that would be of interest to you. We have had several cases of smallpox in town; old Mrs. Dawson died with it. There is but little sickness prevailing at present. Mrs. Bennington's second daughter has the typhoid fever; she has been very sick but is now they think mending. Mr. Bennington is in Baltimore; he has tobacco there which he was somewhat afraid would be appropriated by the rebels to their own use.

Letter written June 26, 1861, by William Byers Tomlinson, age fourteen. (Wylie-Tomlinson Letter Collection)

Well, it is hardly worth while to introduce business matters, and I would not do so only on account of our children. In case of a possible contingency, which I cannot for a moment suffer my mind to dwell upon, our children may not only be left orphans but in a manner destitute in pecuniary matters; therefore, would it not be well to have that war policy secured? Baird said that he had written to you about it, but had not got a reply. I will try and have the matter fixed up if I possibly can if you think it best to do so.

I wish you to write me as often as you possibly can so as to keep me posted relative to all matters which you know I take vital interest in. The children, mother, and myself all write in the most ardent prayer for your safety, prosperity, and triumph over traitors, and after you have achieved all that the most ardent patriot could desire for his country, may you return to the bosom of your family there to enjoy uninterrupted happiness for the remnant of your days, be they many or few. Take good care of your health; do not expose yourself in any way more than is absolutely necessary. Goodbye. God bless you for time and eternity.

Ever yours truly,

Eliza W. Tomlinson

* * * * *

Tomlinson managed to see Eliza and the children one more time before leaving for western Virginia. According to the *Ripley Bee* for July 4, he "made a flying visit" to Ripley on Monday, July 1, a few days before the Fifth and Twelfth Ohio Regiments were scheduled to depart.[4]

* * * * *

Eliza to Tomlinson
Ripley, Ohio, July 3, 1861

Dear Husband,

As I had hardly an opportunity of bidding you goodbye on yesterday, I drop you a line this evening to tell you to dodge all bullets which come your way and to take every precautionary measure in your power to preserve your health. You will probably leave camp in a day or two; please write me as often as you find opportunity, and keep me posted as to every thing which you know would be interesting. You I am happy to say need no incentive from me to discharge your duty to your country as a faithful citizen and soldier; I shall never, I feel assured, blush to own the name before high Heaven which you gave me. Patriotism is something more than a name to amuse old women and children. 'Tis a deeply rooted principle of right, and justice, a love of country which is paramount to all earthly blessings. Life itself is freely offered up on the altar of liberty. I can scarcely realize the fact that any portion of the citizens of this great Republic should turn traitors to the government which has built up their fortunes and their liberty. They surely know not what they do, for most assuredly they will bring down the combined judgment of God and all true patriots upon their devoted heads. I hope that Congress will enter into no disgraceful compromise with traitors to accomplish a peace which would doubtless upon their terms not only be dishonorable but of short duration, but if the combined wisdom of the oration at this late period can adopt any measure compatible with honor to reconcile the discordant elements of sectional strife, I shall hail it as the most welcome boon a God of Mercy could bestow upon our distracted country.

We are to have some kind of celebration here tomorrow. I hardly know what, but there is to be a military parade up at the fair ground. Byers says that you wanted him to go down today. His clothing is not at present such as I would wish him to make the trip in, and I had no time to remedy the want. 'Tis time this was mailed. Goodbye and may God and his good Angels ever guard and protect you from all harm, strengthen your arm in fight, give you the victory, and when war is o'er, bring you home in peace, crowned with glory and honor to enjoy uninterrupted felicity until called up higher.

Ever yours,
Eliza W. Tomlinson

* * * * *

Besides the brief notice about Tomlinson's visit to Ripley on July 1, the July 4 edition of the *Ripley Bee* also carried his first letter to the editor from Cincinnati. The letter's optimistic tone and good-natured sarcasm would disappear from his subsequent correspondence. But he would continue to include the latest information on Ripley volunteers and other regiments. In the meantime, there were two regiments from Kentucky that reminded him of sharpshooters from the War of 1812 hailed in the peppy tune, "Hunters of Kentucky."[5]

* * * * *

Tomlinson to the *Ripley Bee*
Camp Dennison, Ohio, Company H, June 25th, 1861

Eds. Bee:—A few words are sufficient to express all of interest, hereabouts occurring, for, much as fiction may embellish facts, the latter are wanted by the friends we leave behind.

The Camp is more lively than usual. Several regiments have left, and now invest the territory of the worst enemies of mankind, since the days when Cain was a branded wanderer through the earth.

Today, two Kentucky regiments encamped here. They came in in fine style—were received with marked honors, and are a fair specimen of what the rhymester imagined, when he wrote the "Hunters of Kentucky." In our own circle a little incident has happened, worthy of note at home. Comrade Lieut. Ridgway ('Clain) has so demeaned himself as a soldier, that he has been unanimously elected First Lieutenant of the New Richmond Company. Good for him—and it is only a reflex of the estimation in which all your Ripley Boys are held. As a Company, they, I do assure you, hold a permanent popularity equal to that of any company in camp, and which will never be damaged by the official reports after battle.

Another Company has just come in for the 12th, so that our organization will be completed forthwith, and then for "Away down in the land of Cotton."

We just heard that Col. Ammen has been appointed to the command of a Regiment of regulars. It is provoking, but 'tis the duty of a soldier to obey.

Our boys are all well.

—WILL

* * * * *

The Ohio Fifth was finally leaving Camp Dennison. They were en route to Parkerburg, in western Virginia, where General McClellan had deployed other Ohio troops at Grafton to protect a major terminal on the Baltimore and Ohio Railroad. On July 10, McClellan ordered troops already positioned at nearby Buckhannon and Philippi to attack Rebel forces at Rich Mountain. Led by Ohio's Gen. William S. Rosecrans, Federal forces deftly outmaneuvered the Confederates, who scampered down the mountain in fast retreat. On July 14, several companies from the Fifth Ohio joined forces with those under Gen. Charles W. Hill to intercept the retreat of Confederate general Robert S. Garnett in the Cheat River Valley. Once again Union forces swept to victory, leaving Garnett dead in their wake, the Union in control of railroad and telegraph lines, and McClellan crowned with a hero's reputation. President Lincoln called the "Young Napoleon" back to Washington to command the Army of the Potomac, and Rosecrans became commander in western Virginia.[6]

The maneuvers for control of western Virginia were far from over, but the nation's attention soon shifted east to Manassas, Virginia, where the war's first great battle left each side with serious casualties. The war had become a deadly reality, especially for the Union, and Northerners became discouraged by another unexpected and embarrassing loss. Meanwhile, the rhetoric of peace and compromise being touted by politicians like Ohio congressman Clement L. Vallandigham of Dayton became an increasing irritation to Union enlistments. In early July, when Vallandigham visited Ohio regiments in Virginia, angry soldiers bombarded him with stones. With the exception of Vallandigham, however, there was little else for camp-weary soldiers in western Virginia to use as a target for their frustrations. Skirmishing with the enemy continued here and there, but, for the most part, the strategic railroad and telegraph lines of the area were secured. In Ripley, Eliza was wondering how to secure her own diminishing resources. What little she had was too precious to lose, but at the same time, she wanted to give her all to the cause of the just, true, and free.[7]

CHAPTER NINE

~⌒

Into the Hills

How can a good son be neutral when he sees a man with a
dagger at his mother's heart. Country is more than mother.
The neutral is not only a traitor, he is a coward.
—"Brownson's Views of the War,"
Loyal Scout, October 10, 1863

As August swathed the Ohio Valley and western Virginia in stifling
heat, Eliza's anxieties began to boil over. They had been simmering for some
time. Kentucky's allegiance to the Union was unstable, and there were rumors of imminent Confederate invasions into southern Ohio. There was
good news about Union success in the mountains, but Eliza had no recent
letters from her husband and was worried about his safety. He was busy
with a quartermaster sergeant's duties for a regiment on the move. Then the
rains came, and stayed, plunging camp life into deeper levels of misery. Tomlinson, meanwhile, learned of two possibilities for being promoted, one of
which was sure to provide his wife with even more reasons to be concerned.

* * * * *

Eliza to Tomlinson
Ripley, Ohio, August 6, 1861

Dear Husband,

I have received no intelligence from you since you left. I expected you
to have written from the city. I feel very anxious to hear from you, how
you got along, your arrival, etc.

It appears that Wise has fled, and from last accounts was still fleeing. I hope that our boys will catch him and before they are done with him, give him a taste of hemp, which is the most suitable ornament his neck could be decorated with; 'twould be doing him an honor which he richly merits. Honor to whom honor is due, of whatever description that may be. I would not defraud the Devil out of the smallest fraction, but he is a gentleman in comparison to some of the traitors with whom we have to deal, so I hope our boys will give them good measure, pressed down, and running over when pay day comes.

I am happy to inform you that the health of our family is as good as usual; all your friends are well so far as I know. The weather is quite hot. I hear nothing from the west. I wrote several letters to Lowry and Mary telling them to see that my things were shipped here, etc. Why I hear nothing from them I know not. I do not know where the Wylie family is or any thing about them. I know not who to apply to, to attend to our business. I would have written to Williamson, but I know that he is negligent and careless about other persons' interests, or at least has been with regard to anything we have entrusted to his care. I suppose that Frank has sold everything and spent the money. I can now see that we trusted him too far; the temptation was too great for him. Lizzie got a letter from Sam on Saturday night. They were at Gauley bridge, all well, but very tired. They were in pursuit of Wise. I am afraid that he will not be easily caught; they greatly excel in running.

There is no news of any interest here at present. We feel greatly afraid that Ky. will be precipitated out of the Union. If so, we will be in a hot place and will, I am afraid, have to follow Wise's example, but where to flee for safety I know not. I shall trust in the Lord, hoping that all shall be well with us. God bless you and protect you from all evil. Goodbye.

Ever yours in the bonds of affection,

Eliza W. Tomlinson

Please write as often as you possibly can. I feel very anxious to hear from you. Keep us well posted if possible. Mother and the children join me in love and kind wishes for your happiness, prosperity, and success in conquering traitors. Death to traitors, now and forever.

* * * * *

Eliza's scorn for Confederate general Henry A. Wise, a secessionist, member of Richmond's elite, and former governor of Virginia, reflected the prevailing opinion held by many Northerners, and not a few Southerners.

Lack of military experience did not prevent him from pompously parading his troops through western Virginia towns, even though he never managed to stay anywhere long enough to fully engage the enemy. On July 9 he abandoned a march on Parkersburg and withdrew to Charleston. A few weeks later, when Gen. Jacob Cox's troops from Ohio began advancing on Charleston, he quickly retreated a hundred miles up the Kanawha River. A temperamental nature and imperialistic manner did nothing to improve his reputation, and his constant feuding with fellow commander John B. Floyd compounded his ineffectiveness.[1]

In September, Union forces attacked Confederates in tight quarters at Gauley Bridge. With no decisive outcome, the fighting continued at nearby Sewell Mountain. Lack of cooperation between Wise and Floyd undermined Confederate success, and, despite General Lee's reinforcements, Southern troops were unable to win a clear victory. When mid-October rolled around, Rosecrans withdrew Union forces from the area, and Jefferson Davis recalled Wise to Richmond. Lee gave up trying to regain control of western Virginia, and for the time being, Ohioans could breathe a sigh of relief about one threat along their 400-mile border with the South.[2]

Anxieties that Ohio residents had about being attacked from western Virginia had hardly cooled down, however, before concerns about an invasion from Kentucky heated up. This was especially true in the juicy little town of Ripley, which was separated from Kentucky by a mere thousand feet of shallow water across a narrow bend of the Ohio River. Despite a homespun treaty that the town had negotiated with its neighbors on the other side of the river, the prosperous hub of Brown County was still a tempting morsel to Southern raiders. An August dispatch to the *Cincinnati Gazette* from correspondent Whitelaw Reid must have brought sleepless nights to many Ripley residents, including Eliza. She surely read the *Gazette* and other newspapers she sent to her husband and, no doubt, found Reid's recent communication disturbing. According to Reid, Lee's troops planned to winter in southern Ohio, where the granaries were overflowing, horses were plentiful, and everything else they needed was in abundant supply. The fact that Lee's men were in Virginia, far from Ripley, probably did little to allay Eliza's fears, particularly since Kentucky's neutrality was questionable in light of all the aid it sent to the Confederacy. Meanwhile, she continued to worry about the safety of her husband.[3]

But her concerns about Tomlinson's well-being may have been overly solicitous. Instead of putting his life on the line, something he would much rather have been doing, he was still tending to the nitty-gritty details of transporting everything needed to feed, clothe, house, arm, and otherwise provision a thousand men on their way to Buckhannon, Virginia. Each of the nine companies of the Fifth Ohio needed four or five wagonloads of supplies. Additional wagons were packed with medical supplies and other regimental provisions, so that, all together, about seventy-five wagons had to haul everything up and down and around the twenty-eight miles of hills from the end of the railroad in Clarksburg to Buckhannon. Nestled amid gentle hills at the junction of strategic roads, the town of about six hundred people was pleasant enough—except when it rained.[4]

And rain it did, day after day, week after week, well into the fall. Water poured down the slippery slopes of the Allegheny Mountains, inundating towns and valleys, and turning roadways into oozing mud. Nothing much moved—except the churning waters from the constant deluge. It was impossible to walk anywhere without trudging through ankle-deep sludge, and soldiers regaled each other with tall tales about mules sinking up to their ears in muck. By harvest time, the Ohio River was awash with squash, gourds, and pumpkins from flooded farmlands and tributaries. The high spirits of spring enlistments quickly eroded as soldiers pining for home wondered what kind of a sodden mess their country had gotten them into. Eliza's spirits must have been lifted when she finally received a four-page letter from her husband. Every inch of the legal-sized stationery was filled with his penciled descriptions of challenging times in the hills. But nothing appeared to be life-threatening, except for one passing reference at the end to the Snakes.[5]

* * * * *

Tomlinson to Eliza
Buckhannon, Virginia, August 9, 1861

My Dear Wife,

You would surely excuse me for not having written before from this point, if you could but know half what I have had to undergo since Sunday. Orders were given on Sunday, about noon, to issue three days' rations to the men, which were to be cooked immediately, and the regiment, excepting two companies, to prepare for marching. This put an immense amount of labor and care on me, above my ordinary duties. Soon I got the men to cooking, and by night had my "little traps" packed up. Then

I had to see that everybody else was ready and had to visit town several times. By midnight I got to lay down, but it was so hot I could get no sleep worth calling by the name of that "sweet restorer." By daylight I was stirring, and kept so busy that I didn't have ten minutes to dress and eat. By two o'clock the train was loaded, the locomotive screamed, and off we started. Mr. Whitson and the bookkeeper remained at Parkersburg, and I had to go in care of the regiment with only my Dutchman (John) to assist. But he is a good worker, and worth a dozen common soldiers.

On the way the cars (cattle) were so crowded that, with the smoke and cinders, I felt suffocated. I got on the platform (about 16 inches wide), tied my right arm to the step by which the men climb the cars (with my handkerchief), and laid down to sleep. Strange as it may appear, I did accomplish my purpose in catnaps, and found myself wide awake at Clarksburg about three o'clock in the morning. At daylight I walked to the creek, ¾ of a mile, and washed. Here I found Col. Ammen and had a five minutes chat with him. He was rejoiced again to meet me. I answered a few of his eager questions, and away again to business. I had to procure wagons, horses, feed, saddles, bridles, and everything necessary for the regiment, after having to go a mile and back to wake up the Post Quarter Master. It was all "quick," "double-quick" and "run" for hours, in a hot Virginia sun. When I got everything ready, about 10, all but the Col.'s signature to a requisition for horse feed which was essential, I started out to get that, when behold—the whole regiment and baggage train was gone, and more than a mile off! Again I ran to overtake them, got the signature, and returned for my order. Whew! But wasn't it hot!

(I just got so far writing when I was called away on business, up a huge hill, wet with a new and refreshing rain. Now, at ¼ to 9 p.m. I resume.)

Well, I soon caught up with my train, and traveled nearly a mile, when one of my wagons broke down, and I had to stop all hands to get a new king-bolt made in town! Again we start, and make pretty fair time—and at the end of 3½ miles from starting point, resume our journey in just 5 hours from starting! Going down a Virginia Hill, I stepped on a little stone with my left foot. It turned, twisted the ankle, and I was lame. Nevertheless, to keep up appearances I limped as little as possible, walked all that day, and till ten at night, when we stopped at a big manure pile, without food, fire, water, or inhabitants. I slept in the wagon. Early in the morning, with a rather stiff ankle, I started ahead to find water. I found some, but not enough for the regiment, took a wash and a drink, vomited freely, found lots of blackberries, eat fruit, and at the end of 3½ miles, we halted to cook breakfast. I assure you the coffee tasted good. We made this point sometime after noon. A good many soldiers fell by the wayside, fatigued, footsore, weary, panting—the sun heating everything to baking.

Our camp is a pretty place at a distance, but surrounded by a mud hole or slough, like a snake around the neck of a maiden. The health of the boys is good, but it certainly is not owing to the locality. My own is excellent. My first care was to procure fresh beef. By dint of a large amount of pushing and furnishing help, I got a pound to a man for breakfast next morning. I have been constantly engaged till I got a couple of hours to myself tonight, on account of rain and darkness. But I must close for tonight. Tattoo is beating. God guard you and ours!

Saturday:

This morning I resume. Went out to field to see my cattle killed and weighed. Soon it rained—it poured—it flooded everything. It ran through everything, it filled my boots, and at this moment I am wet to the neck. Fun alive—the camp's afloat! But again the sun breaks out and feels like the heat of a furnace. Will soon "dry up."

Yesterday as a company of the Ohio 10th (Irish) were marching here from Bulltown, when about 30 miles from here, they were attacked by a concealed band of murderers, and some stragglers in the rear, which stopping for water, were victims. One man was killed, and three wounded. Our boys will have to be very careful in the order of their marching. I believe we are in the midst of enemies. A splendid large dwelling joining our camp is owned by a secessionist, who has fled with his family. We now use it for an hospital. A very large dwelling opposite the court house is also owned by one who is now a prisoner at Columbus. We hear that the leader of the German Band, 9th Ohio, was waylaid and shot by a party of assassins, four balls entering his head and body at once. A good deal of that sort of thing has been done around here. Our turn may soon come. Yesterday I got a letter from Preston King, and he and Grimes joined in recommending me to the War Department for promotion. I have heard nothing from you. Address: Buckhannon, Va. The Snakes elected me 1st Lieutenant, but I can't get to them.

Excuse "outs" and "doublets," for if this writing on a soap box cover ain't churning, then the opposite would be.

Ever yours,
Will Tomlinson

Whether we shall be attacked here by Gen. Lee is a mooted question. I don't think we will. My love to mother, and all the fondest wishes of a father to the little ones. But I have not written half what I wanted to. Next time I will forget it, so take what little you can get.

Tomlinson's experience as a newspaper editor and publisher was often reflected in his use of printing terms like "outs" (omissions of words) and "doublets" (inadvertent repetitions). The same experience, especially in conjunction with skills needed for running a business, was a valuable asset for carrying out the duties of a quartermaster sergeant. Q. M. Gen. Montgomery C. Meigs insisted that only good accountants and mercantile businessmen be appointed as assistant quartermasters. At least they would know the difference between a requisition form and an invoice, he said. But a quartermaster's responsibilities extended far beyond the necessary paperwork for getting supplies to the troops. *Revised Regulations for the Army of the United States, 1861* specified that the quartermaster's department not only had to provide quarters, transportation, clothing, supplies, equipment, and animals for the army but also had to administer everything from the camp's postal services to the recruitment and payment of spies and scouts. According to one quartermaster, "Everybody (and his wife too, if he has one) goes to the Quartermaster's Department for every thing he wants; and if he does not get it right off, *instanter,* and of the very best quality, no matter what the situation, the quartermaster is straightway branded as an imbecile or a thief, and oftentimes as both."[6]

Even under the best of circumstances, which was rarely the case, a quartermaster's job was almost always frustrating. For Tomlinson, a man of ideas and action, the tedious details involved in securing and keeping track of everything an army needed on a day-to-day basis must have been especially irksome. But in 1861 he lacked the strong party affiliation and political clout in Ohio that would have smoothed his path for securing a post as a commissioned officer. So he drew upon some earlier connections, including New York Senator Preston King, who had founded the *St. Lawrence Republican,* where Tomlinson had probably known him. King was another former Democrat who found his loyalties shifting. A supporter of emancipation, King eventually became a key player in the Republican Party and Lincoln administration. The Grimes that Tomlinson referred to was probably James W. Grimes, also a Republican senator, but from Iowa. Grimes served as governor from 1854 to 1858, when Tomlinson, who was clerking for the Iowa legislature, probably encountered him.[7]

Whether King or Grimes would be able help Tomlinson remained to be seen, but in the meantime there was one aspect of being a quartermaster sergeant that he must have enjoyed: dealing with the recruitment and payment of scouts and spies. Federal troops used them to help track and round up marauding gangs of guerrillas—otherwise known as bush-whackers. According to a correspondent for the *Cincinnati Times,* most bushwhackers were secessionists who had "degenerated into assassins" full of "blood-thirsty hate." Even though they routinely plundered and murdered military personnel and neighbors alike, those who were arrested quickly found themselves released in exchange for swearing allegiance to the Union. Their oaths meant nothing, however, and soon they were terrorizing the countryside again. In the spring of 1861, lawlessness in many areas was so out of hand that some gangs even set up headquarters in county courthouses. The writer of a letter to the *Wheeling Intelligencer* for November 30 of that year estimated that at least one thousand of these predatory "children of the devil" plagued seven counties stretching from Pocahontas County southeast of Buckhannon to the Ohio River on the north.[8]

The Rebel guerrillas that Tomlinson mentions in his letter may well have been the Moccasin Rangers, one of deadliest gangs of bushwhackers. Originally formed as a Confederate Home Guard unit out of Parkersburg, the Moccasins were so savage that the two officers who organized them left in disgust and returned home. Undeterred, the remaining rangers continued their rampages through the hills, often using the sneaky prac-tices of Indian warfare and the wiles of their womenfolk to waylay their victims. Those who lived to tell about their encounters with them char-acterized them as filthy, uncouth renegades who reveled in cold-blooded cruelty and vicious revenge. According to one quartermaster frustrated with their unprovoked attacks on innocent civilians and military supply trains, the bushwhackers used the stealth of a panther to drop their prey and then proceeded to kill for the sake of killing. They virtually controlled the countryside around Buckhannon until July when Federal authorities established a post there and issued a command to track them down and get rid of them by one means or another.[9]

To that end, a group of about fifty Union scouts and spies formed Com-pany A of the Eleventh Virginia Infantry in the fall of 1861 and called themselves the Snake Hunters. These were probably "the Snakes" who elected Tomlinson as their first lieutenant. His duties as quartermaster sergeant would naturally have brought him into contact with them, but the same duties would also have kept him from being able to join them. One way or another, though, whether it was by using his connections to secure a commission through official channels, or by aligning himself with an independent group of scouts and spies, he was determined to be in on some action.[10]

Of course, the best of all worlds for Tomlinson would have been to command his own company of counterinsurgents, like John P. Baggs, captain of the Snake Hunters. "Whisky and the Government is our pride," he is quoted as saying to his men before a fight at Cross Lanes in western Virginia. Such a boast would have strongly resonated with Tomlinson with his patriotic fervor and alcoholic tendencies, and it is not unreasonable to assume that he ingratiated himself with the Snakes not only through his role as quartermaster sergeant, but by also becoming their hard and fast drinking buddy. Their reputations as brave backwoodsmen must have also appealed to his sense of adventure.[11]

Baggs himself had a reputation for being the "most half-horse, half-alligator, and the rest-snapping turtle-est of human beings since . . . Colonel David Crockett." A tall, Ohio hill-country character, the colorful leader of the Snakes claimed to know every trail in the territory. Even more important, he knew what kind of men were needed for his mission: Union loyalists who, like him, had the same skills and rugged nature that their prey did. Using some of the same wily tactics as their enemies, Baggs's men wasted no time in reducing the ranks of the Moccasin Rangers. In June 1862, Col. Thomas M. Harris, to whom Baggs reported, boasted that his men had killed at least thirty guerrillas and captured quite a few more, including Ben Haymond of Braxton County. By 1863, however, the Snake Hunters were accused of being as unorthodox in their methods of reconnaissance as the bushwhackers they hunted, and Captain Baggs was discharged.[12]

The spurious reputation of the Snakes was just one aspect of Tomlinson's affiliation with them that would have worried Eliza. She must also have been concerned about the lonely, dangerous nature of undercover work. She had, after all, lived in Ripley most of her life and had friends who worked with the Underground Railroad. Her family may also have been involved, if only by implicit acquiescence to a conspiracy for good. In many ways, the hazards of being a conductor on the Railroad were the same as those of a scout or spy. Tomlinson could easily end up like the unfortunate Union soldier whose corpse was found with the abdomen ripped open, bowels dug out, and severed head stuffed into the cavity. Even if her husband escaped being butchered, the chances were that he would be killed in some remote mountain wilderness where no one would be around to notice, much less record, his passing. Either scenario was a gruesome reminder of the hazards of guerrilla warfare.[13]

CHAPTER TEN

~o

Curse This Idleness

SUMMER DRAGGED ON, and Tomlinson became disgruntled with camp life and its tedium, broken only by the mutinous conduct of a drunken soldier, the disappearance of two prized possessions, and his wife's letters from home. It seemed that Eliza was witnessing more action in Ripley than he was in western Virginia, and he entertained thoughts of leaving the regiment and raising his own independent company.

* * * * *

Eliza to Tomlinson
Ripley, Ohio, August 26, 1861

Dear Husband,

As I have heard nothing from you since I received yours of the 13th inst., I feel very uneasy about you. There has been no battle, but then I fear that you are sick; you have been much exposed, and your official duties are very onerous, I fear, too much so, for your health. I hope that some situation not so laborious will turn up for you, as you are so tired of Quarter Master business a change would be desirable. We are all in our usual health; both Byers's, and Newt's families are well, as are also all your friends so far as I know. Frank Shaw's have another young daughter; he was, I understand, very much disappointed that they did not have a boy this time. I am happy to inform you that it was all a mistake about Mr. Mitchell being dead. It is true that he was very ill, and at one time they thought he was dead; hence the report.

Last week we had the heaviest rains we have had probably for some years. There was much damage done on the creek bottoms in the loss of property; there were also several persons drowned, among which was one of Norris's Irishmen. City papers state that the loss of property was immense there. There was also a number of persons drowned there.

Last week I received a letter from Mary Lowry. She informed me that Lowry could get no satisfaction out of Frank in regard to our affairs. She says that Frank has gone to the war. The week before he enlisted he got married to Lizzie Himble; I do not know who that is. Mary says that Frank was very careless about our things, letting them lay round every way. Our things have not yet been shipped. Mary says that Lowry had not the money to pay the freight on them to the river. I wrote to Lowry to have them packed and sent as soon as possible. I think it very doubtful whether I ever get them or not. Well, I am not in as bad a fix as many others who have lost their all, and have been driven from their homes by cruel assassins, and are now in a suffering condition.

The Ripley boys are yet at Gauley bridge. I hear that they are about to be ordered to Grafton. Oliver Evans has made up a company and they are to be off by next Thursday. I do not know who all are going. They will stop in camp for a short time when they will leave for St. Louis. When, O when, Great God, shall war cease! And peace and happiness be restored to our distracted country! Not until this vile treason is routed up, and the leaders summarily punished. I fear that this will be a Herculean task, but it is not an impossible one. God is on the side of truth and justice. I put my trust in him and do not fear the result. We shall conquer; do not despair, though the hosts of the enemy fill every valley and cover every hill top, they shall flee before you as the morning vapor before the king of day. Take care of yourself and do not unnecessarily expose your person in any way. God bless and take care of you until we meet in happier times.

Ever yours in the bonds of love,

E. W. Tomlinson

I know not whether you get my letters, but I write once a week. Please write me every opportunity. I am exceedingly anxious to hear from you.

* * * * *

That Tomlinson had been busy with his duties as a quartermaster sergeant went without saying, but there were also other reasons for his negligence in writing—reasons he probably wanted to keep from Eliza. He was recruiting a Home Guard unit from local men who wanted to stay in the area so they could protect their families and homes. Dr. Thomas Maley Harris of Ritchie County was attempting to raise a regiment of such units and had obtained permission to do so from his old friend Francis H. Pierpont, the newly elected governor of the Restored Government of Virginia. The Restored Government, located in Wheeling, supervised the Union-controlled area of western Virginia that would become the state of West Virginia in 1863. In August and September 1861, however, Harris was finding the recruitment of men to be more challenging than he had anticipated, even in counties hard hit by bushwhackers. Tomlinson recognized his own opportunity in the turmoil created by guerrilla warfare and went right to work, minus his old horse, Jeff. By September 28, he had been elected captain of a company of fifty volunteer scouts and spies. Eliza, meanwhile, must have become more suspicious that her husband's military career had taken a dangerous detour.[1]

* * * * *

Eliza to Tomlinson
Ripley, Ohio, September 2, 1861

Dear Husband,

I received yours of the 25th, from which I was happy to learn that you were well. I think that your reason for not having written was rather a poor one. You are aware that if you have nothing else to say other than with regard to your own health and personal matters, it would always be of great interest to me! I hope you will in future write oftener even if you have nothing of an exciting character to relate. I am always anxious to hear from you.

O, what have you done with Jeff? You say that you can hear nothing from your friends the "Snake Hunters." Perhaps it is as well, I think that theirs is a very hazardous mode of warfare. I do not like it at all. A soldier's life is a tiresome one, and they have to exercise a great deal of patience to get along with the monotony of camp life. When they have excitement, it is generally of a thrilling character, such as I hope will soon be unknown within our borders.

The children started to school this morning. Byers is in Mr. Mitchell's room, Belle in Miss Rankin's. I am glad to have them in school once more. For want of anything better to relate, I will give you a specimen of b—a intelligence as related by himself to a lady friend of mine. The gentleman stated that at the age of 21 he could neither read nor write and knew but few letters of the alphabet. At the age of 24 thought that the horizon was the boundary of the world, and a hill not far distant the end or jumping off place of the world. He worked for a farmer about as intelligent as himself, fell in love with his daughter, who reciprocated his flame; planned an elopement, but was afraid to venture upon the Kanawha, lest the river might come to a sudden end and plummet them down nowhere! But as there was no hope of coming round the old father, he concluded at all events to venture upon what to him was altogether an unknown world. So he procured a canoe and his dulcinea and himself tied up all their worldly possessions in a table cloth, and launched forth upon the waters, which carried them down until to his astonishment the Kanawha emptied into a larger and much more beautiful stream than the one which they had left. But strange he came not to the end or jumping off place. Everything was so new, so strange, and his astonishment so great that he kept on passing large towns and beautiful cities until they came to Indiana, where he stopped and located. And now at intervals from labor he managed to acquire a knowledge of the alphabet and learnt to read and write, took up school, prospered finely and soon had a house of his own, on the other side of the jumping off place.

We had quite a fire a few nights ago. Neal's stable was burnt up together with a valuable horse, a large amount of hay. The fire was the work of an incendiary supposed to be the Ceske. It was the best place that they could have chosen to have fired the town. A short time since the Ripley boys had a little skirmish with a company of the evening cavalry. Our boys killed seven men and took some of their traps. We hear a great many rumors which are of an exciting character. I hope that Rosecrans is strong enough to withstand any attack the enemy may make upon him. Be vigilant lest you be taken by surprise. Take care of your self, and may God bless and protect you at all times, and ere long when peace is restored to our beloved country, may you return once more to the bosom of your family, there to enjoy the peace and happiness which your valor helped to win is my unceasing prayer.

Adieu,

E. W. Tomlinson

Capt. Evans's company starts tomorrow. Gen. Thompson and Oliver Lindsay are going in it, and a good many others of our Ripley boys. I do not like to hear of your shooting beaus. I do not think that it is your place to do such work. I would rather shoot a traitor than a poor innocent cow any time.

* * * * *

Eliza was using everything in her power to persuade Tomlinson to stay away from men like the Snake Hunters. She thought she knew exactly what the life of a soldier should be and had no qualms in spelling things out for her husband. After seventeen years of marriage, however, he had probably become accustomed to her lectures on subjects beyond her realm of expertise. In his letters, he seldom, if ever, took umbrage with her pronouncements. Perhaps he developed a deaf ear to them. Or maybe he saw them as oblique and tactless expressions of her concern and love.

Eliza could also be entertaining, and she often went to extra lengths to relate an amusing anecdote or some interesting gossip. Like stories of local color anywhere, Eliza's humorous tale about the Kanawha Valley rube and his Dulcinea revealed a bias common to the time and place in which she lived. Because many Ohioans regarded their neighbors to the south in Kentucky and western Virginia as ignorant and indolent, the illiterate hillbilly in Eliza's story would have been a stock character in Ohio humor. Her reference to the hillbilly's girlfriend as "his dulcinea" further accentuated the discrepancy between the untutored rube from the hills of western Virginia and a more educated Ohioan like Eliza, who obviously knew about Don Quixote's idealized Dulcinea in Miguel de Cervantes's novel *The Ingenious Gentleman Don Quixote of La Mancha*.[2]

On a more serious note, Eliza noted some incidents that were not only close to home but that resulted in the destruction of valuable property and the deaths of seven men. The "evening cavalry" that she mentioned may have been a cryptic reference to slave hunters chasing runaway slaves who were seeking help from the Underground Railroad. The fact that Eliza knew about the incident and reported it to Tomlinson, in addition to referring to the Ripleyites who fought the evening cavalry as "our boys," may indicate that she had a sympathetic connection to Ripley's clandestine operation.

Her letter also included a newspaper clipping with an article about tardy payrolls:

IMPERFECT PAY-ROLLS.

All the must-rolls of the Fifth Regiment, O. V., with the exception of Company A, are imperfect, and have to be made anew. This regiment is entitled to pay from April 20 to August, being four months and two days. There has certainly been great neglect in mustering out the three-months' men. Company B, however, paid off yesterday.

The backside of the article included advertisements for various Ripley merchants, but given the tardiness of the payrolls for the Fifth Ohio, Eliza may have been hard pressed to purchase even the barest of necessities, much less indulge in items like some of those listed below:

Brown stout.
JOS. R. PEEBLES.
Corner of Fifth and Race streets

FLOUR.
150 bbls. White Wheat, made from old wheat;
100 do. Red do.,   "   "   "
150 do. White do.,   "   " new   "
In store and for sale by
    J. F. CUNNINGHAM & CO.,
      N. 20 Front street

OLD GOVERNMENT JAVA CO
FEE—50 pockets of very old Java Coffee.

Old coffee may have been a casualty of Gen. Winfield Scott's Anaconda Plan. In cutting off the South's major routes for importing and exporting goods, the plan made it difficult for midwestern states to access markets in the South. Much of Cincinnati's commerce was linked to New Orleans via the Ohio and Mississippi Rivers, and if Southern suppliers could not get their merchandise to Cincinnati, they could not get it to Ripley. With thirty-seven hundred residents in 1861, the little river town enjoyed a wide range of commercial enterprises that depended on river trade, including four hotels, twenty-five grocers, two breweries, five pork-packing businesses, and five tobacco warehouses. But the war's interference with commerce on the Ohio and Mississippi Rivers and Ripley's lack of direct access to a railroad line left businesses there relatively marooned in a pocket of inland insignificance. When many of the town's able-bodied men signed on to defend the Union, the war also reduced the bulk of its workforce. Camp Ripley, on the other hand, was booming as an important recruitment center for southern Ohio. But at the beginning of September, Tomlinson was still doling out beef to Union forces in western Virginia, where some soldiers could make life not only annoying but hazardous, especially when a character like "Scotty"—a name often given to the "bad man" of a company—acted up. Tomlinson was on the scene to report the incident in another four-page letter using every inch of space. This one, however, was written in ink as he perched upon his newly acquired tripod.[3]

* * * * *

Tomlinson to Eliza
Camp Hope, Buckhannon, Virginia, September 2, 1861

Dear Eliza,

After I had written you on yesterday, closed and delivered my letter, and returned to my tent enjoying a huge nightmare, etc., I this morning got up early, shot an ox, called at the Post Office, and—oh, joyful to my weary heart, there was yours of the 26th just! It may be happiness to you to hear from me once in a while, but yours was ecstasy depicted. My health continues good, and the smallest anxiety of my heart is to get a few shots at the wicked and perverted enemies of our country and flag, rather than at their bullocks. A friend at my elbow says he can find nothing more to write about in this d—d (dried) camp. When now may I?

The weather continues fine. Camp Life is the same monotonous thing. Wake up in the morning, listen to reveille, roll over, try to sleep again, fizzle in the effort, then get up again, comb hair, wash face, throw back crumpled blankets, settle firmly in your shoes, go to work, eat a hearty breakfast, listen to Jewish Brass Band, stand a little grumbling from company commissaries, kill and deal out beef, etc. Then roll over and think if you can, read if your book or papers be not picked up while you yawn, curse the innumerable swarms of flies infesting the tents from reveille to tattoo, listen to camp rumors and rumblings, fight fleas, look over the Army Regulations for form of Pay Roll, consider how the friends and families behind us feel, wonder how they live, wake to dreary miserableness again, eat dinners. Then—and with flies—cover with an old paper, and sleep!

I expect to send this by Mrs. Capt. Hays, of Cincinnati.

One little ripple today occurred. A fellow by the name of "Scotty" (for short), an old sailor, got drunk, drew a knife upon the Colonel, threw him down, abused several of the officers—was tied down and conveyed to jail. Perhaps he will be shot—perhaps not! The penalty is death! If he were an enemy of our government and ourselves, he would be released on a formal oath.

While waiting for above few lines, I was disturbed by a disturbance—went out, found the offense innocence, found a stool, a natural tripod, a thing which I intend preserving. I won it—it was given me. I have it at any rate, and now sit upon the same.

Yesterday afternoon that mean Roman Catholic hound, M. E. Joice, special correspondent of the Cincinnati Times for Camp Harrison and Dennison, and now following us as a sneaking dog follows the bones left by his mastiff master, came into my tent, and, in his own diabolical and contemptible manner, stole my big Virginia pipe. Curse his infernal theology which would on Sunday justify the stealing of an only and valuable pipe!

The Paymaster ain't here yet! When will he? It is to me a question whether government don't intend to repudiate. At any rate it is doing more just now for the traitors, cutthroats, mercenaries, fools, pirates, and idiotic, than they could ever do for themselves.

We hear that in Ohio they are drafting for the Army. Good God! Can such things be? So, however, I predicted. Possibly, in my dissatisfaction, I may leave. If so, I know I could raise another independent company. Good night. God bless you.

Ever yours,
Will Tomlinson

No stated preaching of the Gospel at this station.
Gen. Rosecrans was yesterday at Weston.

Tomlinson's vexation at having his pipe stolen illustrates how important tobacco was to many soldiers during the Civil War. Tobacco rations were common, especially in the South, and Union troops swapped their coffee for tobacco from Confederates whenever possible. Since tobacco was a mainstay of Ripley's economy, Tomlinson was probably well acquainted with its enticements and addictive properties. It is also likely that, in fifteen years of living in southern Ohio, he had adopted a number of other local customs and perspectives, including prejudices against Roman Catholicism. In Cincinnati, where a large influx of German and Irish Catholics threatened the Anglo-Protestant hegemony, feelings ran especially strong.[4]

Many Protestants in the Queen City were alarmed by three trends they associated with Catholic immigrants—a huge increase in the crime rate, particularly in the tenements where many immigrants lived; faster growth in the membership of the Roman Catholic Church than in most Protestant churches; and a strong resistance to the temperance movement by the Germans and Irish, who saw regular patronage of taverns and beer gardens as essential to their social and political life. Relations between Protestants and Catholics were also strained by the German and Irish custom of meeting friends and relatives in saloons and beer halls on Sunday mornings, the traditional time of worship for most Protestants.[5]

Protestants were concerned about safeguarding their religious freedoms from the type of Roman Catholic attitude expressed in 1850 in an address by Archbishop John Hughes of New York. Titled *The Decline of Protestantism and Its Causes,* the address stated that the Catholic Church intended to convert the world, including the United States and its inhabitants, legislatures, Senate, cabinet, and president. "Protestantism," the bishop declared, "is effete, powerless, dying out . . . and conscious that its last moment is come when it is fairly set, face to face, with Catholic Truth." Such a statement would, no doubt, have reignited long-standing embers of hatred and distrust of the Roman Catholic hierarchy by people who had a Scotch-Irish, Presbyterian heritage, like Eliza, or Anglican, border-country origins, like Tomlinson.[6]

Anti-Catholic prejudice in southern Ohio's predominantly Protestant population was exacerbated in 1853 when a Catholic newspaper and archbishop in Cincinnati declared opposition to a law that would strengthen Ohio's public school system. Public schools, according to the Catholic opposition, favored a sectarian system that promoted Protestant values and discounted the Catholic way of life. When Archbishop Gaetano Bedini, the papal nuncio, visited Cincinnati later that year, he became the target of riots, and his effigy was burned in protest by an angry mob of several thousand. Eight years later, of course, Northerners of all faiths would unite to defeat an even greater enemy—the South, with its disloyal, slaveholding secessionists. Meanwhile, Tomlinson was still waiting to get a shot at the enemy, and Eliza feared that the enemy had already taken or killed him.[7]

* * * * *

Civil War soldiers everywhere were anxious to get the latest newspapers, which were sometimes sold from vendors' carts like this one in a Virginia camp. (Library of Congress Prints and Photographs Division)

Dear Husband,

On Saturday night I received yours of the 1rst and 2nd inst., from which I am happy to learn that your health continues good. I am glad that your mind is not so wholly engrossed with matters pertaining to the war (as I at one time thought) as to cause you to forget home ties, etc. The health of our family is about as good as usual, no news here that I know of that would be of interest to you.

It appears from what you say that you do not get all my letters, but only occasionally one. I have written you regularly once a week and shall continue to do so as long as I know where to address you. Do you get the papers which I send you? It seems from your letter that you get Cin. papers; if you get them regularly they come in advance of those which I send. If you do not get the news regularly, I will continue to send you the paper when I think there is any thing in it that would be of interest to you.

This morning brother Newt came down to inquire of me whether Dr. Woodward had given you money when you was last here. He, Woodward, has been telling that you complained to him that none of your friends here would do any thing for you and that he gave you two five dollar bills. I told him that I had no knowledge of any thing of the kind. If you needed or wanted money when you were here, you said nothing about it to me, and I did not believe that you had said any thing of the sort. I know that had you been in need of money, and had applied to either of my brothers, you would have got it, if it had been at their command; they both have given you money and would do it again if necessary. Newt's feelings was hurt that you would apply to Woodward. He tries to make our folks look as little and mean as possible. I know nothing is the matter; if he gave you money, I shall refund it as soon as I can command so much means. Please write and let me know how the matter stands, as soon as you can.

We sometimes hear very exciting rumors about the army in Va. The last was that Rosecrans' army was entirely cut to pieces. What few were not killed were taken prisoners! You cannot imagine my feeling as I describe them; when we ascertained that it was a lie gotten up by Cesesh as an asset to the capture of Fort Hatteras, I then could give vent to my pent up feelings in tears, which lifted the heavy load from my heart. I fear that your patience is oft times sorely tried by many things occurring daily in camp, but I trust for the good cause you are willing to endure in silence many things, which you would otherwise resent. May the Lord and his good Angels ever be around and about you, and protect you from all evil, bring you off conqueror all the time.

Ever yours truly,

E. W. Tomlinson

So you have lost your gold pen or you would not write with a poor steel one. I would advise you to keep everything of any value in your trunk. What has become of Jeff? You never mention him.

Mother and the little ones join me in love to you.

I will send you a paper if I can get one of interest this evening.

Tomlinson to Eliza
Camp Hope, Buckhannon, Virginia, September 10, 1861

Dear Eliza,

With one of the worst pens I ever had hold of, and at about 12 o'clock at night, I sit myself at our Regimental Desk to say that "All's Well." Mr. Whitson told me a few minutes since that he was going to Clarksburg, perhaps to Cincinnati. So I will send this by him, having got tired of trusting the mails. As I have had occasion to say many times in my camp correspondence, I have nothing new to write. But we have an occasional rumor which ripples the surface of current dullness. For instance, we hear that yesterday Rosecrans drove back the pickets of the enemy, pressed on their front, and gave battle with 10,000 against 5,000 traitors. If so, he has whipped them many hours since. On Saturday last I went out to French Creek, where part of our Regiment is encamped, for the purpose of delivering their overcoats. While there Company "D." (Highland Guards) came in with a lot of prisoners, horses, guns, etc. It was a great time with the three companies at that camp. I brought their overcoats. This was joyful. But in the midst of it all, about dark, the news came that our pickets had been fired upon. Volunteers were called for to go out and investigate the disturbance, when of course I was in. We ran nearly three miles before stopping. No enemy, however, gratified me with a chance shot either with my Enfield Rifle or revolver.

Company D. had a most gallant little expedition. In three days, they made seventy-five miles through mountains, hills, valleys, brush, creeks, rocks and mud, three out of the four days being in underbrush so thick, "as you never saw."

We hope here soon to have the chance of doing something. Curse this idleness while our country is imperiled. I want to be at the work I came here to do. Truly it is rather disheartening, to find the people intent only on trading with and plundering the soldiers sent to their relief. If it were not for the cause of government, I would say, let the South go where it belongs.

P. S. While I was gone to Ripley old "Jeff." was sold for $15.00, $5.00 of which I have received.

* * * * *

In a passing postscript Tomlinson finally confessed to the loss of his horse, old Jeff. He did not explain why the horse had been sold. Perhaps he needed some cash to pay back the two five-dollar bills he was accused of borrowing while he was in Ripley. He had also lost his gold pen—or possibly sold it to raise some cash. Camp life afforded countless opportunities for spending money on gambling, prostitution, and drink. In 1862 McClellan stated that the greatest obstruction to his army was "the degrading vice of drunkenness." Gambling also flourished, and prostitution was so prevalent that one out of every dozen Union soldiers in 1861 had some form of venereal disease. For Tomlinson and his compatriots in western Virginia, however, the temptations that grew out of the boredom of camp life would soon take a back seat to more pressing matters.[8]

Military action in western Virginia was picking up. Rosecrans moved troops to Carnifex Ferry on the Gauley River on September 9. The following day the Federals secured the area for Union control. As additional Federal forces infiltrated the Kanawha Valley, some real action at Cheat Mountain was about to take place. There Union soldiers prepared to face Confederate forces headed by Gen. Robert E. Lee. But his brilliant strategy was undermined by feuding subordinates, rugged terrain, and unceasing rains. On September 15 he withdrew and soon abandoned hope of regaining control of western Virginia. Farther east, Gen. Pierre Gustave Toutant Beauregard was still celebrating his victorious command several weeks before at Manassas, and McClellan, fearing that Beauregard's army would move westward and overrun his own, stalled in his resolve to press forward and crush Southern troops. Tomlinson probably had more immediate matters on his mind; he was busy organizing his own campaign against the Rebel guerrillas.[9]

CHAPTER ELEVEN

Mustering Men and Courage

To govern children (and men too)—
commend them oftener than you blame them.
—*Freedom's Casket,* June 15, 1844

As CONFEDERATE TROOPS fanned out in Kentucky and boatloads of Union soldiers floated down the Ohio, one rumor after another made the rounds in Ripley. Eliza did not know what to believe, but she had no doubts that she would be powerless to use the one weapon at her disposal if the Rebels invaded. Meanwhile, she continued to worry about her husband, who, unknown to her, had allied himself with some questionable characters. They were on the trail of Confederate guerrillas in the hills around his company's newly constructed fort.

* * * * *

Eliza to Tomlinson
Ripley, Ohio, September 16, 1861

Dear Husband,

I was disappointed that I did not receive a letter from you on Saturday, as you may well imagine my anxiety is great to hear from you.

Two boat loads of soldiers passed us this morning destined for Gauley or that region. We hear that Beauregard is coming on them there with sixty thousand men. They are determined to retake western Va.; they want salt, they want the whole state for their operations, but I hope that our men will not let them have it. Some two or three Regiments are coming up from camp to spend the week in the fairground; they will be up tonight. The soldiers on one of those boats which went up this morning came off and took breakfast in the market house and vicinity; those on the other boat were not permitted to land, so the citizens handed them provision on the boat. Capt. Evans's company were on board one of the boats.

On last Saturday Ally Evans and Net Campbell got home from Iowa where they had been spending the summer. Ally, according to my direction, called at Mrs. Hendrixes and got my silver plate, which she brought to me all right excepting that Mrs. Hendrix substituted her own forks for mine; mine are much the best and handsomest forks, and as I do not feel willing to make the exchange, I shall send hers back the first opportunity.

Dick and his wife were up last at brother Byers's, but as they did not call over I only saw them at a distance. I forgot to mention in my last letter the death of old Mr. Greg; he had been very feeble for a long time. Death was doubtless a happy relief to him from suffering. Persons who have arrived at extreme old age have few pleasures in life.

I know of no news that would be of interest to you. I hope that you will soon whip the rebels so as to be able to come home and enjoy the blessings of peace once more with your family and friends.

I was very sorry to hear of the death of Col. Low, but we must expect these things. 'Tis reported here that Col. Ammen is surrounded by the traitors; if he is, I hope that he will be able to whip them. We hear so many startling rumors that we do not know what to believe. Please keep me posted as far as you are able as to your situation and movements. Are you well protected from the cold and rain of those mountain regions? I would like to know what provision there is for making your winter comfort. God bless and protect you, give you victory, is the prayer of your affectionate companion.

Eliza W. Tomlinson

* * * * *

It would be sometime before Eliza had any inkling of the dramatic changes in her husband's situation. On September 24, at Bennett's Mill in western Virginia, Tomlinson and fifty-one riflemen from Upshur County were sworn in as an independent company known as the Farnsworth Blues.

On September 28, D. D. T. Farnsworth, adjutant to Governor Pierpont, wrote to the governor from his home in Buckhannon with the information that Tomlinson had been elected captain. The company, Farnsworth reported, had also elected a first and second lieutenant and wanted permission to appoint William Pickens as third lieutenant. In requesting that commissions and supplies for the company be sent as soon as possible, Farnsworth noted that the men were true mountain rangers who had already rendered valuable service in the region where they resided. Col. Harris, who had been scouring the hills for enough men to form his 10th Virginia Volunteer Infantry under General Rosecrans, was happy to welcome his first company of Union men brave enough to step forward in the heart of guerrilla territory.[1]

* * * * *

Captain Kilpatrick to Tomlinson
Buckhannon, Virginia, October 1, 1861

Capt. Will. Tomlinson
Dear Sir,

I have been requested by Col. T. M. Harris to communicate with you upon the subject of having your company mustered into service. He says that you have the opportunity of being Company A, as he has mustered none in yet, but that he will this week. He desires you through me to report to him by letter as soon as possible,

I have the honor to be your humble servant,

R. L. Kilpatrick

Capt., Co. B., 5th Regt.

The following is a copy of his letter to me:

Clarksburg
Sept. 30, 1861
Capt. R. L. Kilpatrick
Dear Sir,

I understand there has been a company raised in Upshur, and that a member of one of the companies of the 5th Ohio has been elected to command it.

I have been waiting to hear from Mr. Sumner and Mr. Darnal, who had taken the matter in hand to raise a company for me, but

1,010
BRAVE MEN
WANTED!

I am authorized by Governor Pierpoint to raise a Regiment of men to consist of

TEN COMPANIES

of 101 men each, including officers. When two companies are formed they will be mustered into service and a camp will be established at or near Morgantown, where they will be armed, equipped and drilled until the Regiment is full and ordered into service.

July 29, 1861.   JAMES EVANS.

This broadside or one like it may have alerted Will Tomlinson to an opportunity for raising his own company. (Courtesy of West Virginia and Regional History Center, West Virginia University Libraries) have not as yet. Will you be so good as to communicate with the Captain in that company and say to him that I would be happy to have him report to me by letter, and I will make arrangements at once to have his company mustered in here. If he will write without delay, he may have his company A, as I have not mustered any in as yet, though I expect to this week.

Very respectfully yours, etc.,

T. M. Harris

* * * * *

On October 15, Farnsworth wrote to Governor Pierpont again to report on the status of Tomlinson's company. He repeated his earlier statement that the company had been rendering "valuable service" but needed more ammunition and other provisions, as specified in an attached letter from its captain. Tomlinson, in his own letter to Governor Pierpont from Camp Pickens, proposed that haste be made in mustering his company of sixty-five men into U.S. Service. The company anticipated being Company A of Colonel Harris's regiment and was steadily increasing and prospering, he noted. The men had built "a large and comfortable building" that was "ready for winter" and was located "within a day's march of the only large camp of the mountain desperadoes." In fact, they were surrounded daily by "concealed spies" and slept with their weapons at hand. "I have so far subsisted my company on individual means and credit," Tomlinson wrote. His men needed winter clothing and better weapons than the "old altered flint-locks, which are, from appearance, the gathered refuse of some grand railroad smash." He signed the letter as captain of the Farnsworth Guards, "alias Mountain Marksmen." Governor Pierpont had already issued and mailed Company A's commissions on October 14, the day before Tomlinson's appeal, but no supplies were on the way.[2]

The so-called comfortable quarters that Company A built were located on land donated by the Pickens family, two of whom were members of the company. Known as Camp (or Fort) Pickens, the outpost was situated in a field overlooking a mountain pass near the village of Duffy, in the shank of Lewis County in western Virginia. The fort was actually just one building that had been constructed from double-thick, hewed logs. It stood two stories high, with portholes around the upper walls of each story. There were no windows, but a door was situated in each end of the cabin, which measured approximately thirty by forty-five feet. Two fireplaces provided both heating and cooking facilities, and one corner of the lower room had a sunken storage area called a "tater hole" for orchard fruit and root vegetables. The upper room, accessed by a stairway at each end of the building, was lined with three-tiered bunk beds that could also serve as platforms for firing guns through the second-story portholes. Each bunk, constructed without nails in the old mortise-and-tenon method, was wide enough to sleep two soldiers. At the center of the room was a rack that held at least a hundred guns and had benches on each end for sitting. Though not luxurious, the cabin was solid, and it fended off bushwhackers until December 1864, when Confederate guerrillas set fire to it. By then Tomlinson was long gone. Early in the autumn of 1861, however, he was proud of his men's capabilities, and others seemed to share in his enthusiasm.[3]

* * * * *

B. Collin (Friend) to Tomlinson
Buckhannon, Virginia, October 16, 1861

Capt. Tomlinson
Mountain Marksmen
Friend Will,

Yours was handed me last evening and I can assure you that I was glad indeed to hear from you and your brave men.

Col. Harris has been here for several days, busily engaged in business connected with the formation of his regiment. I have not had the pleasure of seeing him, personally, but I am assured by Adj. Farnsworth, Mr. Smith, Mr. Whitson, and others that we are all right; and he depends upon you and your company. Mr. Whitson has been appointed by Gen. Rosecrans as mustering officer for Virginia. He will be out in your country in a few days. Mr. Pickens has been with him all this morning, and I suppose has all news for you. I gave my letter to Capt. Kilpatrick; he will inform Mr. P. all he wishes to—he gave me no information. I mailed your letter to your infantry—gave Farnsworth his, and Gov. Pierpont's. I send you some coffee and sugar, envelopes, paper and ink. I think our commissions will be along soon. Hoping to see you soon at your own house.

I am yours to command,
Billy Collin
My comps. to all the boys.

While Tomlinson was focused on getting his company organized, commissioned, and outfitted, Eliza was growing increasingly uneasy about Confederate troops in Kentucky. Gen. Robert Anderson, of Fort Sumter fame, had set up Union headquarters in Louisville but was unable to prevent Confederates from making further inroads into the state. Southern troops began a slow but steady march toward the Ohio River town of Maysville, an ideal launching place for raids into rich, Ohio farmlands. Ripley, just ten miles down river, responded by organizing a company that was part of the 59th Ohio Regiment Infantry and that left for Maysville on October 1. But north of the river people continued to watch the hills on the other side and wondered what they would do if they were invaded. Eliza, whose only weapon was a long Scottish knife called a dirk, thought her only recourse was to hope and pray.[4]

* * * * *

Eliza to Tomlinson
Ripley, Ohio, October 7, 1861

Dear Husband,

Yours of the 29th came to hand on last Friday night. I am happy to learn that you are in good health and also that you have attained unto your wishes in a Captaincy; but you do not say whether you have been received into the army in the regular way, or are just an independent organization. I for my part feel very patriotic, but owing to poverty would much prefer doing something for myself at the same time that I was serving my country. Do you belong to a Regiment?

A great many Ohio troops are going to Ky., which is much in need of our assistance just now. They have had considerable excitement in Maysville. Some eight or ten prisoners have been taken there and sent, past this I suppose, to Newport. There is every appearance of serious trouble in Ky. I hope that they will keep it out of Ohio, but if they should come upon us, I know not where we could flee for safety. I rather guess we will have to stay here and take what comes. The enemy would be entirely destitute of manhood to slay a parcel of women and children, so we will trust to their magnanimity for our safety. Your Dirk came; it is the only weapon of defense about the house, and I should be powerless to use even that.

I forgot in my last to tell you that Lowry wrote that D. O. Finch was nominated for the Senate, and J. M. Walker for Representative. Mrs. Thompson informed me on yesterday that they had got word that Will had been promoted to Capt. and had left Mound City for Louisville, I believe it was, perhaps it was St. Louis. I did not pay much attention, therefore cannot say for certain which. No news that I know of that would be of much interest to you. I sent you the <u>Bee</u> last week. I send you the <u>Gazette</u> regularly every day. Do you get it?

One thing certain—I am confident you will take good care of the men under your control and I hope that they will love and obey you from principle, and not because the discipline requires it of them. A good officer is beloved by his men, and they will follow him any place so long as they retain his confidence. Please give my respects to your men and tell them that they have my prayers for their success in the holy cause in which they are engaged. A God of truth, a God of power, a God of love, a God of mercy, a God of justice will, I am confident, give you a triumphant victory over all the enemies of truth and justice. All join me in the warmest expressions of love to you.

I ever remain yours, etc.,

Eliza W. Tomlinson

J. A. Williamson (Friend) to Eliza
Rolla, Missouri, October 16, 1861

Dear Madam,

I took a letter out of the Post Office at this place today addressed to F. P. Yokauer, which I suppose, judging by the hand writing, to be from you. I regret to have to say to you that Frank died on last Saturday of camp or Typhoid Fever and was buried as an Odd Fellow and a Soldier on Sunday. I have not time to write you any of the particulars of his sickness. I am here—the adjutant under Col. Dodge.

Where is Will? I did hear that he was captain of a company of printers raised in Cincinnati.

I left home the 1st of August and have not seen my wife and babies since, nor do I have any idea when I will.

I think the secessionists will all be driven out of this state within 20 days from this time. If Will is not gone to the war and is at home, let him write to me. If he is gone, write to me yourself, and say how yourself and the children are. My family were well a week ago.

I am very respectfully your obedient servant,

J. A. Williamson

Dear Husband,

Yours of the 15th inst. was received last night. I was very much alarmed, the address being in a strange hand, until I succeeded in opening it. I feared that some disaster had happened to you, but was most happy to learn that you were well and all right. You say that you have built a comfortable house for your men, not a very artistic one I fancy. I should like to see how you look in your quarters, that I might see how you manage your housekeeping affairs and ascertain whether you are provided with the necessary requisites to make you comfortable. I am told that little shanties covered all over with earth are very comfortable.

Col. Ammen is in Cin. on official business. I presume that he will be up tonight. Bent. Norris, I understand, talks of raising a company as soon as he gets through with his road, which will be in a week or two. Cap. Evans's boys who went from here in their pursuit after the enemy, took or captured, I believe they call it, a large amount of provisions, beef cattle, etc., also a large amount of household goods, among which were beds, bedding, splendid quilts, and every thing necessary to housekeeping in the best style. Among other valuables, they took a large amount of silver plate; that is the way to make the rebels pay for their whistle! The boys have sent many of their trophies home to their friends.

On the 7th of this month I wrote to Frank telling him pretty plainly what I thought of his conduct, but poor fellow he was called to answer— at a higher tribunal!—for the deeds done in the body. When he used our money he probably thought that he would be able to refund it before he would be called to account. I answered Williamson's letter telling him when you entered the army, your former, and present rank, etc., but left it for you to tell him your adventures under Hill, etc., over those mountains. I shall enclose his letter.

We are all in our usual health, the children go regularly to school, and I think are improving their time very well. Byers thinks that he has made a fine exchange from Mr. Parker's, to Mr. Mitchell's room. Byers has a fine intellect and, if he has the facility for improving it, will make a talented man. Belle stands number one in the first class in her room! She being almost the youngest child in her room. I am proud of my children and pray that the Lord will spare these sweet buds of promise to me and to their country, to which I fondly anticipate they will not only become ornaments but pillars of strength to bind together and to support this great national government, indivisible in truth and justice.

I wish to know whether you are provided with the necessary clothing to make you comfortable during the coming winter. Have you blankets, comforts, etc.? I know not how to get anything to you, if you need any thing which I can supply. Perhaps you could suggest some plan. (Baird has just received permission for you, if required, to go south provided you do not go before the 1st of Nov. next, and return north of said latitude in or before the 1st of August 1862.)

I hope that you get the papers which I send you. 'Tis little that I can do for you but that little is done most cheerfully. O, that this rebellion was subdued and peace and harmony restored to our distracted country. Take good care of yourself and men. God bless and protect you and give you victory is my prayer. Adieu.

Please give my best respects to the brave men of your company. I hope that they will obtain goodly reward for their loyalty in coming up to the service of their country when attacked by traitors.

Ever yours,
Eliza W. Tomlinson
The Post Master has received no postage stamps yet.

Tomlinson to Eliza
Buckhannon, Virginia, October 28, 1861

Dearest Eliza,

This cold morning I will only agree to fill out one page or less of this letter. I'm freezing. Yesterday I came down from my camp. Things were going off about right, but my Lieutenants were not on the ground. My health continues good, and I feel tough as a mule. As yet I have not got my discharge, though I have my commission. I have been mustered into the U.S. Service, and have the post of honor (the right wing) in the Regiment. The other day I received a letter from Byers, of which I was very proud. I will answer it more fully when I get back. This week I expect to have a scout by which I will probably get a dozen of the most notorious desperadoes and murderers in the country. Through one of my men I have concocted a plan by which, I hope (through a woman in their neighborhood), to secure a valuable prize. My facilities for writing are very poor, being surrounded and continually disturbed.

In an hour I go back to camp, which I will reach about 5 o'clock this evening. Have just heard that a government train of seven wagons were captured yesterday after I left, within eight miles of my headquarters. If so, I expect some hot times by tomorrow evening.

Excuse me. I can't write now—business, rumors, and friends so press me. Goodbye. God bless you all.

Ever yours

Will Tomlinson

Have paper mailed the 23rd, but no letter for two weeks except the one lost last week.

* * * * *

The winter of 1861–62 was unusually bitter, and shortages at the Federal level meant that many soldiers in the field did not have winter survival gear. In mid-October, Governor Dennison had called on the people of Ohio to supply blankets and warm clothing for volunteer troops. Procuring supplies was one thing; getting them to troops holed up in the mountains was another. Tomlinson did not even have adequate writing facilities; the front side of his letter was written in ink, and the back, in pencil. But he was robust and happy. He had finally been mustered into the U.S. Service as an officer. Or so he thought. Exactly what he had or had not been mustered into would become a crucial issue down the road. But he had no way of knowing that then, and meanwhile, he was finally engaged in fighting the enemy. In fact, in the war against bushwhackers, his company was right in the thick of it, though not exactly on top of it. As one frustrated Union commander described the situation a year later, "We have now over 40,000 men in the service of the U.S. in Western Va. . . . [but] our large armies are useless here. They cannot catch guerrillas in the mountains any more than a cow can catch fleas."[5]

A gang of guerrillas known Haymond's Rangers was particularly troublesome in the area patrolled by Tomlinson's company. Some of Haymond's men attacked a Union wagon train within eight miles of Fort Pickens, killing one army courier, William DeBolt, and wounding a second. Shortly after, they killed two more men and wounded another. With the help of a scout and a local woman, Tomlinson thought he could put an end to the attacks. Who the woman was remains a mystery, but the scout he mentioned may well have been William G. Pierson, a local blacksmith described as being a light-complexioned, heavily built man about forty-five years old. Pierson, who was reputed to hang out at a tavern in the small Lewis County community of Jacksonville, had rounded up his own company of rangers, but their activities on behalf of the Union were seen by some as more counterproductive than helpful. If Tomlinson was aware of Pierson's blemished reputation, he gave no indication of it. But as his own sister once wrote, Eliza could see farther into a millstone than her husband could. In writing back to her husband, Eliza included several warnings in six pages of penciled script.[6]

* * * * *

Eliza to Tomlinson
Ripley, Ohio, October 28, 1861

Dear Husband,

Yours of the 18th inst. came to hand on Saturday, giving us the pleasing intelligence that you were in good health. From the fact of your building a fort I presume that you intend going into winter quarters where you are. I fear that you will find it very cold in that region. It will be necessary to make your house as tight as possible, so as to exclude the wind. I presume that it is not much colder there than in Iowa, but that is cold enough for comfort!

Well, we are all about as well as usual, excepting mother has a bad cold, and her cough troubles her considerably. I forget whether I told you that brother Byers's son Jeff was in Cin., attending the medical lectures of that city. I send you the Gazette every day, and the Bee every week; also the Times, and literary papers occasionally. I fear that you do not get all of them. The Times has not come to town for the last week.

A great many boats loaded with troops have passed here within the last week destined for Louisville. I fear that our trouble is only commencing in Ky. You appear to be sanguine to the contrary! But I think that the traitor crew will unite and concentrate all their power to subjugate Ky! They are now driven to desperation; they must accomplish something, so as to enable them to subsist their army at the expense of Uncle Sam, and his subjects, during the coming winter, or they will suffer terribly even unto starvation and death.

I hope that you will not be found napping and so taken in a net by those rebels who infest those mountains. "Eternal vigilance is the price of liberty." This is true now personally as well as nationally. Had our officials been more watchful, or even more energetic when treason was manifest, we should not now have been engaged in this war: We have had entirely too much milk and water; this will never cure treason. No! No! They want stronger medicine than this! They opened the ball! Give them back of their own sort. I feel indignant at the protection given by our Africans to the property of rebels in arms against the very power that protected them. All their property should be confiscated to the government. Let it consist in slaves or what it may. I consider that by their act of rebellion they forfeit life, property, every thing. One word more: I know that you will be careful of your men and not unnecessarily expose them to danger! Could I see those brave patriots I would ask them to take care of their Capt. for my sake and for his children's sake as well as for the good I hope you will be instrumental in rendering to your country.

'Tis passing strange the pay master does not visit you.

I understand that Col. Harris has captured eight hundred Cecesh over here in Ky. not many miles off. The rebels were commanded by Williams. I know not his rank, probably Col. They are bringing the prisoners to Maysville. It was a mistake about Col. Ammen being in Cincinnati. Clain Ridgeway was not here when his wife died, but came soon after. He was not well when he came and was taken down seriously ill with typhoid fever soon after his arrival. He is now well, or nearly so, but is yet here. I presume that he will leave soon. I have not heard any further word from out west. Did you get my letter with Williams's enclosed? What do you think of it? Can it be a forgery? Enclosed I send you a few stamps, the first that I have been able to obtain. The old ones are no longer of any value.

Take good care of your horse. I hope that you will not lose him or have him stolen by those prowling thieves who surround you. I hope that you are abundantly provided with blankets, comforts, and everything which is necessary to make you comfortable. I can furnish you with a couple of blankets and several comforts, but there is no way of getting them to you that I know of. I hope that the ladies of that region will show their patriotism by providing what is necessary to meet your wants.

I remain ever yours truly,
Eliza W. Tomlinson

* * * * *

Given Eliza's lack of military experience, it is interesting to speculate on what motivated her, once again, to lecture her husband on the topic of military leadership. Perhaps she feared that her husband's impulsive nature would lead him astray. "'Eternal vigilance is the price of liberty,'" she wrote, perhaps assuming that Tomlinson would remember the rest of that popular quotation borrowed from the abolitionist orator, Wendell Phillips. Regardless of what he recalled, however, he would have been well advised to heed what Phillips said in his speech to the Massachusetts Anti-Slavery Society in 1853: "Power," he stated, "is ever stealing from the many to the few. . . . The hand entrusted with power becomes . . . the necessary enemy of the people."[7]

CHAPTER TWELVE

Mountain Desperadoes

Men can't be neutral in these times.
—"Brownson's View of the War," *Loyal Scout*, October 10, 1863

As COLD WEATHER SET IN, Tomlinson wrote to his superiors and stressed the urgency of getting winter provisions for his men. Their location in the heart of guerrilla territory also made his request for new rifles and pistols critical, especially since he had undisclosed plans for a raid on Rebel bushwhackers. He seemed oblivious to the potential for disaster of such an operation and probably would have ignored Eliza's warning about his impulsive nature, even if it had arrived in time to change his plans. Eliza, meanwhile, was dealing with the emotional turmoil of hearing good news one week, no news the next, and distorted news day after day.

* * * * *

Eliza to Tomlinson
Ripley, Ohio, November 4, 1861

Dear Husband,

I received a letter from you on last Friday—the date I disremember, and cannot lay my hand upon it just now. I am happy to learn that your health continues good. You anticipated a brush with the enemy. I hope that our boys got back those wagons and army stores and gave the villains a good whipping into the bargain. You speak of being cold. I fear that you have not got sufficient warm clothing. If so, I would do anything in my power to supply your necessities; but I do not know how to get anything conveyed to you.

On Saturday night I received a letter from Will Lowry in which according to my request he sends me your final card. I enclose the letter, but as you have had such bad luck with my letters, fear to send the card until I hear further from you.

You say that you got a letter from our son Byers. I did not know that he had written, but as I had often told him to do so, he wrote one or two which he showed to me which I commented upon, not much to his satisfaction, so I suppose he thought that he would not subject himself to my criticism.

I received a letter from Williamson in reply to one I wrote him. All we entrusted to Yokauer's care is lost; he has left nothing that can be got. He says that he left the Brooks' notes and mortgage in the hands of Hoyt Sherman. So he can foreclose the mortgage and get a good title to the land. Mr. Sherman was willing to take the deed and give up the notes and mortgage, but he could not do so and get a good title, as several judgments were on record against you, so he has to foreclose it at his own expense. He will bid the property off at the full amount of the debts and costs and will then give up the notes and mortgage. Williamson says that he made an arrangement with him to this effect. I was not aware that you were indebted to any one in Des Moines. Williamson says that he will write you shortly; that note he says he marked it paid and laid it away before he left.

Should you remain in your present quarters during the winter I hope that you will make your house as comfortable as possible. It would be a good plan to paste those papers which I send you on the wall.

We are all in the enjoyment of our usual health. I have no further news of interest that I can think of at present. I hope that you and your command in any contest with traitors may come off victorious, without any loss on your part. Dodge the bullets, and hustle them back with fatal aim.

Mother and the children join me in the warmest love to you. Do not be rash in risking your person. I ask this knowing your impulsive nature. May God guard and protect you from all evil.

Ever yours,

Eliza W. Tomlinson

I send you three papers today, the Gazette, Enquirer, and Times.

* * * * *

On November 3, in a letter to Colonel Harris from Camp Pickens, Tomlinson wrote that his company was engaged in "active and essential service" and was "generally in good health." His men had almost finished the buildings for their accommodations but needed clothing, especially since much of their service was done at night, when guerrillas were on the prowl stealing horses. But Tomlinson protested that no sooner had his men captured the "thoroughbred guerilla secessionists" who were guilty of everything from horse stealing to shooting Union men, and from inciting treason in the countryside to collaborating with Southern spies, than they were released by Col. S. H. Dunning of the Fifth Ohio at Buckhannon and sent back to terrorize their neighbors and spy on Union troops. "It is not right," he wrote, "and I must either send my prisoners

Confederate bushwhackers, such as these from an illustration in an 1861 *Harper's Weekly*, infested the hills around Camp Pickens in western Virginia. The mountaineers are described as being tall, muscular, and hardy. (Courtesy of West Virginia and Regional History Center, West Virginia University Libraries)

at once to the devil, where they belong, or to some more secure place than the Post at Buckhannon, as now commanded. What am I to do?" The last question, however, was purely rhetorical, and he was quick with an answer. Since many "mountain desperadoes" went home at night to get provisions from their wives, why not, he proposed, "take such women prisoners, and burn their harbors, or, at least, possess ourselves of their food and cooking utensils?"[1]

What Tomlinson did not tell Colonel Harris was that he and some of his men had already taken matters into their own hands. But Harris was quickly informed, and two days later, on November 5, he wrote Governor Pierpont that he was worried about Captain Tomlinson's company. The captain's men had killed some secessionists in their vicinity, including Porter J. Arnold, a prominent citizen, and, Harris wrote, there was much excitement about it. He had yet "to learn the particulars" but would do so in the next few days. Meanwhile, Harris enclosed Tomlinson's letter of November 3 so that the governor could see what was needed by his company, which then included eighty-four men.[2]

Later in his letter, Harris recounted the attack on a Union wagon train by Ben Haymond, the appearance of Arnold's dog on the scene, and the refusal of a Jacksonville tavern keeper to help the wounded Union teamsters. "Circumstances such as these and such as Capt. Tomlinson recites in his letter no doubt caused his men to take the law into their own hands," Harris wrote, in seeming defense of Tomlinson. Yet, in his very next sentence, Harris began distancing himself from Tomlinson and the actions of his men. "You see," Harris explained, "he is serving on his own hook not being under orders from any one. He claims to belong to my Regt. but I have no authority to control him. He may require to be under the authority of some one more prudent and judicious than himself." As for Haymond—from what Harris understood, he had been captured. But the two oaths of loyalty he had already sworn to the Union had done nothing to stop his plundering and shooting of Union soldiers. "I understand he boasts of a specific number probably one dozen which he says he has killed," Harris wrote, adding that there was too much leniency in the policy that allowed such men to go free.[3]

The challenge involved in controlling an independent company of mountain marksmen stationed on a lonely mountain outpost in heavy guerrilla territory may have been more than Harris was equipped to handle at the time. The former medical doctor had no military experience but was determined to launch an ambitious military career by raising his

Will Tomlinson's commanding officer in western Virginia, Thomas Maley Harris, as photographed sometime between 1860 and 1865. (Library of Congress Prints and Photographs Division)

own regiment. He could not afford to have his early efforts besmirched by an unfortunate incident involving the captain of his first company. Nor could he afford to disregard any successes that could be attributed to men under his command. He had to find out exactly what happened and tread carefully around a controversial incident that would eventually become known as the Jacksonville murders. Eliza, meanwhile, also had serious concerns about Tomlinson.[4]

* * * * *

Eliza to Tomlinson
Ripley, Ohio, November 12, 1861

Dear Husband,

Your last which was written on the 28th contained the intelligence that you were going out on a scout, and also that you were going after some rebels who had captured a number of our wagons containing army stores. You may possibly form some faint idea of the anxiety of mind which I have endured since the reception of the aforesaid letter a week ago last Friday: I fancy a thousand things: one moment you are sick, the next a prisoner. Again I see you wounded or killed, and in the power of fiends who take pleasure in torturing you in the most barbarous manner. All this is folly you say; but I cannot control my imagination within the limits necessary for my own happiness.

Our family are all in the enjoyment of their usual health. Young Deboalt returned from the Gauley region of Va. night before last. He says that our men have the enemy surrounded, so that it is not possible for them to escape; they will now be compelled either to fight or surrender: no possibility it is thought of their running this time.

I send you eight or ten papers every week. I now send you Harpers Weekly, every Saturday, the Bee on Friday, and occasionally the Times and Enquirer; the Gazette every day. I hope that you receive them.

When I last wrote you, I sent you Lowry's letter, but thought it best not to send your final card until I should hear from you. You are probably not in a situation to make use of it at present. I cannot think of any news that would be of interest to you. You will learn more from the papers than what I can tell you.

I hope that you will not be rash. The enemy is subtle and will employ all their arts to entrap you. Beware of pretended Union men, and women, too: their loyalty may be only assumed for the purpose of gaining your confidence so as to get you in their power. Oh dear, I do so ardently wish for this war to come to an end. It does appear so cruel and barbarous for men to be killing each other like wild beasts. 'Tis heathenish.

I have just heard that on Sunday night last the enemy, some one thousand strong, entered Guyandotte whilst the citizens were at church, cruelly murdered them, pursuing them with demonic fury into the river, slaying all before them, and then burnt the town to ashes. This news may probably be false, but there was a letter received here this morning stating the above as facts. Please write immediately.

I ever remain yours affectionately, etc.!

Eliza W. Tomlinson

* * * * *

The version of the skirmish at Guyandotte that Eliza heard showed how twisted the account of an event could become by the time it reached the eager ears of loved ones back home. Located on the edge of Huntington, where the Guyandotte River emptied into the Ohio, the town was a cesspool of outlaws and renegade Rebels. Most were only too happy to join some Virginia Border Rangers intent on harassing Union recruits

Most of Eliza Wylie Tomlinson's letters were written in pencil, like this one in which she expressed fears for her husband. (Wylie-Tomlinson Collection) quartered nearby. Some of these recruits were in church when the Rebels drove them into the river and killed several of them, including one young man who swam back to shore in the act of surrendering. But no townspeople were harmed, much less killed. And it was the Union forces, not the Confederates, that burned the town—in reprisal for the raid on Union troops.[5]

It seemed that Federal forces everywhere were finding out how resistant the Rebels could be. The Union presence in Kentucky was shakier than ever with Confederate general Albert Sidney Johnston on the scene, and east of the Blue Ridge, at Ball's Bluff near Leesburg, Virginia, poor strategic planning by Union commanders made sitting ducks out of hundreds of troops as they tried to retreat back across the Potomac River and got stuck in the middle under fire. News of the bloodbath sped across the country on the newly completed, transcontinental Western Union lines. It took an act of courage just to read the newspapers.[6]

Around the same time, Tomlinson may have found his own courage faltering as his leadership was being impugned. Colonel Harris had completed his inquiry into the Jacksonville incident and reported back to Governor Pierpont. Harris, described by a neighbor as "an honest and sincere man" who conducted a thorough investigation but never changed his mind once it was made up, had formed several conclusions. In his letter of November 15 to the governor, he acknowledged the two-faced loyalty of one of the men who had been shot, but he could not justify the "manner in which the thing was done." Harris wrote that the Jacksonville men had been taken from their houses and "deliberately murdered." According to what Harris discovered, the Union raiders were led by William Pierson, a "malicious and vindictive man," who "got Capt. Tomlinson to take a few of his men and do this wicked deed" while "under the influence of liquor." But, Harris wrote, Union men in the area had been living in terror and dread ever since Capt. Tomlinson had received a commission from the governor. Furthermore, according to Harris, Tomlinson's company had been unable to increase their numbers "on account of the bad character and unpopularity of their Capt." Since the men in Tomlinson's company had now been mustered into U.S. Service and had yet to elect new officers, Harris told the men that Tomlinson was no longer their captain and had no authority over them.[7]

Harris's statement that Tomlinson's men had been mustered into U.S. Service may not have been accurate. Perhaps he misunderstood or had been misinformed. Or maybe he saw a fast and easy way to get rid of

Tomlinson, who would have been a convenient scapegoat for an expedition that went horribly wrong and might interfere with his rise to the top. Whatever his reasons for telling Tomlinson's men that they were without a captain after being mustered into U.S. Service, Harris himself was not commissioned by Governor Pierpont until December 13, and it was not until the following March that the Tenth Virginia Infantry Regiment officially came under the federal command of U.S. Brig. Gen. R. H. Milroy of the Cheat Mountain District, Department of Western Virginia. Company A, formerly under Tomlinson's command, was not mustered into U.S. Service in the Tenth Virginia Infantry until March 13, 1862, one month after its new captain, Morgan A. Darnall, was commissioned. In the meantime, Harris had moved his headquarters to Randolph County after wintering at Camp Pickens, which Tomlinson's men had completed in the fall of 1861.[8]

Ironically, on November 1, 1861, Tomlinson finally received his discharge from the Fifth Ohio, thus completing the process enabling him to be commissioned as captain of Company A in the Tenth Virginia Infantry. Within days of his discharge from the Fifth Ohio, however, he was relieved of his duties with Company A by Harris, leaving him without a commission or any official military affiliation. Eliza's warnings about his impulsive nature must have come back to haunt him when he left Camp Pickens that November. It was an ignominious ending for his military service, even though exactly what had happened on the night in question—October 30, 1861—remained contested.[9]

Accounts of the incident—including the alleged date of its occurrence—vary, but according to one account, the evening in question began unraveling into a disastrous sequence of events when Tomlinson ordered a few of his men to assist William Pierson and some other local volunteers on an unspecified mission. Pierson led them to the village of Jacksonville, where they arrested Porter M. Arnold, William Francis, and William Brake, who were then marched outside of town on the Walkersville Pike and shot without warning. Brake was killed outright, but Francis faked being hit and escaped. Arnold, who had tried to outrun his assassins, was shot several times and died a few days later. Pierson and Tomlinson, with their men in tow, then made their way to the home of George Blair, who was shot point-blank when he opened his front door. Francis, winding his way through the mountains, managed to reach Weston and notify military authorities. Two men from Tomlinson's company, Enoch

Cunningham and Christian Simons, were identified as being part of the gang that attacked the Jacksonville men.[10]

On November 19, Governor Pierpont issued a proclamation offering a reward of three hundred dollars for the apprehension and securing of Pierson, Cunningham, and Simon—or one hundred dollars for the arrest and delivery of any one of them. A few days later, Harris wrote that Pierpont was "misinformed in the facts of the affair." Harris quoted Blair as having stated that "the only way to put down the union Spirit or the Union party would be to drag them from their nests and kill them and burn them." Brake, he maintained, was "a traitor in disguise" and may well have been "carrying a Secret Express" to the Southern army, and Arnold was "a bad man having counseled and incited his fellow citizens in a public speech to engage in guerrilla warfare." Pierson, Harris noted, was not a secessionist but should be one. It was Pierson who induced Captain Tomlinson "to have two of his boys detailed as scouts," Harris explained, and they obeyed him, even though they "did not know what duty they were going upon" and did not realize that they were under no obligation to follow such orders since they were already mustered into U.S. Service and had no captain at that point. "They were simply a congregation of U.S. volunteers without any organization," Harris wrote. Harris stated that Tomlinson was "odious to the whole company on account of this brutal act and to none more so than the boys Simons and Cunningham," and Simons, he said, was willing to swear that he did not fire on anyone during the incident. After Harris informed the company of "their true condition," they voted unanimously "to invite Tomlinson to leave, which he did at once." The Governor, Harris argued, should not only publish the facts as he (Harris) presented them but offer a reward for the apprehension of Pierson and Tomlinson.[11]

Local law enforcement officials were hesitant to get involved in a situation that aroused the ire of so many area residents. But on November 29, a captain in the Third Virginia Regiment wrote to Governor Pierpont requesting information on where he could collect the reward for arresting Cunningham, Simons, and Pierson. The three were imprisoned in various locations to avoid further incidents. A public letter written by Pierson on November 28 stated that he, Cunningham, and Simons, were in jail on false charges arising from information provided by Owen F. Francis of Weston, a Southern sympathizer. Moreover, Pierson, asserted, he had been sent as a guide by General Rosecrans to arrest the men in

Jacksonville, who were known secessionists and had resisted arrest. Meanwhile, J. Holt, a resident of Bennetts Mills, where Tomlinson's company had been mustered in and which was just a few miles from Camp Pickens, had written a long letter to Governor Pierpont about the incident. According to Holt, Pierson had been hanging around Camp Pickens since troops came into the area. The home guard unit that became Company A was actually in the process of organizing a few months before "a man by the name of William Tomlinson came to the neighborhood," Holt said. He added that Tomlinson had said he was from Cincinnati and was authorized by Pierpont to raise a company. Then, according to Holt, Tomlinson persuaded the men in the company to elect him as captain. Holt was pressuring local magistrates not only to arrest Pierson and Simons but also Tomlinson, who, he said, was also guilty of taking a rifle and valuable horse from Camp Pickens when he left for Wheeling.[12]

In the mountainous terrain of western Virginia, where loyalties to family clans ran wide and deep and the choosing of sides often pitted one family member against another, it was next to impossible to distinguish people who could be trusted from those who could not. Internecine warfare was especially treacherous around Camp Pickens, an area sometimes called "Little Dixie" due to the number of families who had relatives in the Valley of Virginia. Opinions differed on the loyalties of the men killed in Jacksonville. Holt maintained that none of them had said or done anything to support or encourage the "present infamous rebellion." Colonel Harris, on the other hand, was convinced that Arnold, Brake, and Blair were all involved in aiding and abetting the enemy. There were also varied impressions of Pierson. Harris regarded him as "a vindictive malicious man" capable of inhuman deeds. But before the war, he was known to be a peaceful citizen. In light of all the conflicting opinions about the local men involved in the incident, it is interesting that no one, absolutely no one, stood up for Tomlinson—the only one not from the area.[13]

There is no record of Pierson, Cunningham, and Simons ever being tried, and they were exonerated of the charges against them. Cunningham and Simons were mustered into Company A of the Tenth Virginia Infantry Regiment in March 1862, and Pierson became a scout for Col. Nathan Wilkinson, who regarded him as "an energetic and reliable Union man." On the morning of September 20, 1864, as the forty-seven-year-old Pierson stepped out on his back porch to wash, he was fatally shot by assassins who had apparently been hiding in a cornfield. A rock not far from the house had the following words inscribed on it: "Don't follow us or you will get what Pierson got."[14]

Col. Thomas Maley Harris continued to rise through the ranks, and on March 12, 1867, he was commissioned as brevet major general for his heroic service in the capture of Fort Whitworth in the Battle of Petersburg. After the war, he served in various public offices, but what he became most remembered for and what he spent a large portion of his time and energy defending was the role he played in the trial of the conspirators involved in the assassination of President Lincoln. Harris, who was described as having a "stern disposition" and a temper with a short fuse, was handpicked by Secretary of War Edwin M. Stanton to serve on the military commission that tried the conspirators and sentenced four of them to death, including Mary Surratt. Some commissioners thought she should have received a more lenient sentence because of her age, sex, and the questionable circumstances regarding the degree of her guilt. Harris, to the contrary, believed "she was the most guilty of all," stating later on that she ruled the roost that hatched the eggs. Because Harris refused to join several commissioners in signing a petition requesting that Surratt's life be spared, he was often blamed for her death. The controversy arising from his role in her sentence plagued him for the rest of his life.[15]

An interesting footnote to the tragic episode from the perspective of Tomlinson's former association with Harris is that the Supreme District Court justice who issued the writ of habeas corpus that would have made it possible for Surratt to have a new trial, one by civilian authorities, was none other than Andrew Wylie Jr., Eliza's first cousin. Andy, as he was called, was the son of her father's brother, Andrew Wylie Sr., the first president of Indiana University, and had been appointed to his office by President Lincoln. The writ of habeas corpus that Justice Wylie issued in the wee hours of the morning was promptly suspended by President Johnson, however, and Surratt and three other conspirators were executed the same day.[16]

As for Tomlinson, he not only made it back home but wasted no time in writing Governor Pierpont to request clarification of his status. In a letter dated November 18, 1861, from Ripley, he wrote how utterly surprised he had been when Colonel Harris visited Camp Pickens and informed him that his commission, which had been signed and issued by the governor himself, was no longer valid and that a new election of officers must be held. In the meantime, he was told, the company was not under anyone's control. "As we were hourly in the front and face of danger, and as such an anomaly as a company without a commander was entirely new to me," he wrote, "I concluded to retire until I could consult with you." The former captain was also concerned about how the men in his company were to be paid and wanted the governor to know that the winter quarters at Fort Pickens were completed and could comfortably accommodate one hundred fifty men. He concluded by asking Pierpont to send him a reply at Ripley so it could be forwarded to him in western Virginia, where he intended to fight, as a private—if not a commissioned officer—until peace returned.[17]

CHAPTER THIRTEEN

~

Disarmed

One half of those who are born, die before they attain the age of seventeen.
—"Interesting Facts in Brief," *Freedom's Casket,* June 8, 1844

THE WINTER OF 1862 was a difficult time for the Tomlinsons—and the country. About the time that Tomlinson was dismissed from the military, he came down with a "disease of the lungs," which was probably some form of bronchitis or pneumonia. His illness was given by the family as the reason for the end of his military service. Letters from him and Colonel Harris, however, reveal that his discharge was actually precipitated by his involvement in the deplorable Jacksonville affair. If Eliza ever learned the truth of the situation, she never mentioned it in her letters. More than likely, she never knew much, if anything, about what really happened during her husband's star-crossed interlude as captain of an independent company of counterinsurgents in the hills of western Virginia. She may not have cared all that much since she soon had more pressing concerns. Byers was also ill, and his father was not around. After recovering, Tomlinson had gone back to work in Cincinnati. But his recent humiliation in the military, his damaged health, and the depressing war news made it hard for him to see any rays of hope, as indicated by the following fragment of a letter he apparently wrote to Eliza early in 1862.[1]

* * * * *

Tomlinson to Eliza
Cincinnati, Ohio, January 1862

Now that I have filled two pages, what more can I write? Oh, yes—Belle is again going to school. I feel a gleam of sunshine once more. For her sake at least I will try to cast out many a bitter thought, and stop repining.

There seems nothing of importance to speak of except the high water. Many a poor family is turned out homeless, penniless, naked and hungry. The other day I walked out to the place where that memorable railroad accident befell us. Just beyond it is all a vast lake, with many tops of trees barely visible. The river is also close to the Johnson house, on Plum. A good many have been drowned. The most painful accident of this kind to me was the drowning of my esteemed friend Geo. P. Buell. He was one of the editors of the Cincinnati Times. It was Mr. B. who spoke in the Seceeder Church last year for Douglas. He was physically and morally brave. He was very talented and highly educated, but poor. Blessed be his memory.

You ask about whether Webb has succeeded in settling our pay matters? I have not seen him for more than a week. I gave him the necessary documents, but he has not reported. Somehow I feel that the State intends defrauding us. I have now but slight hopes of success. Was my communication put in the Bee? I now wish I could get work in that office. Do you hear anything about the old horse "Auditor?"

My health is much improved

Ever yours,
    Will Tomlinson

* * * * *

Tomlinson never did work for the *Bee*'s editor, who was probably the old "horse Auditor" referred to in his letter. But the *Bee* for January 23, 1862, did include a letter to the editor from Tomlinson. If he could not fight on the ground, he could at least charge forward with his pen.

* * * * *

Tomlinson to the *Bee*

CINCINNATI, Jan. 14.

EDS. BEE:—In these days of great expectations, the daily news is searched with avidity by all classes and ages, for in this mammoth game of "bullet and bragger," who of all mankind but has a personal interest in the stakes?

It was my intention to write something of local matters in the city, but the deep shadow of impending events, pregnant with the fate of this nation, and the future liberty of millions make all minor considerations tasteless for discussion.

Therefore permit me to relieve myself, and talk on this theme, and then something else may come up. It is useless to disguise it, and a growing distrust prevails as to either the capacity or fidelity of the Administration in its higher departments. After spending hundreds of millions of dollars—after arming over six hundred thousand of the strong armed brave hearted fathers and sons of the free North—after nine months of weary camp life and drilling—after burying our dead who have thronged the threshold of the king of terrors by tens of thousands, from hospitals and mountain sides and wooded valleys, what have we to show for offset? An enemy more confident and hellish, a chapter of great blunders, and two important and shameful defeats. Why all this? When Congress, representing the sovereignty of the People, inquires at the proper Department, that body is, in effect, coolly told that it is none of their business—and so it goes. Are we already under a military dictatorship? But pass over the growling. Where is our remedy? It is in an advance on the whole line. If we cannot whip the devilish traitors with our present means and preparations, then we never can do it.—Strike with the strong arm—onward with a purpose! Give to our army the sort of work they so ardently covet. Let us hope that the dawning day is here, full of glorious sunshine. Disembarrass our cause of the negro incubus, by leaving that question to be settled between master and slave.

Hoping that the same paper which contains this may have the felicity of setting forth in glowing capitals a great Union victory,

I remain yours,

WILL

* * * * *

Tomlinson's ardent support of suppressing the rebellion and simultaneous restriction of the "negro incubus" to a "question to be settled between master and slave" was not an unusual stance for Union loyalists who still saw the war as a struggle over the dissolution of the Union rather than the elimination of slavery. Although Tomlinson had published antislavery sentiment as early as 1844, his views about the "Negro question" were complex and evolving, like those of many white Northerners who feared that a large influx of freed slaves would not only undermine their economic security but also "Africanize" their race. Whites in the Border States like Ohio were especially prone to such fears. In Ohio the number of "colored people" had already increased 187 times from 1800 to 1860, when the census counted 36,673 colored residents out of the state's total population of 2,339,511. In the same period the state's white population had increased 51 times. But statistics were far from Tomlinson's mind with the approach of spring and the children's birthdays.[2]

* * * * *

Tomlinson to Eliza
Cincinnati, Ohio, March 10, 1862

Dearest Eliza,

I send herewith a pair of birds and cage. It is a birthday present for our daughter, and I hope it will please not only her but all of you. Yesterday the cage met with a little misfortune, having fallen from a nail in the yard fence. The floor of a part of the second story is busted out, but Byers can fix it in a few minutes. For the present I like it best as it is, for it gives the birds more room. The front left hand corner post is also loose. It can be fastened by a little more glue.

About next Monday I will send Byers his birthday present, as you suggest.

My health is improving some. I have no news other than what you see in the papers. As I understand the new order of the President forming corps de armee, to be governed by a Council of War of five generals, Mc-Clellan is left clear out of all command. I hope that this interpretation of the mystery may prove correct, though I think it would have been much preferable, and more dignified in the head of this still great nation to have boldly said to him: "Get Thee hence—you have been well weighed and found altogether too light for the purpose."

But I must be in a hurry, and get that cage to the boat.

In haste, yours ever,

Will Tomlinson

* * * * *

A present of canaries in the midst of war could be seen as a bit extravagant. Perhaps the absent father wanted his children to have something that would remind them of him and infuse the long, drab years of the war with a note of joy. He may also have hoped that Eliza would recall times when their love for each other was more like a robust melody than a long, plodding march. Whatever his motives, Tomlinson's gift soon provided a bright motif for the family's letters, even in the darkest of times.

* * * * *

Eliza to Tomlinson
Ripley, Ohio, March 18, 1862

Dear Husband,

Since I wrote you Byers has been quite sick. He is some better this morning. I do not apprehend any danger in his case, but if convenient to you, I would be glad to have you come up. Byers would like to see you, as would also the rest of us; it is a considerable length of time since we had that pleasure. Should you come up, please bring Byers a few nice apples. He thinks that he could eat some roasted; two or three lemons would not be amiss. Should you not be able to come up, you can send these on the packet. Byers has no appetite and has not eaten anything since he has been sick. He has taken no nourishment excepting what he has taken in a fluid state, so that he is quite weak. His fever is broke now, and I think now with careful nursing he will get along.

Belle is doing finely. Mother is feeble. I feel about as well as usual excepting that am considerably fatigued nursing the sick. The birds are doing fine; they are very much admired. I know of no news that would be of interest to you.

Ever yours, etc.,

Eliza W. Tomlinson.

Do not be alarmed. The reason I write for you to come up is that we would like to see you, but should it not be convenient for you to do so, please do not discommode yourself by coming.

Eliza to Will
Ripley, Ohio, March 19, 1862

Dear Husband,

I am sorry that you did not come up on the packet last night. Byers is quite ill. I hope that you will come as soon as you receive this. Inflammation of the lungs is the trouble. I hope for the best, but I cannot longer disguise the fact that he is dangerously ill.

Ever yours,
Eliza W. Tomlinson

We have blisters on Byers' breast, wrists, and ankles. They have raised well.

* * * * *

On March 23, 1862, a few days after Eliza's letter, Byers would have been fifteen years old. But the severity of his illness and unpleasantness of its treatment must have left him with few fond memories of that particular birthday. The blisters raised on his body probably indicated that he was being treated for pneumonia through a procedure known as "cupping." Two methods were used to produce blisters as a "counter irritant" that was supposed to reduce pain and promote healing by drawing the blood to the skin, away from the inflicted area. The first method used a suction cup pressed against skin to induce blisters. In the second, a glass or metal cup was filled with burning alcohol and then pressed against the skin. Another counter-irritant used for treating lung disease was the direct application to the chest of hot plasters consisting of moistened mustard or belladonna spread on cloth. Although today these methods seem primitive and needlessly painful, the fact that both of Eliza's brothers were on the scene as university-trained physicians suggests that Byers was probably receiving standard medical care for the time. Whether or not it would keep him alive was another matter.[3]

* * * * *

Dear Husband,

I am happy to have the pleasure of informing you that Byers is improving daily. He came downstairs this morning and has been down all day fixing up specimens for his instrument the greater part of the time. He ran out of glass so he will have to desist until he is able to go up the street and have some more cut. Belle started to school again this morning. I was almost afraid to have her go on account of the whooping cough, but I suppose if she would take it now, she will have it at any rate no matter what precautious we take to prevent it.

Those three lemons came to hand and were very acceptable. I am inclined to believe that both of those birds are females. Eddy has never uttered a note excepting peep, peep. Maggy twitters a little some times. The males bring higher price; hence, I think the imposition. I may possibly be mistaken; we shall ascertain ere long. Byers is somewhat fatigued and has lain down upon the lounge. It will take some time for him to regain his strength.

Mrs. Kerr is getting better. We have had two beautiful days, yesterday and today. I suppose that we may look for rain again tomorrow. My paper did not come to hand on Saturday. It will be out the first of March. I would be glad to have it come on at least as long as the war lasts. No news of interest that I know of.

I ever remain yours, etc.,

Eliza W. Tomlinson

* * * * *

Now that Tomlinson was in Cincinnati, he was sending Eliza the latest newspapers, instead of the other way around, when he was in western Virginia and Eliza sent the papers to him. Newspapers were obviously a daily staple for the Tomlinsons, wherever they were, and with Byers in recovery mode, Eliza would have more time for keeping up with the latest publications, including the hometown paper, the *Ripley Bee*. Its April 3 issue included an advertisement for a photography studio calling for five thousand babies to have their pictures taken at thirty-five cents each. Next to it was Tomlinson's column on current events, which opened with a reference to an incident at Pike's Opera House in Cincinnati on

March 24. In response to an address by abolitionist Wendell Phillips, an angry crowd threw eggs and stones at him, and general pandemonium broke out, forcing Phillips's friends to rush him incognito from the scene.[4]

Tomlinson's major focus, however, was on the somber farewell that the city of Cincinnati had given to Capt. George Whitcom, who was killed at the battle of Kernstown, near Winchester, Virginia, on March 23. Whitcom was one of five color-bearers shot down in succession in what would later become known as the first significant engagement in the Shenandoah Valley Campaign. Union troops defeated Stonewall Jackson's force of more than four thousand, but for Tomlinson the battle would always be remembered for the loss of gallant comrades like Whitcom. Compared to him, Parson Brownlow—Tomlinson's next item of interest—paled as a rather pathetic example of patriotic sacrifice. The former Methodist minister and colorful newspaper editor was the only U.S. senator from the South to stay loyal to the Union and was eventually arrested by the Confederacy. But his flair for aggrandizing his martyrdom made him a hot potato for Confederates, and they dropped him at the doorstep of Union lines in early March. Meanwhile, a visit to Cincinnati by the captivating Gen. Tom Thumb was providing a welcome diversion to wartime news and gave Tomlinson an opportunity to engage in some fun.[5]

* * * * *

Correspondence of the *Bee*

Cincinnati, April 1
Nothing very exciting has happened here since the "Opera mob," excepting it may be the City Democratic Convention, this moment in session.

Funeral of Capt. Geo. W. Whitcom.
On Sunday last was exhibited the all pervading devotions of our people to the cause of our country, in the extraordinary honors paid to the remains of Captain George B. Whitcom, of the Fifth Ohio, who was shot through the head on the Sunday previous in the battle of Winchester.

During the forenoon the body was laid out in State, in Skaat's Hall. With the crowd I passed along the Hall, and looked upon what was mortal of my late gallant comrade.

In a moment rushed back memories of the scenes and trials of the past few months, both in camp and on the march—in peaceful Ohio and hostile

Virginia Mountains. How vividly arose again the scene of the presentation of that flag into his hands as its custodian for the regiment—that identical flag which he died in waving before the very jaws of their guns. Others of his brave color-guard had fallen before him, and as he straitened [*sic*] his manly form he received the fatal bullet about an inch below the left eye, close to the nose. As he reeled his dying words were "BOYS, KEEP UP THE COLORS!"

The funeral was very largely attended by the military, Odd Fellows, Police City Council, and Citizens. Religious services were held in Christi Chapel, Rev. Mr. Fee, formerly stationed at Ripley, presiding. Fully twenty thousand people bordered the route of the procession evincing their deep interest in the event and a desire most fittingly to do every possible honor to the remains of the fallen brave.

We deposited the remains in the beautiful Spring Grove Cemetery, first reciting and performing the impressive ceremonies of the beloved order of Friendship, Love and Truth, and closing the Last sad scene with three volleys of musketry.

PARSON BROWNLOW.

This celebrated Parson, of the bang-up-jam-down, unterrified order, is the boner of the day. He is enjoying his release gloriously, and has met with a much more cordial and substantial reception than he had ever anticipated. He speaks at the Opera House on Friday night. Tickets 50 cents, the entire proceeds to be for his own benefit. The Committee having the affair in charge defray all expenses from their purses. As the Parson is now very poor, this delicate mode of relief for the exiled Patriot and editorial hero is unexceptional.

GEN. TOM. THUMB.

This young gentleman has been the curiosity of the past week. His carriage, with footmen in livery drawn by those "weeney-teeney" Shetland ponies, daily passes the principal corners. The carriage is about the size of a market basket on end, and the horses but little larger than a good-sized St. Bernard dog.

ABOUT WAR POLICY.

It is known, from sources well-posted and entirely reliable, that if Gen. McClellan dilly-dallies a few days longer (say six) without a decisive advance on the enemy, he will be unconditionally displaced in disgrace.

He is now where he can no longer hold back other commanders in their forward movements, and assuredly he will have to move promptly, or retire on his laurels as the most magnificently puffed military humbug of this or any other age. Let him at once come up to the policy of attack, pursuit and destruction of the enemy, and, if himself be faint-hearted, we are content to trust the brave army under him for a victory which will echo joyfully from the Rappahannock hills to the hearts of freedom-lovers throughout the world. We've been fooling and fooled long enough—let the bloated monster of American treason be pricked to the raw, whether in Eastern Virginia or any other part of God-forsaken cotton dom.

By next week you will need all your lungs for lusty cheers over a once-again conquered fee. Breathe freely—the hush is ominous—the storm is about bursting!

Yours,
Will

* * * * *

Three weeks before Tomlinson's column for April 1, President Lincoln issued War Order No. 3 officially demoting McClellan from general in chief of the Federal armies to commander of the Army of the Potomac. McClellan had taken a ragtag assembly of downtrodden regiments and transformed them into an impressive instrument of war, but he was unable to deploy them effectively in the face of battle. Along with McClellan's demotion, the president also shuffled commands in the West and began requiring that all generals report directly to the new secretary of war, Edwin M. Stanton. The former Ohio Democrat was known as a curt politician, and he quickly gained a reputation for being a hard-nosed but efficient administrator of the war department. He also became a staunch Republican and one of the president's biggest supporters.[6]

But many Northerners were still highly skeptical of Lincoln's leadership, especially when it came to his proposal before Congress to institute the gradual, compensated emancipation of slaves in the Border States. In June 1862, an Ohio congressman, Samuel S. Cox, told the U.S. House of Representatives that the rapid migration of blacks across the Ohio River would result in a state composed only of congressmen and Negroes, which, he said, would be "punishment enough." Rampant racism had already ignited mob violence and race riots in Cincinnati in 1829,

1836, and 1841—and was threatening to do so again. With racial tension mounting, Tomlinson must have been glad that Eliza and the children were back in Ripley. His long hours at the *Cincinnati Gazette* would have left little time to spend with the family anyway. As he worked through the night, he must have wondered what fate would have befallen him if he had stayed with his old regiment, the Fifth Ohio.[7]

CHAPTER FOURTEEN

Hatching New Hope

Have ye poverty's pinching to cope with?
Does suffering weigh down your might?
Only call up a spirit to hope with,
And dawn may come out of the night.
—Eliza Cook, *Democratic Standard*, July 16, 1850

IN THE WINTER following Tomlinson's severance from the military, the Fifth Ohio was at Romney in western Virginia, Paw Paw in western Maryland, and the Battle of Kernstown, near Winchester, Virginia. The Union's victory there in March came at a cost of nearly six hundred casualties, including forty-seven from Tomlinson's old regiment. Among them was Caleb Whitson, whom Tomlinson knew at Camp Harrison in Cincinnati, when Whitson was elected as regimental quartermaster and Tomlinson, quartermaster sergeant. The two would also have crossed paths in western Virginia, where Whitson, then a lieutenant, assisted Colonel Harris in swearing in companies for the Tenth Virginia Infantry Regiment.[1]

As winter dissolved into spring, there was news of Union victories along the Mississippi. Gen. John Pope opened a key stretch of the river with his success at Island No. 10, near New Madrid, Missouri. But carnage at Shiloh, with casualties amounting to 13,047 for the Union and 10,694 for the Confederacy, shattered illusions about a quick ending to the war. Early April also brought news from President Lincoln's desk when he signed a congressional resolution to bring about the gradual emancipation of slaves in the Border States. Anxieties among white Northerners along the Ohio River escalated as they considered the impact of thousands of freed Negroes rushing across the river. Many Ohioans were also upset by the inflammatory rhetoric of Ohio congressman Clement Vallandigham, who had been branded by Republican editors as the most detestable congressman and Copperhead in the country. One Republican senator from Ohio even accused him of belonging to the Knights of the Golden Circle, a secret organization supposedly working to overthrow the Union. Among the newspapers trying to discredit Vallandigham as a traitor was the *Cincinnati Gazette,* where Tomlinson was still working as a compositor.[2]

By the end of May the South was regaining momentum. Stonewall Jackson had routed most Federals from the Shenandoah Valley, and the month of June opened with an even more significant turn of events for the viability of the South's war efforts. The wounding of Gen. Joseph E. Johnston at the Battle of Seven Pines east of Richmond brought Robert E. Lee to the forefront as he assumed command of what would become the Army of Northern Virginia. The South also benefited from General Mc-Clellan's reluctance to attack during the Seven Days Campaign at the end of the month, leaving Richmond secure for the Confederacy and striking a severe blow to Union morale. The month of July began with President Lincoln's call for 300,000 more troops and his approval of a number of far-reaching congressional acts that included raising the federal income tax and approving a transcontinental railroad. Tomlinson continued his commentary on current events in his correspondence for the *Ripley Bee* and in his letters home. His morale rose and fell with the latest developments on the battlefront, his and Eliza's financial affairs in Iowa, and his family's well-being.[3]

* * * * *

Tomlinson to Eliza
Cincinnati, Ohio, April 4, 1862

Dearest Eliza,

It is not because I have any particular news to impart, or a surplus of time on hand, or any other sufficient reason why I write, excepting that you may be uneasy to hear from me. My health is better than it was previous to my late visit. I have been working every day and have now a prospect for a regular situation, for some weeks anyhow.

I inquired about those birds, and the man tells me they will not sing in breeding cages. By separating them temporarily I suppose the thing may be tested.

I have just been to see the body of Sergeant Johnson, of the Fifth. He fell at Winchester, being shot in the breast. The remains of many others are arriving. My old friend Quartermaster Whitson had his leg accidentally wounded so that amputation was necessary.

I suppose Byers keeps on improving, or you would write. You must excuse me for not writing as much and often as you desire. This thing of working away in the night, does not leave me, at least, in the mood to scribble in the forenoon. It is as hard work almost as plowing.

I will send the Gazette again next week, when I raise a dollar Saturday. Crawfords are anxious to have me board with them. As they could accommodate us if you should occasionally visit the city, I may change.

But as it is now only five minutes to starting time of the boat, I must hurry, and can then hardly get this aboard.

Ever yours,
Will Tomlinson

* * * * *

Besides working at the *Gazette,* Tomlinson was still churning out his correspondence to the *Ripley Bee.* In his latest column he described the shameful treatment the bodies of some of his fallen comrades from the Fifth Ohio had received, but he was also callous himself in recommending how the government should deal with former slaves. His humor at the end of the letter probably refers to two events that happened in early March: the defeat of Stonewall Jackson at Kernstown by Gen. Nathaniel P. Banks and the engagement of the U.S.S. *Monitor* against the C.S.S. *Virginia* (formerly the U.S.S. *Merrimack*) off Hampton Roads, Virginia. Neither vessel scored a victory, but the battle itself marked the beginning of modern naval warfare.[4]

* * * * *

Correspondence of the *Bee*

CINCINNATI, April 8

This morning is such a mixture of weather—a Western Virginia mountain drizzle with a city fog—a struggling chill with steam heated pipes—that is anything but mentally exhilarating.

MORE MILITARY FUNERALS

On Saturday morning last the bodies of fourteen more of the dead of the Fifth Ohio reached this city. They were all packed in a wagon by the Express Company having them in charge—some of them standing endwise—and thus disgustingly taken through our streets to the stables of various undertakers. After this all possible honors were bestowed by our citizens on the remains of the fallen brave. Sunday seemed almost exclusively devoted to funerals. Farewell, comrades—kindly earth covers what was mortal, but in the hearts of a grateful country—in the memories of heroism—among the proudest reminiscences of this great battle of Freedom—in prose and verse, and in tradition and history—ye still live with things right and glorious!

THE WAR TAX

By the morning papers you will notice that Congress is reducing the War Tax Bill into shape. With its details I offer not criticism. But there is a general principle that should be at once declared by the highest authority and promptly acted on, which is to make the rebels feel more fully and directly the weight of their great crime. If there be no Constitutional power to confiscate property for treason, let a heavy and peremptory tax be laid on their plantations, and all persons and property there abouts. Let the penalty of non-payment be a forfeiture of title, and provide by speedy process for absolute sale, as delinquent property and grant the purchaser a title similar to a patent on any other Government land. But what will you do with the slaves? Well—as slavery is a creature of *local* law, and local authorities have lost all their power and virtue through treason, and as the statutes of the general government become supreme in such circumstances, and they do not recognize the "institution," why, our power ends with the letter of the law, and, as "other persons," they may be treated and treaty-ed like the Indians—export and isolate, or employ or put out as wards subject to guardianship. However, as you probably comprehend the idea, I will refrain from explanations.

THE MISSISSIPPI GUNBOATS

Nothing more brilliant and but very few things more important, have taken place, than that of our gunboats, the <u>Carondelet</u> and <u>Pittsburg</u>, running the rebel gauntlet at Island No. 10. It has given to Gen. Pope the means of crossing the river thus preventing the rebels from planting batteries of heavy guns, which might have dislodged our forces from New Madrid.

By this time next week the enemy will have been driven from Island No. 10 and vicinity, or we shall have been ingloriously whipped. At least such seems now to be the probabilities.

PERSONAL

I was pleased the other day to meet your gallant townsmen Lieutenants Ligget and Ridgway. May these brave boys of Scary, of Carnifex, and a dozen important skirmishes, be saved from rebels, and the tongues and spittle of all secesh women.

PUBLIC INSTITUTIONS

As leisure time may afford, I propose sending you some interesting statistics about various public buildings, organizations, etc., which will not be met with in other places.

JOKES

Apropos to affairs in Virginia, <u>Yankee Notions</u> says: "Drafts are being made in Virginia. Our <u>Banks</u> will meet them promptly, and then wont [*sic*] there be a <u>shelling</u> out?" From ditto: "What our Naval Schools are much in need of—<u>Monitors.</u>"

But excuse haste—'tis "high noon"—the boat bell rings—so I "dry up," and the weather clerk wets down.

Yours,
WILL

* * * * *

With Byers still in recovery mode and the birds propagating, Eliza was still tied to the house. Once Byers and the weather improved, she and the children visited Tomlinson in Cincinnati and even managed to bring back a few treats.

* * * * *

Eliza to Tomlinson
Ripley, Ohio, April 15, 1862

Dear Husband,

I have nothing special to write about. Byers continues to improve but is not yet able to enter school. The rest of the family are as well as usual. I informed you about Newt's going down to attend upon wounded soldiers. They went by rail from Cin. Lizzie got a letter from him last night written at Vincennes. They were all right. Fine weather today; it comes so seldom that it makes a person's heart glad when we do have a pleasant day. Eddy has just commenced to sing but not very loud. Maggy is sitting. I do not know how long it takes for the eggs to hatch. No word from the west.

Please give my best respects to Mrs. Crawford.

Ever yours, etc.! In haste,

Eliza W. Tomlinson

Eliza to Tomlinson
Ripley, Ohio, June 3, 1862

Dear Husband,

On last evening we arrived here all safe and found the folks all as well as usual. The boat was in such a hurry that we did not get all our flowers put off, but it will be all right I suppose when she comes down today. Whilst I was absent Newt got a letter from Allen forwarding the tax receipts; according to Newt's order, he says that the houses have been sold several times for the taxes and now the charges upon the same amount to some one hundred and forty dollars. This astonishes me! But the extra charges from year to year mount up. He says that he can get nothing from Lowry, who says that he has been sick. Allen seems to think that there is a poor prospect of getting anything of him. The tenant who formerly lived in the other house is also owing for six months or more, and he thinks it is a doubtful case whether we get anything of him. He thinks that the one who occupies it at present is good. Allen advanced the money for the redemption of the property and wishes a draft sent him for the amount which is within a few cents of one hundred and twelve dollars.

I have not seen Newt since I came home and therefore do not know what he says about it. I have between thirty and forty dollars, say $35, but this will go but a little way in making up the bill. How shall I raise it? As Lowry cannot pay his rent, we cannot afford to find him a house for nothing; therefore, I think that we had better try and get a paying tenant. I am sorry for the unfortunate, but we cannot live keeping them in a tenement free of charge.

All your friends are well so far as I know. The birds are all right. You had better see to those two lots which you spoke to me about; they may also be sold for the tax. There was no letter here for me from you. I think you said that you sent it by someone coming on the boat; they forgot to deliver. I wish you would save up what money you can to meet this. Please write and advise me in this strait.

I ever remain yours affectionately.

Please give my love and respects to Mrs. Crawford and family.

Eliza W. Tomlinson

The carpet was on the boat.

Byers (Son) to Tomlinson
Ripley, Ohio, June 3, 1862

Dear Pap,

I am well. We had a great time up on the boat. We had a piece of canvas 18 ft long and printed upon it in large letters, was [Richmond taken with 42,000 prisoners.] The Kentuckians did not seem to like the news, but the Ohioans gave us cheer after cheer. We had a small cannon aboard, which we fired on our road up, and before we got to Ripley, they had their brass cannon belching forth its thunder. At dinner I went up to feed the dog, but his string was laying there untied, and he was gone. I hunted the boat all over but could not find him. It is now time to send this so I must quit.

Goodbye,

W. B. Tomlinson

* * * * *

Byers had clearly taken some care in writing to his father. He used lined stationery, and at the top was a printed cartoon of the North's first mili-

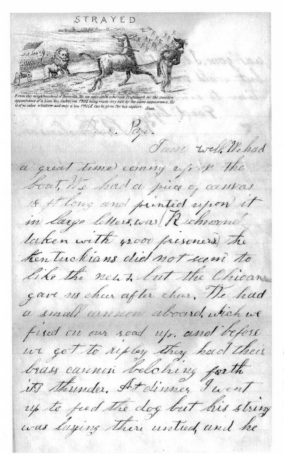

This letter, dated June 3, 1862, was written by William Byers Tomlinson on stationery depicting one of the Union's first heroes, Gen. Nathaniel Lyon. (Wylie-Tomlinson Letter Collection)

tary hero, Gen. Nathaniel Lyon, who kept the St. Louis arsenal out of Confederate hands in 1861. Despite his special stationery and careful penmanship, however, Byers was misinformed about the number of prisoners taken on June 1 at Seven Pines or Fair Oaks, east of Richmond, Virginia. Although each side had about forty-two thousand troops and at least five thousand casualties, the battle was strategically inconclusive. Even though Eliza jotted a quick note on the back of her son's letter, she did not correct him, but she did take time to explain what may have happened to the dog.[5]

* * * * *

The *Magnolia* was favored by the Tomlinsons for traveling and sending mail between Ripley and Cincinnati, shown in the background. It also delivered the Ripley cannon free of charge in December 1862. (From the Collection of the Public Library of Cincinnati and Hamilton County)

Eliza to Tomlinson
Ripley, Ohio, June 3, 1862

I suppose that some of the Cin. boys untied the dog before we left as Byers took up a plate of scraps from the dinner table soon after that time.

Tomlinson to Eliza
Cincinnati, June 5, 1862

Dearest Eliza,

Was glad to hear of your getting home all right. It surprises me much what Allen wrote you. As to Lowry, he has evidently played false, and is unworthy of our sympathy, no matter what his distress. He should have informed you that the taxes were <u>not</u> paid, even if he could not pay them. The amount is enormous and must be two-thirds made up of premiums to land-sharks who have bid them in. However, I suppose this must be paid. You are unfortunate in tenants and gents. I will save what money I can for you. You may rely on at least a dollar a day for the next 90 days. That much I feel sure I can average for that time.

Your brother Byers called up to see me this morning. I am sorry to see him so poorly. He goes up today and I send this with him. It is time to have it at the boat.

I was glad to get that letter from our son Byers. And I want our daughter to write. I feel like a new and better man since your pleasant visit.

Ever Yours,

Will Tomlinson

* * * * *

Tomlinson may have felt like a new man, but he was obviously still ruminating about the past. The posture of humility he assumed in his next letter to the editor actually glorified his participation in antiguerrilla warfare in western Virginia. He probably welcomed an opportunity to dispel any deprecatory rumors that may have been circulating around Ripley concerning his service record. The allusion to his own "practical" experience would also have boosted his credibility in assessing current military operations.

* * * * *

Correspondence of the *Bee*

CINCINNATI, June 5

Though it is some weeks since I last wrote you, yet the humor is not on me. However, as these are stirring days, let me dip my oar.

THE LATE NEWS

After the evacuations of Manassas, Yorktown, Corinth and New Orleans, it was natural for editors, or "any other man," to anticipate at least speedy victory in the open country over a concentrated enemy which could not and dare not fight behind their bomb proof casemates and strongly mounted earthworks. This I merely hint, however, as a vague surmise of one who has no command, and whose military education consists in a rather practical, though short campaign, among the mountain guerrillas, known as "Moccasin Rangers," and the banded murderers of "Ben. Haman's gang."—Why is not the navigation of the Mississippi now opened? We have the sources and the mouth of that river—why do we lay at anchor near Vicksburg? Why for months feed secesh mosquitoes on Union blood, awaiting the evacuation of Fort Pillow? Why exhaust our men in constructing parallel entrenchments, only resulting in nauseous evacuations and the undisturbed "skeedaddling" of our "erring brothers?"

But the "Very Latest News" shows an agreeable, though slight break in our past policy. Gen. Pope is let loose among 'em, and don't he take the gentleman cow by the horns? As his simple report, he, as the result of a few hours' real work, with sleeves rolled up, sends back to the army "10,000 prisoners and 15,000 small arms." That's the sort of "infallibility" I believe in a "Pope" manifesting. Even if he did once make a speech rather disrespectful toward Buchanan, of Wheatland, let you and I dear Tom forgive this sin of the past, and help spread out the starry folds of glory all over him.

And there's Gen. Mitchell. What a change, to come down from his astronomical studies of firmamental splendors to the practical extermination of lousy secesh! But "sich is life." And, like the good old Methodist, under the exciting sermon on the creation of woman—"thank God for the slight variation."—He, too, is reported to have taken about 5,000 prisoners. And another thing he's done, quite remarkable—he's got some of those sneaking cut-throats, the guerrillas, and has telegraphed to Stanton for the privilege of hanging them!—Good. And the "true and the bold" Edwin responds by lightning—"swing 'em up!" Better. Bully for the trio, and for Fremont, and Jake Ammen, and all hurrah for every man who does his whole duty in this fight, by positively "pushing the enemy to the wall."

THE TAKING OF RICHMOND

Before this gets in print we shall surely have Richmond. The signs are all cheering for a speedy settlement of our great troubles. Then won't we be a happy people? "Reveling in the Halls of the Montezumas" was tame, compared with our forthcoming Fourth of July in the land of Dixie. Hope the commanders will not on that day forbid the playing of our National Airs, out of regard to the fastidious tastes of town vixens in a conquered city, as was done at Norfolk.

One of the numerous letters recently captured in the New Orleans Post-office, I wish you to copy the following. It strikes me as a masterful painting of domestic despair.

A SAD BUGLE

Extract from a Letter dated New Orleans

April 21, '62

* * * <u>Mon Cher Ami</u>—Will the long life <u>never</u> end? Weary am I of sighing—weary of dreaming by night, and weeping by day, for my own husband. <u>O, mon Dieu! mon Dieu!</u> In this world will men never be kind? In the tomb will the true God forgive the brothers who, in the dark hours of this world's life sought each other's blood?—I suffer! Is death coming? Each crash of the iron guns below the city makes a widow or a childless mother. I would shriek, and drown the sound. It is useless. <u>Hereafter,</u> husband—my own—hereafter may we meet. * * *

ADA

There can be no real treason in the heart which gushed forth those sweet, sad words of love, of prayer, of heavenly faith. Oh, how many other sad hearts and lonely hearths and aching voids—how many mangled, living and untimely dead—how vast the flow of misery and poverty and vice—how awful and terrible the ravages of hunger to other lands beside our own loved shore—all caused and let loose upon a world innocent of offence in the premises, to gratify the base and damnable ambition of those hell-born politicians who first fired upon our flag at Sumter!

WILL

* * * * *

Mindful of the power of melodrama, Tomlinson saved the sad letter from a New Orleans widow for the last item in his column. Besides appreciating the pathos dripping from the widow's words, his readers would, no doubt, have imbued the letter with an extra dose of sympathy in recalling a situation that had been widely publicized and criticized by Northern and Southern newspapers alike. After the Union took control of New Orleans, Gen. Benjamin Butler, head of the military government there, attempted to halt hostile behavior toward Federal soldiers by the city's denizens, especially women. He ordered his troops to treat any New Orleans lady who "insulted or showed contempt" toward them in "word, gesture or movement" to be treated as a "woman of the town plying her avocation"—in other words, as a prostitute. Tomlinson, appalled that a grieving widow could be mistreated in such a way, decried the "hell-born politicians who first fired upon our flag at Sumter." Tomlinson's own wife, meanwhile, was more concerned with the increasing melodrama of their affairs in Iowa. But first she had to give her husband a little pep talk and provide the latest news on everyone's health, including their son Byers, who complained about the deleterious effects of studying.[6]

* * * * *

Eliza to Tomlinson
Ripley, Ohio, June 7, 1862

Dear Husband,

Brother Byers delivered your letter yesterday morning. I was happy to learn that you feel better and are hopeful for the future. Never despair. There is doubtless a bright future for the hopeful and energetic; perseverance overcomes what appears to be impossibilities.

Our family are in their usual health. Byers has not yet started to school; he complained so much of his head that I thought that it was probably best not to force him to go contrary to his inclination. He says that when he is in school his head aches badly and study confuses his brain. As this term will soon be out, I think that it would be best not to start him until next term.

I feel very uneasy about Brother Byers. I think his case requires particular attention; this is what I am afraid he will not devote to it.

A few weeks ago I again wrote to Mrs. Wylie telling her that I needed the money which they owed me and that I should look to her for it—Will being a minor at the time and acting for her—she of course was responsible. I waited a long time on her convenience; only, it appears, to be insulted for my kindness. Did Will ever pay any debts for you? It was so contrary to his principle to pay his own debts that I cannot believe that he ever paid anything for you; in fact; I did not know that you were owing anything. What shall I do with them? Nellie says probably truly that her mother has no property, but I know that she has money at interest in the hands of her brother in this state, for she told me so herself. It is evident that they wish to defraud me out of the rent! Please write to Will and tell him that he must settle it with me. In Nellie's letter soon after we came here, she said that Will rented of you and that he settled with you, and not me. Will is a rascal I have long known and now believe the rest of them to be no better in principle. Newt I suppose has sent a draft to Allen for the amount which he called for. I gave him $30, only retaining a trifle for present necessities.

Take care of your health. Did the dog go back to Mr. Crawford's? The birds are doing well but do not propagate their species.

I ever remain yours affectionately.

Write. Enclosed please find Nellie's letter; return it when you write.

Eliza W. Tomlinson

I wrote Allen that if Lowry should not pay what he owes, to require good security from him and also for his future continuance in the house. Return Nellie's letter to me.

Tomlinson to Eliza

Cincinnati, Ohio, June 13, 1862

Dearest Eliza,

I owe you many apologies for apparent neglect in writing you for the last few days. But the reason justifies me. I have been working steadily since the day after you left, and owing to the weight of trouble taken off my mind by that event, I have been able to sleep later in the mornings, and so resting as to work constantly and feel better. My health is much improved.

As to our financial matters, I can promise you a great improvement. I wrote you that you might depend on $1.00 a day for 90 days. I will make it good if my health continues. I may not send in every letter, but it will reach you in the aggregate. Last week, you know, I worked but half the week and was at some extra expense; but in the end it will prove a gain. I again feel like living and striving to the utmost for you and the children. I feel under many obligations to Brother Newt for advancing you necessary means at this time to disencumber your property. I will make it all good to him to the uttermost farthing.

That letter from Nellie was written by her under wrong impressions as to Will's dealings with me. He has not only never paid me any house-rent, but owes me nearly the full value of my team and carriage and a few dollars borrowed money in addition. I was not in debt in Des Moines, and the only claim of any significance was that security debt for John Hyde, who employed the lawyer to attend to the case. I owe some lawyer's fees there, which is all I remember, and I know he has not paid <u>those.</u>

As I cannot take time in one morning to write you, and the children, too, just tell them that I will answer them soon. That letter of daughter's is a model of perfection for one so young. I want her to continue. Write as often as convenient and fully, without reference to my answers.

Ever and only yours,
Will Tomlinson

Eliza to Tomlinson
Ripley, Ohio, June 16, 1862

Dear Husband,

We are all in our usual health. I have been attending examination in Belle's room during this day—have just come home. Belle stood a good examination, as much as any one in the room. She will doubtless be presented to a higher room next term. Belle says that she lost or left her picnic gloves in the City. They were long, new gloves extending up to the elbow. The last she remembers of having them she says was laying them on the washstand at Mrs. Crawford's. If she left them there, please send them up by Mrs. Evans. Belle's bird has laid three eggs. I hope that she will have better luck this time than what she had before in sitting. There is no news that I hear of more than what you learn by the paper.

Your friends so far as I know are all well. I learn that Bony Lindsey has again come home sick or at least worse than what he was when he last left. He has not been anything but sick for the last six or eight months, and if he does not quit fooling in this way, his will soon be a hopeless case! He should by all means get his discharge. Please give my love to Mrs. Crawford and the girls.

I ever remain yours truly,
Eliza W. Tomlinson

This letter by Sarah Isabella Tomlinson (Belle) was probably written in 1862. (Wylie-Tomlinson Letter Collection)

Belle (Daughter) to Tomlinson
Ripley, Ohio, June 16, 1862

Dear Pap,

We are all Well. Mother got your letter last night. We are glad to hear that you are getting Well. Last week the boy did not leave us a bee and mother sent me up to the bee office and Mr. Sniffens asked the boy if he left a bee at Mrs. Tomlinson's and he said he did not and then he asked him if he sent a bee to Mr. Tomlinson and he said yes, so Mother thinks that it ain't Mr. Sniffens' fault. My bird has got feathers on it. It is all yellow except two or three black feathers on each wing. I am going to give it to Mag because she has been so good to me. Pap I want you to write me another letter. Give my love to the girls and tell them to write to me.

Goodby Pap from your affectionate daughter,
Sara I. B. Tomlinson

Belle to Tomlinson
Ripley, Ohio, June 17, 1862

Dear Pap,

We are all well. Our examination came off yesterday. I only missed one question. I expect to be in Miss Mitchell's room next year. Maggie is laying and has four eggs. I hope she'll hatch some birds this time. My pink gloves left in Mrs. Crawford's I think. I want you to write to me. Give my love to the girls.

Goodby Pap,
I. B. Tomlinson

Eliza to Tomlinson
Ripley, Ohio, June 17, 1862

On yesterday I did not get my letter sent up in time for the mail. I suppose that Eliza Evans will remain in the city all week. If she was not married, what a fine time she could have in enjoying herself, but I suppose that she feels better as she is. I got your letter last week, but would

An envelope from Will Tomlinson to his wife, Eliza. Note the absence of postage and its routing by the steamship *Bostona*. (Wylie-Tomlinson Letter Collection)

like to hear again from you this week. There is nothing transpiring here of much interest that I am aware of.

Ever yours,
Eliza W. Tomlinson

* * * * *

The end of June was a quiet time in southern Ohio, but east of Richmond the costly Seven Days Campaign resulted in more than twenty thousand casualties for the Confederates and close to sixteen thousand for the Union. On July 1, the Battle of Malvern Hill brought the campaign to an end, but no one knew exactly what the outcome was or how it would affect the course of the war. What eventually became clear was that McClellan had failed to pull off a decisive victory once again. When the *New York Times* ran a story on July 4, however, even that was ambiguous, as indicated by a lengthy headline: "From Gen. M'Clellan.; The Great Battle Continued Through Seven Days. IMMENSE LOSSES ON BOTH SIDES. Terrific Onslaught of the Rebels on Our New Position. Final and Overwhelming Defeat of the Enemy. Death of Stonewall Jackson and Gen. Barnwell Rhett. Gen. Magruder Reported to be a Prisoner. Gen. McClellan Safe and Confident in His New Position. Arrival of Considerable Reinforcements. OFFICIAL ADVICES FROM

GEN. MCCLELLAN." Tomlinson must have had that headline or another one like it in mind when he dashed off an emotional note to Eliza.[7]

* * * * *

Tomlinson to Eliza
Cincinnati, Ohio, July 3, 1862

½ past 12 Noon

My dearest Eliza,

It is not only in great haste, but with a soreness of heart and depression of feeling unutterable, that I scribble you a line to tell of our heavy calamity as a Nation. Our Noble and well-appointed army before Regiment has not only been <u>repulsed,</u> it has been dreadfully <u>beaten—whipped!</u> Gen. McClellan has retreated 17 miles, and got under protection of the gunboats. The rebels stood the fire of even those terrible ministers of death for two hours, and then retreated. We have lost <u>all</u> our siege-guns. We have 2,000 prisoners, including Gen. Magruder. The loss on both sides is awful. The fight lasted four days. It is estimated that the rebels lost most, from the destructive gunboats. No time for speculation. I fear we have been betrayed. O, God of Nations! Save us or we utterly perish.

CHAPTER FIFTEEN

Attacks from Within and Without

Guide me, O thou great Jehovah, pilgrim through this barren land;
I am weak, but thou art might;
hold me with thy powerful hand.
—"Guide me, O thou great Jehovah," William Williams, 1745

IN 1861 the military took control of the telegraph to prevent the publication of strategic information that could undermine the war effort. By July 1862 the telegraph had been shut down so many times that Tomlinson mentioned it only in passing in the following letter. But no telegraph meant no breaking news, a situation that may account for Tomlinson's outdated assessment of McClellan. When the final reports of the Seven Days Campaign near Richmond did reach the Midwest, Tomlinson's estimation of McClellan must have plunged. In spite of complicated choreographies, thousands of troops, and dozens of battles that presented McClellan with countless opportunities, the only decisive outcome was that he was clearly not up to the job. He repeatedly miscalculated the enemy's strength and failed to act when circumstances were propitious for a Union victory. It was also clear that no army could stay viable for long with such horrific losses. By the time casualties for both sides were counted, some 30,000 men had been killed or wounded.[1]

Meanwhile, there was additional cause for alarm in Cincinnati. Racial tension erupted in violence when black strikebreakers took the jobs of Irish stevedores and roustabouts for less pay. Irish workers attacked blacks on the waterfront, shouting, "No damned niggers should work on the levee!" Seven days of rioting followed, and the mayor's deployment of seventy-five volunteer guards with Winfield rifles did little to quell the unrest. Many African Americans fled the city as white supremacists resorted to brutal suppression. Violence within the city soon paled before the prospect of imminent attack from across the river, however. John Hunt Morgan and his raiders were on the move in Kentucky, and by July 14 they had reached Cynthiana, fifty miles south of Cincinnati and even closer to the abolitionist stronghold of Ripley, where nerves twitched in preparation. Governor Tod rounded up what troops he could and sent them across the river to repel the Rebels. Tomlinson yearned to be part of the action, despite his health, his personal battle with alcohol, and his wife's concerns.[2]

* * * * *

Tomlinson to Eliza
Cincinnati, July 5, 1862

Dearest Eliza,

I have but a few minutes in which to write, as I want to send this by the Bostona. I know that you will excuse me if, under the circumstances, I should have to cut it very short. I did think of putting off till tomorrow a job which I could then finish up much more satisfactorily. But perhaps I may try it over again then.

My health is improving, and in a few days I expect to enjoy my usual hale condition. As to matters spiritual and reformatory, it is with a heart swelling with gratitude to our merciful Father in Heaven that I can announce to your anxious bosom—"All is well." I think that I appreciate the weak points of offense as well as defense. But trusting in Him who is able, and planting my feet firmly in the Rock of Ages, I shall at least know that my own fault will be the only cause of another downfall. I feel more fully than ever the import of that poetic prayer:

"Guide me, O Thou Great Jehovah,
Pilgrim through this barren land."

The Fourth was a very pleasant day, though rather warm. We worked all day excepting some two hours about suppertime. I have heard of no accidents.

The telegraph has been entirely closed to war news since day before yesterday. Something may come today. I have faith that McClellan can now hold his own, and in a week he will have re-enforcements embracing a large part of the Western Army. With 200,000 veteran volunteers, well equipped, he will drive the enemy before him like grasshoppers before a hurricane. The generalship displayed by him in the six days fighting before Richmond places him, in my estimation, the greatest military commandant of all history. Neither King David, Caesar, Napolean, Wellington, Scott or Jackson ever saw such fighting, ever bore up against such crushing odds, or fought a field fight six consecutive days.

But I must hurry to the boat. Enclosed find $10. I hope I will be in better working condition the coming week. How did the children like their letters?

Ever yours,
Will Tomlinson

Tomlinson to Eliza
Cincinnati, July 15, 1862

Dearest Eliza,

This morning I got up more than two hours before my regular time so anxious was I to hear from you. But the mail has been brought to the office, and nothing for me. The reason for this neglect I cannot imagine, unless that you are sick and cannot write. In that case daughter could take your place, for she writes a good letter. I wrote you a week ago last Saturday, enclosing $10, but the boat was just starting as I reached the landing. I sent it up Monday a week ago by the Magnolia. Why have I not heard from you about the money? Did you get it? I have some more in my pocket book for you, but I shall wait to know if the first ten has got into the right hands.

I ought to have had two letters in the last "Bee," but it seems that they care not a copper either for me or my letters, as they have sent me no copy of the paper. Such treatment disgusts me, and if you should happen to see Tom please tell him so frankly. My letters on the war as published I should like to have preserved, but such carelessness or contempt is more than I feel like subjecting myself to unnecessarily.

The state of affairs over in Kentucky is rather excited. Let me warn you of Ripley to be on the lookout. There are plenty of men ready to pounce down on it for its plunder. At any rate let Byers have his gun and ammunition in good order, so as to help us in case of necessity. I thought some of again going with the service. I am assured of conscription if the military committee of the Brown Co. District should recommend me. But on more mature reflection my conclusion is to wait events. If the government takes some positive and proper measure to <u>crush</u> and absolutely <u>subjugate</u> the enemy, then I may again seek danger and the battlefield. But the way it is we are only, as children say, <u>playing</u> at war.

I wish you would try and get me a copy of last week's Bee.

A heavy rainstorm is now pouring down. We need it to clear the sultry atmosphere. It has been very hot for some days.

My health is improving and now I feel quite stout again. Last week I had three chills.

Otherwise, also, all yet goes well with me. Thank God who is willing and able to save, strength to resist temptation and refrain from the ways of evil has been given me.

There is a continuous riot every day now between the Irish and the negroes. Nearly all our police force is gone to Lexington, so that paving stones may be thrown with impunity. Mrs. Dick has not yet heard from her husband, who was captured at Port Republic. She has written to Jeff. Davis about him. Some maliciously hint that her clairvoyance is a humbug, or she might at a glance soon know all about him.

Tell Byers I want him to write to me. I hope he is not too lazy, and surely he has nothing to be afraid of.

I wish you would write every Saturday so that I would get the letter Sunday morning.

Love to you all.

Are there any companies being raised in Ripley?

Ever yours,

Will Tomlinson

Eliza to Tomlinson
Ripley, Ohio, July 15, 1862

Dear Husband,

This is to inform you that we are all in our usual health. Your last, of Saturday week, was received on last Monday night; for the enclosed money I thank you. I am happy to hear that your health has improved. From last night's paper it appears that treason is working itself off in guerrilla warfare in Ky. I hope that our boys will capture Morgan together with all his infernal gang and make an example of them such as will strike terror to all remaining traitors. Milk and water has been effectually tried so as to prove its want of efficacy. A little hanging at this stage of the disease would doubtless result most happily. The children were delighted with those letters which you wrote them.

I received a letter from Lowry written on June 29th in which he says that, on the day before, that city was the scene of a horrid murder, committed by A. N. Marsh, City Marshall. The murdered man's name was Michael King. It occurred in Sherman's building. Marsh stabbed King, who died in half an hour.

Lowry says if we knew the causes which have prevented him from paying promptly we would not think hard of him. He says that he saw Allen and talked the matter over. Allen told him that he would give him three months to pay what was due, for which he is to pay him at the rate of ten percent. He says that within that time he hopes to be out of debt. Lowry says that he has made inquiry about your files of bound volume of paper. I could hear nothing of them. Probably you could think of some one who would hunt them up for you. I expected a letter from you last night but it did not come.

I ever remain yours, etc.,
Eliza W. Tomlinson

O that policy, what is to be done about it?

Eliza to Tomlinson
Ripley, Ohio, July 16, 1862

Dear Husband,

I know that I did wrong in not writing you on last Monday, but I delayed until Tuesday thinking that you would write me on Sunday (that being a leisure day with you). I had just written to you before the reception of yours, confirming that, and so did not write, thus causing you anxiety, for which I am sorry.

As to your again entering the army, I hope that you will not do it unless the enemy should come on us here at home, in which case every man should defend his hearthstone and the loved ones which surround it to the last.

I send you last week's Bee. There is but one communication in it from you; probably he had not time or space to insert the other one last week. Your communications are highly appreciated by all who I have heard say anything about them.

When you send me money, would it not be the safest plan to send it by mail. You know best.

Ever yours, etc.,

Eliza W. Tomlinson

Eliza to Tomlinson
Ripley, Ohio, July 18, 1862

Dear Husband,

Yours of last Tuesday came to hand last evening. Thank you for that money. I shall now be able to renew that policy unless you should again enter the war, in which case I should be compelled to drop it, sacrificing all which has been paid. As I said before, I hope that you will keep out of it; you would not now be able to endure the hardships of another campaign. I do not feel any less patriotic than when you first enlisted in your country's service, but you cannot but be aware that your constitution has received such a shock in your Va. campaign that it would be as bad as suicide for you to undertake to go through the same or equal hardships to what you have done.

We are in our usual health. We have had quite exciting times here yesterday, last night, and today. Word came on yesterday that Morgan and his band of robbers and murderers were marching on to Maysville. Some said that he was not more than eight or ten miles distant from that place. Last night a boat came down from Maysville at twelve o'clock for volunteers to help defend that city. The alarm bell was rung and the citizens rallied to the rescue. Several boatloads I believe went up; they have not yet returned. It is now 6 o'clock P.M. There was a report came down today that Morgan was within a short distance of the city. We know not what to believe. There are so many rumors afloat, I think that he (that is Morgan) will hardly have the audacity to come here. It is true that there is a great deal to induce him to come here. We have what he needs: flour, pork, and other provisions in abundance. Also three banks—money is what they are after. But I must close lest I should not get this in the mail

Ever yours, etc.,

Eliza W. Tomlinson

We have pickets all round and also over the river.

* * * * *

On July 19, Morgan's men skirmished with Union troops near Paris, Kentucky, just north of Lexington, on the road to Maysville. Tomlinson was soon in hot pursuit of them; before leaving he used a torn, half sheet of paper to jot a quick note to his wife. It was sent from a village that, ironically, lay a short distance across the river from Ripley.[3]

* * * * *

Tomlinson to Eliza
Minerva, Kentucky, July 21, 1862

Dearest Eliza,

With only time to write a note of a line. All well. Getting along fine. Penetrate further tomorrow. Don't know when I will be back.

In great haste—

Will Tomlinson

* * * * *

Years later, Tomlinson's son, Byers, would capture his reflections on Morgan's Raiders in an essay that would one day be published in a history of Ripley. In explaining how townspeople never knew when or where the raiders would strike, Byers wrote that the excitement usually began with "a series of lantern flashes from the Kentucky hills signalling the approach of the Confederates." Or sometimes, Byers noted, "from out of the dark shadows of the Kentucky willows a skiff with muffled oars would shoot silently for the Ohio shore." Soon men would be shouting throughout the town as church and schoolhouse bells rang, and every boy and old man would be summoned to the marketplace, where they would be ordered to cross the river. There they would march or wait, depending on the latest reconnaissance. It was important to remember, Byers wrote, that the Home Guard volunteers were not in the U.S. Army and had no rights under the rules of war when they entered enemy terriotry. In July 1862, they never caught up with Morgan, who took his raiders and headed back to Tennessee. Tomlinson returned to work at the *Cincinnati Gazette* and resumed his correspondence for the *Ripley Bee*. In his latest column he even managed to get a few words in about the way the Home Guards acquitted themselves in the recent scare.[4]

* * * * *

Correspondence of the *Bee*

CINCINNATI July 28.

We have received an interesting letter from our correspondent "WILL," and regret that it came to hand too late for this week. We make one or two extracts however:

Your recent military demonstrations in and about Ripley have brought great relief and honor to a much slandered and persecuted class—I mean the Home Guards. Your promptness and efficiency has become the talk of the whole State, and I have reason to know was highly appropriated by Father Abraham and Uncle Ned. And here, by the way, can't you give us a little dash of the chivalric and daring in the part taken by the Ripley Flotilla on that memorable occasion. Surely the way those hosses did work, and how that flatboat dodged friendly bullets and blank cartridges—how those 3 cent banners waved from stern to stern? Get Lieut. Martin to draw it in Dutch, you puff it, and let's have some record thereof in the archives of sleepy Gideon.

RECRUITING.

I would suggest to the powers that be that our boys in the ranks now and for the last year battling for our country, have some claims to be considered when promotions are being made. They can't leave guard in the enemy's country and come home to buttonhole a Committee.—Nor do they like to personally push themselves forward in any way. Those men have experience, and are ready to put companies and regiments and battalions in immediate fighting order. I would just hint that the Military Committee and Governor might make it profitable to the service to take at least one glance in the direction of the old Twelfth Ohio.

PERSONAL.

Our old friend "Bony" Lindsey has been here for some days. Yesterday he received his discharge, on account of affection [*sic*] of the heart caused by exposure in the service last fall. I am glad of his release.

Have just met Capt. Will Shaw, who is, I understand on furlough from Mayor of R. Also the irrepressible Jim Guy, laughing and—anything that's funny. If we just now had the serene countenance of the patriarch "Ike" we'd be about "set up."

WILL

Tomlinson obviously enjoyed mentioning some of his old buddies from Ripley. He was also probably missing the days when he had his own printing shop and could take time to josh with friends while he got everything "set up" for the next press run. Words were the printer's mainstay, of course, and printers loved to engage in wordplay using the trade's jargon. The more irreverent, the better—as in the following attempt at humor from the *Dubuque Herald:* "Jim, put Gen. Beauregard on the galley; and then finish the murder of the negro you commenced yesterday. Set up the ruins of Guyandotte; distribute the small pox; you need not finish that mutiny; put the mumps in the paper this week. Pitch the pi into hell, and then go to the devil and he will tell you how to dispose of that dead matter." As a compositor for the *Gazette,* Tomlinson may not have been in a position to order an apprentice around or tell a lowly printer's boy (devil) to dump old type (pitch the pi) and ditch outdated copy (dispose of dead matter). But he still had ink under his nails and printing in his blood. He must have wondered if he would ever be master of his own press again. Meanwhile, he was still dependent upon the editor of the *Ripley Bee* to get his words in print.[5]

* * * * *

Eliza to Tomlinson
Ripley, Ohio, August 4, 1862

Dear Husband,

I am happy to inform you that we are in our usual health. There is no news that I know of which would be of interest to you.

I was sorry that your last week's to the Bee came too late to admit of its being published in full. What was published was good—emphatically so, and gave general satisfaction. I have not received a letter from you since you left, but from the one Belle received from you, I am happy to learn that your health has improved much since you left.

I saw Bony Lindsey on Saturday; his countenance looks more cheerful and hopeful, and although far from being well, he looks altogether like another man. He feels that he is a free man, but doubtless as patriotic as ever. He never would have got well in the army; he may not get well as it is, but he stands a better chance for it. One thing injures Bony—he is quite intemperate. I am sorry for it; he is a clever fellow aside from that.

The weather has been quite sultry, but today we have had a fine refreshing shower, which has made quite an improvement in the atmosphere. 'Tis now cool and pleasant.

From the Bee you have probably learnt that the good people of Ripley swore the Russellville rattlesnakes and let them go. I suppose that they could not do otherwise as there was no one appeared against them.

Please give my best respects to Mrs. Crawford and the girls. Belle has written a little letter to you, and one to Jennie, which I enclose. If you see proper, you can give Jennie hers. Belle writes poorly as yet, but I think by encouraging her to write letters, she will improve in the mechanical part of it. Please write and tell me how you are getting along, etc.!

I ever remain yours affectionately,

Eliza W. Tomlinson

Belle (Daughter) to Tomlinson
Ripley, Ohio, August 3, 1862

Dear Pap,

I received your letter this morning. I am glad to hear that you are well. We are all as well as usual. Mich has commenced to singing, two of Maggie eggs hatch out, and I do not know whenever anymore will come out or not. I will tell you.

Monday morning—last night another bird came out so that she has three. We have just had a very fine shower and the air is cool and pleasant. I do not know what makes our pears so late this year, they are not beginning to get ripe yet.

They have not got their company made up far to go to the war yet. Pap you wanted me to tell you how many letters there are in all the words in the English language. There are 26 letters in the alphabet so I think that must be the number.

Your affectionate daughter,

Sarah I. B. Tomlinson

Excuse my bad writing. I hope that you can read it. I have written a letter to Jennie and it will be in your envelope. Please give it to her and with it my best love. Write to me. Goodby Pap.

Eliza to Tomlinson
Ripley, Ohio, August 8, 1862

Dear Husband,

I have just received yours of yesterday; also that $15, both sent by Mr. Jolley. He handed them to Jeff Wylie, who he came upon last evening on his return from Columbus. He got an appointment as surgeon. I thank you for the needful, which you was so thoughtful and provident as to send me.

I am sorry to learn that you are not very well. I think that a mustard plaster applied to your breast would be of benefit. Our family are as well as normal. Your friends are all well so far as I know. No news of interest; you are better posted in that respect than myself.

Baird handed Byers the enclosed note on your policy for you to sign; the amount to be paid this year is $19.92. He says that they also sent a war policy, but this I hope you will not take steps to make it necessary for us to have anything to do with. Should you determine (which God forbid) to enter the army again, it would probably be best to drop the whole thing; in such case the presumption is we could not keep it up.

There was a small table or stand stood by our bed when I was down, but filled up with large amount of papers. If it is yet in the room, throw the papers to one side or put them in the press and furnish it with stationary. I think that it would answer for ordinary purposes. I should like for you to remain at Mr. Crawford's if you can accommodate yourself to do so. Should I at anytime go down, I would much rather stay where I am acquainted, and another item—in their house you will not be subject to the petty larceny of servants and others from which you have hitherto suffered.

Belle's bird hatched five eggs; she had seven eggs in all, two did not come out. She has a nice brood. I hope that she will raise them. Please inquire of the cost of a small wire cage. Lizzie wants to get one, but does not want to pay a big price. Please visit soon and return me the enclosed note. The weather is quite warm, but there is a pleasant breeze stirring.

I ever remain yours truly,
Eliza W. Tomlinson

Dear Husband,

I hope that you are well and that all goes well with you, but as I have not heard anything from you for some time, I thought that it would not be amiss to again drop you a line this morning.

Byers is doubtless with you; he went down to see you day before yesterday. As I had not warning of his going, I had not time to fix him up or to get anything prepared to take along. As the school takes up next Monday week, he said that if he did not go down now, he could not do so for a long time, so I let him go. I hope that you will not think that I did wrong in letting him go.

Mother has just this moment come in with yours of yesterday, written in Camp Dennison, so you have not seen Byers. I feel uneasy about him. I suppose that he is wandering about some place; he would probably go to Mr. Crawford's. You have doubtless come across him ere this. Please send him home tomorrow or at farthest next day. He has no clothes with him but what he has on. At any rate I think that he can get his visit out by the time I mentioned. Jeff. goes down to his appointment tonight. We are all as well as usual. Belle's birds are doing finely. If you can get those cages, send them up by Byers.

I ever remain yours affectionately, etc.!

Eliza W. Tomlinson

I wish you to talk to Byers about the matter you mentioned in your letter; however, I think that he is not sufficiently advanced in his studies to commence the study of a profession. Newt says that he is not. He will probably commence some new studies next session and will need some new books. I wish him to go through a thorough course and to be master of his profession.

* * * * *

July and August brought repeated calls by the federal government for more recruits. The new Militia Act not only conscripted state militia, but also allowed blacks in the Southern Department to enlist and be trained as guards. Volunteers in Ohio once again responded to their country's call, but the state fell short of its quota even as threats across the river took on new urgency. After whipping the Federals at Richmond, Kentucky, E. Kirby Smith took control of Lexington and declared his intention to install a Confederate governor in Frankfort. In addition, the South's recently minted commander of the Army of the Mississippi, Braxton Bragg, was also in the Blue Grass State and planned to unite his forces with Smith's in Ohio. Even with 60,000 new Federal recruits gearing up for action in Louisville and Cincinnati, Northerners along the Ohio River were alarmed. Cincinnati business came to a standstill on September 2 as martial law became the order of the day.[6]

* * * * *

Tomlinson to Eliza
Cincinnati, Ohio, September 2, 1862

Dearest Eliza,

Martial Law prevails. Business generally suspended. I could not get away to be with you in this hour of peril. I trust all will be well, though I anticipate the capture of Ripley and all therein. Tonight I go with a party of mounted scouts into Kentucky to see the enemy. Probably this city will have fallen into the hands of the enemy before you receive this.

Will write on return.

Yours, aff.,

Will. Tomlinson

Goodbye, little ones.

CHAPTER SIXTEEN

~⌇

This Sea of Passion

"My son, hold up your head, and tell me who was the strongest man?"
"Jonah."
"Why so?"
"Cause the whale couldn't hold him when he got him down!"
—*Hickory Sprout,* October 3, 1844

OHIOANS LIVING ACROSS THE RIVER from Kentucky saw some of their worst fears realized at the beginning of September 1862 when John Hunt Morgan and his hard-riding raiders joined forces with Gen. Kirby Smith's army of twelve thousand in Lexington. Their strategic objective: invade Ohio. Gen. Lewis Wallace quickly organized a defense for Cincinnati and its two sister towns across the river, Covington and Newport. Business was suspended to free up volunteers, and men from the city and surrounding farmlands thronged the streets with the weapons they had on hand, from picks and spades to old muskets and hunting rifles. A thousand African Americans, in what became known as Cincinnati's Black Brigade, dug trenches and built fortifications south of Newport and Covington. Cannons were mounted on hills, steamers were outfitted as gunboats, and a pontoon bridge was hastily constructed across the Ohio. Women baked meats and biscuits to feed thousands at the Fifth Street Market. Churches, warehouses, and other large buildings provided temporary shelter for the motley crowd as they milled around waiting for orders.[1]

The homespun volunteers, known as Squirrel Hunters because they never had to shoot twice at the same target, were issued a certificate of

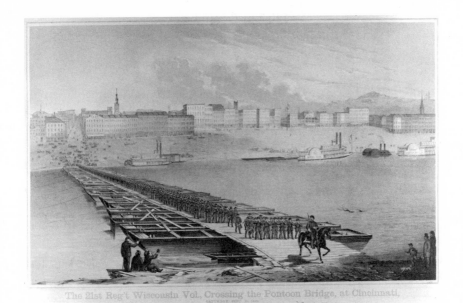

The 21st Reg't Wisconsin Vol., Crossing the Pontoon Bridge, at Cincinnati,

In September 1862 when Confederate forces threatened Cincinnati, William Byers Tomlinson was among the Squirrel Hunters who crossed the Ohio River on a hastily constructed pontoon bridge. (Library of Congress Prints and Photographs Division)

discharge by Governor Tod in 1863. Nearly thirteen hundred of the 15,766 volunteers were from Brown County, including fifteen-year-old Byers Tomlinson. It must have been an exciting time for him, even though he probably saw little action. Fanning out in the hills along the Kentucky side of the river, the volunteers stirred up more dust than Confederates. Drenching thunderstorms turned dusty trails into soggy bivouacs, and the threat from Kirby's army never came to pass as the Rebels retreated to Lexington. Ohio volunteers sang rousing choruses of "John Brown's Body" as they headed back across the pontoon bridge. Then so many of them disappeared into the city's taverns and establishments of ill repute that it took persistent prodding from local residents to dislodge them and send them on their way. Byers soon returned to Ripley, but Eliza had yet to hear from her husband.[2]

* * * * *

Dear Husband,

Not having heard anything from you since I received yours of the 15th & 14th inst., I feel very uneasy about you! I had hoped that ere this the company to which you belonged would have been disbanded or at least you would have left for the pursuits of civil life. Your occupation as compositor would exempt you from any such service. I fear that the fatigue and exposure has been too much for you! You should not have undertaken it.

Our family are in their usual health. Brother Newt is some little better; our son Byers has complained of his spinal column hurting him ever since he drilled so much. School commenced again last week, but as Jolly's company drill today out at Phil Jolley's, there is no school in Byers's room, giving the boys an opportunity to go. Byers went, notwithstanding my opposition; he is too young to endure the hardship of severe drilling! This is a critical time of life with him, but he does not realize it. He grows so fast he is like a mushroom which springs up in a night and cannot endure the noontide heat.

I received a letter from Mrs. Williamson from Des Moines a few days ago. She says that Mr. Williamson was then at home, being the first time he had visited his family for more than a year. She during that time had visited him once. He is colonel of the 4th Iowa Infantry; it is in Gen. Curtis's command, stationed at Helena, Ark. She says that the 23rd Reg. was then in Des Moines. Milton Walker is 1rst lieutenant in Company B; Gus, and John Walker are privates in the same company; Albert Hull is Adjt. of the Regt.

Mr. Williamson does not know what Frank did with our property; those bundles of papers cannot be found. Frank was an unprincipled villain; his wife is no better. She utterly refuses to give Mr. Williamson Sis's bird, to whom I gave it. She says that she would not give it to me if I was there! I would give her a trial for it were I there. Leggitt is wounded. Baird has gone to bring him home if possible.

Ever yours, etc.!
Eliza W. Tomlinson

* * * * *

As Eliza grew impatient with swindlers in Iowa, the impact of a tremendous upheaval on September 17 just outside of Sharpsburg, Maryland, was still being assessed. There, in an idyllic setting of rolling farmland flanked by blue hills and a gurgling creek on its way to the Potomac River, twenty-three thousand men were killed or wounded in what would become the war's bloodiest day of battle. Tomlinson's old regiment, the Fifth Ohio, had been among the hard-fighting units that drove Confederates out of the woods around the Dunker Church. Eleven men in that regiment were killed, thirty-five wounded, and two listed as missing. The forty-eight casualties amounted to well over one-third of the 180 men from the regiment. Tomlinson must have wondered who among his old comrades had fallen and whether he would have been among them if he had stayed with the Fifth instead of raising an independent company to fight guerrillas in western Virginia. That choice had brought his military career to an end, but he was alive, unlike the thousands whose blood oozed from the cornfields, lanes, and woods at Antietam.[3]

For the North there was some consolation in a strategic victory that produced a significant turning point in the war. The victory not only enabled Lincoln to redefine the war but to recast the kind of Union that would be forged from it. On September 22, the president announced the Preliminary Emancipation Proclamation. It stated that "all persons held as slaves, within any state, or designated part of a state, the people whereof shall then be in rebellion against the United States shall be then, thenceforward, and forever free." Many people were unhappy with such a bold step, and bitter controversy ensued. Fears about being invaded by large numbers of Negroes loomed large in the minds of many Ohioans. "Suppose," Ohio's ex-senator William Allen stated, "that the contemplated emancipation should be inaugurated successfully. Seven or eight hundred thousand negroes with their hands reeking with the blood of murdered women and children would present themselves at our southern border demanding to cross into our State as Ohio's share of the freed slaves. Then would come the conflict between the white laborers and the negroes."[4]

The war was being redefined as "a damned abolition war," according to one Democratic newspaper in Ohio, and that made Lincoln "as much of a traitor as Jeff Davis." Other Ohioans thought the Emancipation Proclamation had not gone far enough, but fears associated with abolishing slavery carried the day, and the Democratic ticket swept to victory in Ohio's state elections for the first time since 1853. The Emancipation Proclamation was not the only factor that contributed to Democratic success in Ohio, however. The state's Union ticket had also been hurt by Lincoln's proclamation on September 24 announcing the suspension of the privilege of the writ of habeas corpus. The proclamation also specified that any person guilty of disloyalty by aiding, abetting, or giving comfort to the Rebels would be subject to a military trial.[5]

When Democratic Peace candidate Clement L. Vallandigham ran for reelection to Congress from the Dayton district, he lambasted the Lincoln administration for not adhering to the Constitution. He also attacked the enforcement of abolitionism and aggressively solicited antiwar protest. Although he lost the election, many Ohioans agreed with the slogan published in the *Cincinnati Enquirer:* "The Constitution as it is, the Union as it was, and the Negroes where they are." For a while, even the *Cincinnati Gazette* was at odds with Republican policy. At one point, the *Gazette* editor not only noted his own lack of confidence in the Lincoln administration but criticized it for a "want of pluck" that had brought the country "to the verge of ruin." Within weeks he confessed the error of his thinking, however, and claimed that his confidence had been restored. But not all Ohioans had turned the page with him, including Tomlinson, who vented his frustrations in two letters for the *Ripley Bee.*[6]

There are no letters from him to Eliza for most of October, all of November, and the whole month of December. Perhaps he was visiting Ripley regularly and had no need to write. It is also possible that he and Eliza were estranged or that some letters are missing. At any rate, other than a few notes to the children, the only letters from Tomlinson during this period were to the *Ripley Bee*'s editor.

* * * * *

Correspondence of the *Bee*

CINCINNATI Nov. 1.

There is but little encouragement to write you of this week. The backbone of the strategic "anaconda" is dislocated, and our generals seem at a loss where to find the enemy in force. Our arms in the last few months have met with more disgrace as well as imperishable glory than in all our previous history. But the disgraceful chapters generally date back to commanding officers.

For instance—what is to equal the pusillanimity of our recent defense of Cincinnati:—With breastworks, siege guns, field pieces—with twenty-six hundred cavalry—with ninety thousand well armed infantry—with the Pea Ridge heroes to lead the raw troops—with squirrel hunters swarming like bees around a disturbed hive—with abundance of resources of all kinds—yet mortifying to acknowledge from 5,000 to 7,000 rebel soldiers under Gen. Heath take up a position within easy cannon range of our cities and troops—stay as long as they please, and march back at their leisure, with the loss of only about a dozen of their sick and stragglers captured, and two or three killed.

But it's all of a piece with the heartsickening and lukewarm records of other fields—of Harper's Ferry and Cumberland Gap—of Buell and McDowell. Where and when is it all to end.

Business seems to be quite lively, considering that the river is so nearly "dried up."—Send us down a slight sprinkle to water the crows on Four mile. Yesterday I had the pleasure of meeting "Doc." Ross, Ike Vorhees, "Jim" McMillin, "Bill" Armstrong, and W. Thompson, of Ripley. They had quite an experience in reaching this far. They came to Four Mile bar on the <u>Lavina Logan,</u> light-draught steamer. There they took yawl passage and at Pendleton took the Omnibus, then the cars and then—feeling that they might take at least one drink without seriously incommoding navigation above—imbibed "zweilager." Pilots Bobo and Kuntz of the <u>Logan</u> assure us that that boat will "make the riffle" on a return. Capt. Robinson, of the <u>Parthena</u> seems to have faith in the signs, for an early rise in the river, which when it comes will set him afloat in the Pittsburg trade. Our Ripley merchants will find Capt. Robinson and his boat worthy. I mention him thus because we were for months together in the 5th Ohio.

I wish the "Bee" would wake up a little, and rout out a lot of other editorial sleepers who don't talk half strong enough. Has "Old Abe" really got fast in the quicksand of military glitter? Let him be extricated, and the Nation saved at once. If there is anything left of good in the warehouse of Providence for this country let President Lincoln as our authorized agent go in and wheel it out. If the Administration can save us let it be done and speedily. Weary, bleeding, dying—let no military incompetence or traitor sympathies further deplete and utterly ruin this glorious country. I understand that Gen. Ammen has been placed in command at Covington in lieu of Gen. Crittenden.

Yours,

WILL

P.S. Capt. "Billy Shaw" sends his best to ancient friends, good fellows and the "Bee" from C & R's Grocery.

With elections over and winter coming on, people wondered what the two thousand battles fought since the war's beginning added up to—besides the staggering losses and hostilities that would need generations to heal. The Emancipation Proclamation would also bring about great change. Yet in the face of all the loss and uncertainty, a few signs of hope emerged. In early November, Lincoln finally relieved McClellan of all command. From the eastern peninsulas of Virginia to the rolling hills of Maryland, McClelland had constantly overestimated the enemy, shrunk from taking risks, and failed to act and seize the day. In addition to his ineptitude on the battlefield, his popularity with soldiers and conservative Democrats and his promotion of newspaper attacks on Secretary of War Stanton were undermining the war effort of the Lincoln administration. Quick to follow in McClellan's retreating footsteps was Don Carlos Buell, who also preferred "soft warfare" that spared the enemy as much as possible, as opposed to the aggressive destruction of the enemy pursued by Ulysses S. Grant. Many people, including Tomlinson, were thrilled to see the Union war machine sharpen its teeth.[7]

* * * * *

Correspondence of the *Bee*

CINCINNATI Nov. 12.

EDS. BEE.—It is a critical time in which to write of "men and things." Events hasten, toe upon heel, and if not advancing, at least whirling in such a style that the prophet is at fault and the chronicler in a sweat.

But of facts accomplished we may speak with comparative safety.

McClellan, Buell, Wool, McDowell, Porter—all relieved. good:

Our armies, East, West, and South advancing on the enemy, with orders to "push him to the wall," corresponding with fighting propensities in our commanders.

Better!

The prospect is that our armies will not go into "winter quarters" but keep up a vigorous campaign during the winter months in the "Sunny South," drawing in the lines, tightening the cords, squeezing to an available compass the ranks and status of rebeldom.

Best!

Our President is waking up to his duty, becoming alive to his responsibility, is no more the tool of West Point aristocracy, or educated imbecility.

Bravo!

Our people are filling with a spirit equal to the hour—they are becoming sensitive on their losses in family blood and national treasure—they are driven to the corner and badgered into fight—they are using strong words, mean hard work, their blazing eyes dens to the roused lion—the fatal spring will in a moment come, dragging or casting off all temporary grapplings and hindrances. They will take down with them all Generals, all powers, all obstructions—even a hesitating Administration. They are in earnest, and "mock at fear." Who shall hinder?

We are only beginning to feel what it means to have our children and brothers and friends, our hopes and bones in unnamed graves—our crippling, wounded, hobbling thronged highways and lonely country places our victims of disease sadly plodding with weary limbs the pavement o'er which their boyish limbs so lively skipped.

The masses fast realize that the liberties which their fathers won, are in jeopardy—that the nation bounded by its ten thousands of miles of seacoast is in peril—that its flag which so many years proudly proclaimed our glory on every land, in every sea is being ravished and dishonored—that the grapple of the cut-throats is at our very vitals.

Jubilate!

And we are going to arbitrate a compromise all along the line wherever appears an enemy, bayonets for pens and rifles for advocates and artillery for traitors. Treason is a crime—murder an offense.

We are no longer to suckle and nourish outlaws at the bosom of the Goddess Truth, and Loyalty is to be a standard value.

When the people rise let shoulder strapped hucksters, penny-wise demagogues and great ghouls who batter on murdered Virtue and strangled Freedom, take heed and vanish.

Then again shall we have peace, happiness, home prosperity. Then may we praise the God who has brought us through. But if we fail, then to those who have opened those flood gates of blood, this sea of passion, this devastation and desecration, and who show us naught but vacant homes and countless graves, and despair and anarchy exceeding the agonies of the damned, as the proceeds of the struggle—happy to them were the fate of Judas!

Vox Populi—Vox Dei!

Our too kind President is now learning new lessons to some purpose. He will no longer select a lady's palfrey for an artillery wheel horse, nor use a stage coach for speedy traveling.

WILL.

Eds. Bee—There's lots of funny things said and done even in these times when hostile armies meet in battle shock, and tread the wine press of brave blood. One thing which just now pumped up a smile from the rather seriously disposed countenance of "Will" was an anecdote to the purport that a boarder was one day observed picking out something from the dish before him.

"What have you got," asked this fellow.

"O, only a little bark," was the reply.

"Well," responded No. 2, "it's my opinion you'd better not hunt longer or you'll find a big growl."

It's so apropos to Old Abe fingering over the Pot-omac pie of generals.

But it seems the old gentleman found neither "bark" or "growl," but this mongrel howl; says the correspondent of the N. Y. Herald.

"The moment that they fully realized it, all those soldiers, animated by one universal impulse, ran after him some weeping aloud, and shouted in the most appalling manner—Fetch him back! fetch him back and 'Oh, come back to us, McClellan!' Many of them were melted to tears, and after cheering him again and again, joined in the universal supplication 'Come back to us! Come back to us McClellan!'"

Now, dear reader, you won't scold me for a slight smile at such a scene. Even though it was a whole army of brave soldiers boo-boo-ing right out and melting into sympathetic brine. Then that "universal impulse."—Did you feel that "airthquake" up on Red Oak? I couldn't keep from forgetting the lines of the immortal bard of—some place. Was it not Sir Walter Scott, in some unwritten work, who described a scene between a mother and daughter somewhat thus:

"She screamed in horrid accents wild,

My daughter! O, My daughter!

Come back! come back!

You know you hadn't orter."

I had some notion of getting you up a little bagful of fun about this and other things, but in these days of checks and coppers have to save a little for small change.

WILL.

* * * * *

Tomlinson's own daughter was nine years old when he wrote the following note to her. He also wrote to Byers—with some good news about his latest invention.

* * * * *

Tomlinson to (Daughter) Belle
Cincinnati, Ohio, December 10, 1862

Dear Pet,

It is 2 o-clock in the morning, but I will send you a line. I got a letter from your mother yesterday. Don't be uneasy about me, as I am getting along pretty well. I will soon have to use specs, as the gaslight and new type have affected my eyes.

Enclosed I send you a letter from Jennie, which I have had for over a week. Hope all's well at home.

Your aff. "Pap,"

Will Tomlinson

Tomlinson to (Son) Byers
Cincinnati, Ohio, December 12, 1862

Dear Boy,

This morning I sent you a lot of papers; hope you got them.

At noon I met Capt. S. W. Johnston, of Kansas. He is just from Washington City, and returns there on Monday.

Incidentally, speaking of my family, I mentioned your bullet invention. And what think you? He had gone on to Washington to get out a patent for a cannon ball (invented by a client of his) on precisely the same principle. But his ball rounds off at the point, like a solid ball with a hole drilled through it. His had one great defect, which is supplied by yours, and perfects his. I refer to the solid plug which comes next the powder.

He proposes on certain terms (himself furnishing necessary funds) to return to Washington, and take out a partnership patent. He waits you to furnish a model, either in lead or wood, and description of the claims sought to be secured by the patent. I would suggest to you that you employ Mr. Belchambers to aid you in making the model and specifications. Also describe the style of the mould for the ball. Send to me, if possible, by the packet, as soon as you can, informing me by letter of its arrival. He is sorry that the notice of it was published and suggests that you keep very quiet about it, and thinks the invention worth to you your weight in gold.

I am well. Sorry to hear that Lizzie and Mag are so bad. Do they not know any one?

Love to all. I send this in a hurry, by Hayden Thompson. Write me as soon as possible.

If I get any more war news, I will send by same. In great haste,
Yours,
Will Tomlinson

* * * * *

There is no indication of whether or not Tomlinson spent Christmas in Ripley with Eliza and the children. But as 1862 drew to a close and the new year dawned, he was nowhere to be found.

* * * * *

Byers (Son) to Tomlinson
Ripley, Ohio, January 10, 1863

Dear Father,

I am well and so are the rest of the family, and I hear you are the same. Mag is a great deal better. Sam is going back to the army in a few days. I am going to school again; our teacher, Mr. Coon, went up to Pennsylvania and got married during the vacation. I have taken up the study of philosophy in school.

We had a snow here the other day but it is now raining. I looked for that model both on the Bostona and wharf boat but could not find it. The clerk on the Bostona said it had been put off on the wharf boat at Cincinnati; if it is necessary I can get another one made. Have you heard from Johnston yet? I see by the paper that Williamson is distinguishing himself in the southwest. I suppose that many of our friends and neighbors from Des Moines have been killed and wounded in those great battles which have been fought lately.

Goodbye,
W. B. Tomlinson

Eliza to Tomlinson
Ripley, Ohio, January 10, 1863

Dear Husband,

Byers has told you that we are all well. There is no local news that I know of. I presume that you are aware that Sid Leggett was killed at Murfreesboro. This is a sad vicissitude and will be hard for Mrs. Leggett to bear up under. Alas, alas, many hearts will be made to bleed, many hearths will be made desolate, ere the conclusion of this war, which I fear will not soon be over.

Please write and let us know how you are, how you are getting along, etc.

I had written thus far when the whistle blowed on Saturday. Byers did not get up in time to have it mailed. This is Monday and our health continues good; the weather beautiful. No news that I am aware of more than what you are already apprised of.

Ever yours, etc.,
Eliza W. Tomlinson

That $1.00 by Collins came to hand, thank you. Sam Pangburn and some others of the boys started back to camp on Saturday night.

Eliza to Tomlinson
Ripley, Ohio, mid January 1863

Dear Husband,

It is now four weeks since we received a line from you, why is this? We are and have been very uneasy about you! Do write or come up. It is now near about the time you promised to be here at any rate. I know of nothing of interest further than what you learn before we do from the papers. The war clouds appear to be breaking. Light shoots at last on the horizon. There now appears to be a goodly prospect of this unholy rebellion being crushed out. God grant how now.

I ever send yours, etc.,
Eliza W. Tomlinson

This letter was written January 24, 1863, by William Byers Tomlinson, age fifteen. (Wylie-Tomlinson Letter Collection)

Byers (Son) to Tomlinson
Ripley, Ohio, January 24, 1863

Dear Pap,

We are all well except Belle she is not very well, she has not been able to go to school for some days past. We are begining to be uneasy about you for we have not heard from you for a long time. I have been going to school ever since I came up from the city. I am studying Latin, Philosophy, and Algebra. We had a great snow here a few days ago it was near two feet deep, but it is nearly all gone now. Have you heard from Johnston yet or has he got back, I would like to know his success. I have nothing of interest to write about. Did that man send a drawing of my ball to the Scientific American, if he has not I would like to have it done. Good bye.

W. B. Tomlinson

Tomlinson's Friend to Eliza
Cincinnati, Ohio, January 29, 1863

Mrs. Tomlinson,

I have just rec'd your note as I am on the point of leaving for George-town, and have but a moment in which to answer. Mr. Tomlinson left for Nashville Saturday week, as nurse, on a hospital boat chartered by the Governor. He was well at the time; expected to be back in two weeks. Previously to leaving he had been working regularly in the Gazette office. There are several of your letters waiting for him at the office.

Regards to all, and excuse haste.

Very respectfully yours,

S. H. Cook

CHAPTER SEVENTEEN

~⌢

Nursing the Wounded

Man's inhumanity to man makes countless thousands mourn.
—"Man Was Made to Mourn," Robert Burns, quoted in "The Life of a
Prisoner," *Freedom's Casket,* June 15, 1844

AT STONE'S RIVER, Tennessee, on the night of December 30, 1862, closely encamped enemy troops alternately serenaded each other with popular songs like "Yankee Doodle" and "Dixie" before singing "Home Sweet Home" in unison. Soldiers from the North and the South wanted to be home, but at dawn the next day, Confederates caught Union soldiers off guard at breakfast. The four days of battle that followed brought staggering losses to both sides. The Rebels were forced to retreat, however, and Lincoln credited Rosecrans with saving the nation from a defeat that would have destroyed it. But the Confederacy was far from being vanquished. Many of the 7,543 Union soldiers wounded at Stone's River were put on hospital boats heading north on the Cumberland River. Confederates seized three of the boats, crammed all of the wounded onto one ship, and burned the other two. Tomlinson was apparently among those trying to help the hundreds of injured soldiers. After returning to Cincinnati, he was not only depressed by what he had seen but disappointed in Eliza's reaction to his latest project—another plan for obtaining a military commission.[1]

* * * * *

Dearest Eliza,

Yesterday I returned from Nashville, having been absent nearly four weeks, most of the time being blockaded, first from going up the Cumberland, and then from coming home. So long in the midst of wounded, dead and dying, the effect of the trip has not been such as to throw off that gloom which for months I have felt consuming up all hope, and love and inward life. Though in your answer to a former allusion which I made to this state of feeling, you only added bitterness to what was before almost unbearable, yet I have no censure. In your letter just after the return of Byers you intimated as much as if you wanted nothing more to do with me if I persisted in my project of organizing a negro brigade. I have studied it all over, and though a favorable response from Washington was received, I have not yet actively engaged in the enterprise. What my future steps in regard to it may be I can't say; but my Southern trip has convinced me that under the present order of things our Government is virtually defunct, never to be restored. Our own imbecility and indecision has brought upon the world this awful and heavy curse.

But it is no more use, however, for me to talk or to do. I feel broken down in hope and purpose. If we could once again gather our little family circle and be to ourselves, I might yet rouse up energy enough to make things comfortable. But I have none to cheer with a word in the struggle against despondency. The visit of my boy was sunshine o'er the gloom for a few days.

This is the third letter I have commenced. Perhaps I may finish it. The others are best in the flames.

Next week I will send you some money.

Will Tomlinson

Saturday morning.—No packet left yesterday, so I add today that I feel some better. It is a beautiful morning. I have just received from the painter a very fine little picture. I will have it framed and forwarded early. It was made according to my order for her, and pleases me very much.

* * * * *

The enlistment of African Americans as soldiers was a volatile issue for both sides during the Civil War. Each side employed blacks as laborers to support military operations, but neither was eager to let them enlist as bona fide soldiers armed with weapons that would be used to kill whites. In the North, however, the pressure to muster in troops of contraband slaves and freed blacks was much more persistent. A few Union generals had already tried on their own to organize African American troops before the Militia Act of July 17, 1862, authorized President Lincoln to enlist them "for any military or naval service for which they may be found competent." Soon after, Massachusetts Infantry Capt. Thomas Wentworth Higginson formed the First South Carolina (Union) Infantry, the first black regiment to be raised from scratch. But it was the implementation of the Emancipation Proclamation that made massive enlistment of African Amerian troops possible.[2]

When President Lincoln signed the proclamation into law on January 1, 1863, he not only reformed military enrollment policy but instituted an act of justice that redefined the war and the American republic. As a legal document, the proclamation first and foremost delcared that slaves in any state in rebellion against the United States would from thenceforward be forever free. It also provided for the protection of that freedom by the federal government and for the right of freed people to work for decent wages. It even had international ramifications in making the ownership of another human being not just unlawful but unethical and immoral. It did not, however, eliminate racial prejudice against African Americans. Many Northerners who opposed slavery believed blacks to be inferior. In the military, black regiments still needed to have white officers, and Tomlinson wanted to be among them. Yet as the winter lull settled in, he was in Cincinnati, where he seemed to be mending his relationship with his family.[3]

* * * * *

Eliza to Tomlinson
Ripley, Ohio, February 23, 1863

Dear Husband,

We are somewhat better in health than when I last wrote. Belle is yet not very well; therefore, I thought not proper to let her go to school today. I have nothing of interest to communicate that I can remember at present. I am out so little that I know scarcely anything of the gossip of the day.

Mag has entirely recovered excepting that she is not yet quite so strong as what she was before she was sick. Your friends are all well so far as I know.

Please give my best love and respects to Mrs. Crawford and daughters. I presume that Eliza will remain at her father's during her husband's absence or continuance in the war.

When are you coming up? We should be glad to see you.

Ever yours, etc.,

Eliza W. Tomlinson

P. Cornell (Friend) to Tomlinson
Columbus, Ohio, February 26, 1863

Dear Capt.,

You will excuse me for not answering your kind letter sooner when I tell you that I am just able to sit up. I came very near getting a wooden overcoat. When I got home on Thursday night my head and face was so swollen that my eyes were shut. I was as blind as a bat and my brains felt as if they would jump out of my head. The folks sent for the doctor and he stayed all night with me. For two days he did not think I would live, but the disease changed for the better. The swelling went down after three or four days and I am getting better slowly. I began to think that my trip to Nashville was very unprofitable. Capt. Tom, I have got the blues. This staying in the house almost gives me the horrors. As soon as I can get out I will see about that matter you wrote about.

When I got home I found a notice from the U.S. Mustering Officer that I was mustered out. But I expected it, for you know I have no Regt., and I could not hold my position without a Regt. You must excuse this short letter, but I am weak and cannot sit up long at a time. Please answer soon and give me all the news.

Your Friend,

P. Cornell

My love to the Parson. Tell him to write to me. Yours, P. C.

* * * * *

The matter that Tomlinson wanted his friend Cornell to see about may have involved organizing a company of African Americans. Such an undertaking

THE COPPERHEAD PARTY.——IN FAVOR OF *A VIGOROUS PROSECUTION OF PEACE!*

This editorial cartoon from the February 28, 1863, edition of *Harper's Weekly* shows three Copperheads ready to attack Columbia with her Union shield and sword. (Library of Congress Prints and Photographs Division)

was dangerous in southern Ohio, where embittered Democrats like Clement Vallandigham were inciting violent attacks against officials sent to arrest deserters. On March 5, a mob of civilians and soldiers retaliated against Copperhead agitators by destroying the office of the *Crisis,* a newspaper published in Columbus by Sam Medary. Medary was as virulently opposed to the war and Lincoln administration as Vallandigham, and the two were generally regarded as the primary leaders of antiwar and anti-Lincoln propaganda in the Midwest. Tomlinson had never been a Copperhead, but he still could not embrace the Lincoln administration, especially when its stance on raising black regiments in the Border States thwarted his plans.[4]

* * * * *

Tomlinson to Eliza
Cincinnati, Ohio, April 9, 1863

Dearest Eliza,

I received yours last night. My leg is about well. I don't drag it any more. But that pain in my right breast is worse. I have had to quit work for the last two weeks. I am going to try it again today, but feel almost smothered. The weather is beautiful. The election went off all right every-where. The traitors are rebuked by the genuine patriotism of the people. The government will be sustained, and if the President will only let our armies march on to meet the armed rebels in front, be assured that glo-rious spring victories await us. Lincoln is now the only man or power in the way of a speedy and glorious universal triumph.

We have three cases of the smallpox at Crawford's. John has it. Oth-erwise the family are well. I think Mrs. Evans is glad that her husband is a prisoner.

Yesterday morning Bob Peters and his lady visited our house. I had just got up, and found them in the parlor. I was so alarmed at finding them so exposed, that my embarrassment must have been very visible. I didn't know whether at once to warn them away, or wait for the family to do so. The fact is, the house ought at once to have been closed. I afterward explained to Mr. Peters.

Mr. Bell has been down here to engage coal. I think it the wrong end of the line to come to. It is doubtful whether he succeeds.

I have not seen Newt, but probably shall on taking this letter to the boat.

Ever yours,

Will Tomlinson

Lincoln has backed out from raising negro troops in the border states. He is an old worn-out dotard on this point.

Tomlinson to Eliza
Cincinnati, Ohio, April 15, 1863

Dearest Eliza,

I know you must have suffered much surprise and disappointment at my not writing you according to promise. But I have hitherto been afraid, perhaps without reason. But on arriving at Crawford's, after passing sev-eral times through the house, I found three cases of smallpox. This dis-ease seems so peculiarly mysterious and easy of communicating that I dare not send you anything from my hand, though I have had it. I have read of bankers catching it from handling bills exposed to the contagion. I will, however, risk it now. John Crawford is still quite bad. As to my own health, it is improving. Last week I was very bad with the pleurisy. For four days I kept mustard poultices on my breast till it is raw in blis-ters. My leg is well again. Your brother Byers knew best.

Enclosed I send you $2.00. I will write you again on Saturday. I wrote you a letter last week, but did not send it. Hereafter you may rely on greater punctuality. I have not seen Mr. Wilkes, but sent him Daughter's letter. I suppose you have read Gen. Burnside's Order. It reaches Ripley, and I hope will be lived up to. Exciting and good news may be looked for soon from Rosecrans. Halleck will soon be removed. Lincoln won't take negro regiments from the border. But I must to go bed.

Who is John W. Thompson, of Ripley, who so abused that place in the Enquirer last Sunday? He says he is a discharged soldier from the 34th Ohio.

* * * * *

Not everyone was a fan of Ripley, as Tomlinson's last comment indicated. John W. Thompson had abused Ripley in the *Cincinnati Enquirer,* a leading Democratic newspaper aligned with the *Crisis,* published in Columbus by Sam Medary. Medary persisted in referring to African Americans as "niggers." According to him, slavery was constitutional, and the abolition of it was not. Around the same time, Copperhead propagandists in Cincinnati were stirring up Southern sympathizers who were sending provisions to friends across the river. On March 23 at a rally just outside the city, one of the key speakers was Vallandigham, who provoked resistance to Lincoln's commanding officer of the Department of the Ohio, Gen. Ambrose E. Burnside. On April 13, Burnside issued Order No. 38 specifying that anyone found guilty of committing acts "for the benefit of the enemies of our country be tried as spies or traitors and, if convicted, suffer death." The order also made it clear that any expression of sympathy for the enemy would not be tolerated and that anyone committing such offenses would be arrested with a view toward being tried as a spy or traitor. But the order did not deter Vallandigham, who spurned it as an infringement of freedom of speech. The heated atmosphere surrounding the controversy was bound to erupt in violence sooner or later. When it did, Tomlinson managed to keep his head down and met with no harm. But others were not so fortunate.[5]

* * * * *

Tomlinson to Eliza
Cincinnati, Ohio, April 19, 1863

Dearest Eliza,

I agreed to write you yesterday but this will reach you as early as if written yesterday. My health is improving and I hope soon to be able to work full time. We have had a "hot old time" here tonight—all about the irresponsible nigger. Several men, of color and colorless, are badly hurt. About six o'clock to-night three negroes, well dressed, were passing along Walnut Str., east side, between 5th & 6th, when some white rowdies, in front of a coffee house, used toward them most infamous insults. The negroes passed on, when one of the rowdies followed, attacking. The negro, with a brickbat, mashed the head of his assailant. He did right. Other incidents I will give you again; but I find the papers are getting a fuller report, and drop the subject.

Monday morning—This is a beautiful morning. Today I will go to work. By the boat I send you some papers. One of them is the paper Mr. Perry sent for. Next Saturday I will send you ten dollars. Mrs. Evans is at Ripley. John is getting along finely, so Mrs. C. tells me.

The war news from Nashville is quite exciting. Grant will not reach Rosecrans an hour too soon. We are bound to have some big fighting soon.

But I must finish up this, and hurry down to the boat.

Love to the children.

Ever yours,
Will Tomlinson

Eliza to Tomlinson
Ripley, Ohio, April 22, 1863

Dear Husband,

Yours of Sunday, together with that package of papers, Belle found thrown over the fence in the yard upon coming from school on yesterday. I would have written you on Monday, but delayed hoping to receive your promised letter, intending to answer next day. I was prevented writing yesterday on account of attending Mrs. Copple's funeral, not getting back in time to write for yesterday's mail.

Mrs. Copple was a sister of Mrs. Bennington and stayed at her house. She was a very fine woman, but had seen a great deal of trouble. Her husband some four years ago converted his property into money and left for parts unknown, taking with him a bride woman from Manchester, since which he has not been heard of. His wife has fallen a victim to his cruelty and injustice. She was acquainted with Mrs. Crawford.

I am very glad that your leg has got well and that your health has improved. I hope that it will soon be altogether restored. I received those $2.00 last week; thank you it was very acceptable. Belle wants to know whether you have had an opportunity of giving Mr. Wilkes those roots which she sent by you to him.

Last evening Mrs. Allen informed me that Mrs. John Evans was at her house. I called up this morning but she was not in, so I did not see her. You did not say whether any others excepting John had the smallpox. Please give my respects and best wishes to Mrs. Crawford. No news here that I know of which would be of interest to you.

I ever remain yours, etc.,
Eliza W. Tomlinson

Eliza to Tomlinson
Ripley, Ohio, April 28, 1863

Dear Husband,

I received yours of the 26th inst. last night. Thank you for those $10.00. It was very acceptable. I am happy to learn that your health is improving. I hope that this pleasant weather will do away with that pain in your side altogether. You speak of your eyesight having failed of night; from the symptoms I think that you are probably bilious and that in all probability a dose or two of anti-bilious pills would remedy that matter.

Our family enjoy their usual health. On Sunday night Bony Lindsey and Mary Vohres were married. They are going to live down at the vineyard. I hope for her sake as well as his own that he will now quit drinking. Miss Jane Porter was married to Jim Howard the Cecesh!—on last Thursday. I presume that you remember him; he lives over the river, opposite this place. She is his third wife. He has not borne a very good reputation as to virtue, but some persons will look over a multitude of sins for the sake of getting a husband.

We are sorry to hear such a report of Mr. Wilkes. As to that John W. Thompson, I know nothing about him—never saw him. Our son Byers says that he heard that in the first place he belonged to some artillery from which he deserted, has again joined the army many times and as many times deserted. And is now a deserter. In person he is tall and large. Byers would have written an account of all that he has heard relative to him this morning but had not time before going to school. I will have him write by tomorrow's mail. Our neighbor John Lafabre opposite has sold, bought a farm and gone to the country to live. Marcus the Miller bought him out and moved in yesterday.

Belle's bird is sitting on five eggs. Byers has just come home at recess; he will write you a few lines. No news of interest. Please write as often as you can, at least once a week. I would like that you would send me Harpers Weekly after you are through with it; it is an interesting paper.

I ever remain yours, etc.,

Eliza W. Tomlinson

Byers (Son) to Tomlinson
Ripley, Ohio, April 28, 1863

Dear Pap,

I am well and so are the rest of the family. We were all very glad to hear that your leg had got well. You ask in your last letter who John W. Thompson is. I will tell you what I know about him. He used to belong to some artillery regiment which he is reported to have deserted. The next that I knew of him he belonged to Evan's company of Zuaves. He was in town when you were here and for some time before and perhaps is yet. He is tall and slim, and I think he is an Irishman. He is the man that came to the market house, the time of that raid on Maysville, with an old saber and nothing else. He came here—to Ripley—slandering Capt. Evans, and saying he was a traitor and had a contract with Bragg to sell the town of Ripley into his hands. I expect that Captain Evans could give you a pretty correct history of him.

I have finished that clock that I was making when you were here. Instead of making it run by water, I fixed weights and a pendulum to it. It would run well enough if it were not for my having to make knots in the hands. I need not say well enough either, for it is not satisfied with quick time, but must do double quick. It goes twice as fast as it ought to, but this could be remedied easily if I was not tired of working at it. I am glad to hear of John's recovery.

Goodbye,

W. B. Tomlinson

If you want to write to Evans about that man, he is in town, and you pray know where to direct your letter.

Eliza to Tomlinson
Ripley, Ohio, May 5, 1863

Dear Husband,

I am happy to inform you that we are all in the enjoyment of our usual health. Yesterday's mail brought no letter from you—hope you are well.

In my last I forgot to tell you what a fine time we had here at our Union meeting on Friday week ago, but you have doubtless heard all about it: Dr. Darcy is a fine speaker and handles the subject of treason, butternuts, etc., boldly! Gov. Tod also is a good Union man, but I think is a little more tender of the feelings of his friends the butternuts. He may be a great man, a talented man, a learnt man, a patriot and all that sort of thing!—but surely he is a great egotist. Big man Me is prominent throughout all his remarks. But this is no doubt all right, a certain amount of self esteem is necessary to constitute the great man. Tod is a good Jackson Democrat, therefore is all right.

Last Friday evening Dr. Bradford lectured in the Methodist church. He handled the traitors without gloves, commencing some 25 or 30 years ago, giving the rise and progress of treason until the present period. He threw such light upon the subject, I think that all butternuts present must have felt very much ashamed of themselves and their party. We need a few such speakers as Dr. Bradford to canvas the state; it would have a better influence than all the papers in the land. The truth when spoken by a Ryan and a slaveholder would do much good in the cause of the government. Dr. Bradford is a good impromptu speaker; he makes some very fine points, and happy illustrations.

I have got that fine picture of yours taken by Minner, I did not like that old gilt frame, so I had it put in a new one. The Sunday School children have a celebration or rather exhibition tonight in the Methodist Church—admittance 20 cents, children 10 cents—the proceeds to purchase a new library.

Ever yours, etc.,

Eliza W. Tomlinson

* * * * *

While Northern loyalists were cheering each other on in Ripley, Union officers dressed in civilian clothes were monitoring Copperhead meetings throughout the state. At a rally in Mt. Vernon northeast of Columbus on May 1, they heard Vallandigham say that the war was being used to liberate blacks and enslave whites. Lambasting the Lincoln administration and Order No. 38 for curtailing basic rights, Vallandigham claimed that he answered to a higher order, Order No. 1, the U.S. Constitution. Then he announced his outright repudiation of Order No. 38, saying that he "despised it, spit upon it, trampled it under his feet." A few days later, Burnside sent the 115th Ohio Regiment to arrest Vallandigham at his home in Dayton. When a military commission arraigned him for violating Order No. 38, Vallandigham tried to refute the legality of his arrest and trial, but on May 16 he was found guilty as charged and sentenced to "close confinement in some fortress of the United States."[6]

After spending three days in Fort Warren in Boston Harbor, Vallandigham, with a commuted sentence from President Lincoln, was sent to Rosecrans to be transported beyond Union lines. On May 25 Vallandigham was deposited in the Confederacy, but his arrest had already triggered a riot in Dayton on May 5. His supporters wrecked the office of the *Dayton Daily Journal,* and after setting fire to the Republican newspaper and the building that housed it, they prevented firemen from putting out the raging flames, which quickly spread to several other buildings in the center of the city. Burnside's troops brought the situation under control and established martial law by 10 o'clock that night, but the propaganda that the situation generated was not so easily quelled. Democratic newspapers across the country denounced Lincoln for abrogating freedom of speech and the press. Even Republican editors were critical of the president for such a strategic mistake. Eventually Lincoln answered his critics with the following question: "Must I shoot a simple-minded soldier boy who deserts, while I must not touch a hair of a wiley agitator who induces him to desert?" No doubt Tomlinson applauded Lincoln's strong stand regarding

Vallandigham and the Copperheads. But "the great crushing news of the day," the Union's defeat at Chancellorsville, left him despondent over the administration's "imbecility" in managing the war effort.[7]

* * * * *

Tomlinson to Eliza
Cincinnati, Ohio, May 7, 1863

Dearest Eliza,

I am happy to write you that today I am considerably better. This afternoon I worked, but tonight put on a "sub," so as not to tax my strength too much. Your last was a pleasing, whole-souled, old-fashioned letter that it has cheered me greatly.

But as the current news is of such vast importance, I have no doubt but you would like to know what I think about the state of affairs. That mob at Dayton, in which home traitors played such havoc with a loyal printing office and other property, was last night followed by one of the same stripe at Hamilton, Butler County, some 25 miles from here, on the railroad to Dayton. They destroyed the freight depot and cars and started to destroy the R.R. bridge, when loyal citizens enough intercepted them to prevent the success of the attempt. And all about that infamous traitor Vallandigham. But our troops are after them. How long before we have similar scenes in Brown County?

But the great crushing news of the day came on us at noon, like a pall over hope—like a shroud for liberty, a sexton digging the grave of our country, a cloud of ghouls howling and gloating and tearing at the tombs of the patriots who left us the legacy of this glorious government.

O, but this is terrible. Our brave army again outgeneraled and defeated by inferior numbers, and our killed and wounded numbering over 10,000. Hooker, whom we familiarly spoke of as "Fighting Joe," alarmed at the shadow where he had so bravely faced the substance, is suddenly, in the darkness of night, seized with pain, and again the splendid army of the Potomac has to <u>steal a shameful retreat</u> to whence they came, leaving a large portion of the wounded to the tender mercies of the enemy, with exhausted medicine-chest and unwholesome commissariat. Why it so is or can be, God only knows, unless Administration Cabinet imbecility or worse be at the bottom of the disaster.

My old regiment, the noble Fifth Ohio, has been most terribly used up. The particulars have not yet reached us; but one company (K) had 17 killed. Two of my old personal friends are numbered with the uselessly slaughtered. How many more such will appear in the long roll soon to appear I fear to contemplate and dread to realize.

What is to come of it? That is the momentous issue—the question of the future, of which we have no Daniel to prophecy or Jeremiah to weep. Who shall tell? O, that at the head of this great people we now had a man instead of a joke, with strong and loyal surroundings—anything thus approaching would be a blessing rather than the cormorant curses now wrapping the vitals of our government as a pest-house robe.

Can we recover? The people, honest, loyal and fearless, would say "yes, we can and will." But it is very little they can do. We must join together our voices as the millions and swear to our rulers that the power of the People—all its resources—shall forthwith be called into play and vigorously used to crush out and utterly and speedily overcome the enemy in every shape.

But as what news comes tonight you will get in the same mail with this, and you can draw your own conclusions therefrom, I will no longer wait for dispatches, but close, knowing that nothing can be darker than the hue of our present fortunes.

Mrs. Crawford's family are all well. John does not yet make his appearance, though will. Matchmaking has been vigorously prosecuted in the parlor between a gentleman (divorced) named Smith and Mrs. Belle Maguire.

Ever yours,
Will Tomlinson.

This moment a dispatch says that Hooker only retired to receive forty thousand re-enforcements, explaining the sudden rise in the river endangering the pontoons, and his connection, as reasons, etc. Not whipped yet, thank God.

Another item. We have captured Grand Gulf, with Jamison, etc. Breathe lightly, gentle hope—all may yet be well.

Again, yours—goodnight, all.

* * * * *

With his hopes for Union victory somewhat restored, Tomlinson wrote to his daughter on May 21 and asked her to write to him and describe "any little incidents" she might have seen at a fire in Ripley a week or so before. According to an article in the *Ripley Bee,* the fire came close to engulfing the town's main street before "a few resolute and unflinching men and boys" mounted the top of a house in the fire's pathway and used water pumped from the town's cistern to douse the flames. Three buildings were destroyed and ten or twelve families dislodged. No one was injured, however, and the cause of the fire was attributed to a defective flue from a wood stove. In the same letter, Tomlinson inquired about his daughter's health and her progress in school, adding that he hoped that the "blockheads" in her class were not holding her back. His own health was not so good, he wrote, but there was nothing in particular that ailed him, even though he felt "stiff like an old Ripley dray-horse in the pork season."[8]

What really ailed him was the diaster at Chancellorsville, where, he wrote, "so many tens of thousands of our men" were killed and wounded "for no adequate result, as they were at Fredericksburg." He blamed the fiasco on a number of factors, including the negligence and drunkenness of Union soldiers who had no pickets out and were boiling coffee when Stonewall Jackson attacked them with 40,000 Rebels. According to Tomlinson, the Yanks ran without scarcely firing a gun, leaving guns, knapsacks, overcoats, and everything to the enemy. "It has almost made me hate a Dutchman," he wrote, since that corps was composed of Germans. But Tomlinson also blamed Halleck, the Union general in chief who, he wished, would "soon need a coffin ordered." Halleck's mismanagement of military affairs at Chancellorsville resulted in seventeen thousand casualties for the Federals. Northern morale was crushed. "My God! my God!" Lincoln exclaimed, "What will the country say?"[9]

Such strategic losses provided Copperheads with more fuel to keep the fires of dissatisfaction burning. In fact, the Copperheads in Indiana were getting quite bold. In his letter to his daughter, Tomlinson also described a recent incident in Indianapolis. A train full of Southern sympathizers had "fired into the 'Soldiers' House.'" But Union soldiers planted cannon at each end of the depot and searched all passengers. They captured 1,500 revolvers, which, at $20 apiece, were worth $30,000, Tomlinson wrote. It was "a good lick" to the Copperheads, he added, and "every man who fired at the Soldiers' House ought to be shot or hung."[10]

Meanwhile, events in Ohio were moving in another direction. John Mercer Langston, an Oberlin College graduate and well-known African American, had been lobbying Governor Tod for permission to raise a black regiment and had visited Cincinnati in his statewide appeal for black volunteers. Tod had already granted permission for the recruitment of Ohio's African Americans for Massachusetts regiments, and on May 27 he finally petitioned Secretary of War Edwin Stanton for permission to raise a Negro regiment in Ohio. On June 16, Stanton granted that permission, and the 127th Ohio Volunteer Infantry Regiment (later the Fifth Regiment, United States Colored Troops) came into being. More than five thousand colored volunteers from Ohio would serve the Union, making the Buckeye State second only to Pennsylvania in the number of African American troops who served the Union.[11]

Despite the willingness of black volunteers, most white Ohioans still had mixed feelings about black soldiers. Many whites believed that African Americans were inferior in social, intellectual, and military abilities. To make sure that the great experiment of using Negro troops was off to a good start, Federals required that the officers of African American regiments be white. One white soldier eager to secure a commission with the 127th Ohio was Tomlinson's friend Sam Evans from Aberdeen, Ohio, just east of Ripley. After accepting a lieutenancy with a black regiment, Evans wrote to his father that he would be paid $100 per month for his new position. From his perspective, A Negro was "no better than a white man" and would "do as well to receive Rebel bullets" and "save the life of some white men." His father was not pleased that his son had accepted such a "degraded position" and wrote that he "would rather clean out S__t houses at ten cents pr day" than take his son's position at its rate of pay.[12]

If Tomlinson were still interested in leading a regiment of African American troops, his chances of doing so were slim. A military panel interviewed candidates about their military experience and qualifications for such appointments, and even prospects who were political favorites or popular with African American troops failed to obtain commissions. Tomlinson carried a serious handicap even before putting in an application. Black regiments were still highly controversial, and any officer responsible for one assumed a position loaded with political dynamite. Tomlinson's involvement in the Jacksonville murders in western Virginia had probably left him with a questionable reputation and military record. Whatever his future entailed, it would, no doubt, not involve a military commission.[13]

CHAPTER EIGHTEEN

~

Close to Home

Give the rebels peace and you give them independence.
—*Loyal Scout,* October 10, 1863

BY THE SUMMER of 1863, people in both the North and the South were weary of war. Northerners were disheartened by the ineffectiveness of Union commanders and the audacity of Confederate officers in leading raids into Pennsylvania. But a few bright spots emerged. The South rejected Vallandigham as an "alien enemy," West Virginia became the thirty-fifth state in the Union, and the Yanks scored critical victories at Vicksburg and Gettysburg. In Ripley, meanwhile, Tomlinson's sixteen-year-old son, Byers, was finding it difficult to enlist support for a local militia company, and a neighbor was suspected of aiding the enemy. On May 28 the *Ripley Bee* ran the following story:

> On last Friday, Wm. Norris, of this place, was arrested by an officer and squad of soldiers, from Cincinnati, and taken to that city and committed to prison on some accusation of disloyalty. We do not know what the specific charge against him is, but have heard from one who visited him in prison, that the charge on the book of the prison is that of being a rebel <u>officer</u> within the Union lines. This is absurd—probably a mistake has been made in entering it on the book, as it is well known, that Mr. Norris has resided here for years, and has very seldom been absent—never for any considerable length of time since the commencement of the war.

Norris was evidently regarded as one of Ripley's "most esteemed and prominent citizens," but not by Tomlinson and his son, who understood the gravity of Norris's offense.[1]

By mid-June skirmishes between Yanks and Rebels were coming dangerously close to Ripley. Fighting broke out across the river in Maysville, and a few weeks later Morgan and some twenty-five hundred cavalrymen crossed the Ohio into Indiana. They then turned east toward Cincinnati, where General Burnside imposed martial law on July 12. Governor Tod reactivated the Squirrel Hunters in thirty-seven counties, and the town of Ripley had its new three-inch, rifled cannon armed and ready for defense. Eliza's brother Newt had contributed five dollars to the $785 that sixty-eight residents paid for it the previous year, including ammunition. The town had also installed a large bell to warn residents of imminent invasion.[2]

As Morgan swept through the Ohio countryside, people hid everything from livestock to silverware, and militia units cut trees to block the roads. But corralling Morgan was no easy task. After making a few fake passes at Cincinnati, the dashing Kentucky highwayman outmaneuvered Federal forces and divided his men, sending some to Ripley to see if they could cross the river there. But the river was high and ferries were closely guarded, so they rejoined their compatriots in neighboring Adams County before heading east across the southern part of the state. Along the way, they tore up railroad tracks and took whatever they could find, from store merchandise to household goods and prized horses. Federals finally apprehended several hundred of Morgan's troops near Pomeroy in late July, but many escaped across the Ohio to West Virginia. Not until July 26, in Columbiana County in northeastern Ohio, were the legendary guerrilla leader and his remaining cohorts finally captured.[3]

* * * * *

Tomlinson to Eliza
Cincinnati, Ohio, May 31, 1863

Dearest Eliza,

My general health is improving. I worked four days last week. Byers' letter came duly to hand, but daughter has not yet favored me with one of her pretty notes. I have been out in the country all day, at Mr. J. D. Fosters. He is the old press maker and foundry agent from whom I purchased the Iowa Statesman office. His family is a very interesting one, Mrs. F. being one of the most amiable of women. Her married daughter,

The Ripley cannon, now preserved in front of Union Township Library, was purchased in 1862 by townspeople for protection from Confederate raiders. (Courtesy of Ron Ralston, Photographer, for the Union Township Library, Ripley, Ohio)

whom I knew as a child eight years ago, is an excellent performer, and she gave me some piano music. Her son George is about the age, though not so large, as Byers. He amused me a good deal in describing the battle feats of a valiant rooster of which he is the proud owner. This bird has killed seven antagonists and looks able for as many more.

I walked over the old battleground (3 miles back of the city) where we had such a bloody time with the Indians in Wayne's time. It is said that many trophies are still being found, such as hatchets, tomahawks, etc.

The first news we had of the arrest of Mr. Norris was in your letter. It is no use, or I would try to call on the man, not the traitor past. By the way, I understand that a petition for his release was gotten up and numerously signed, Chambers Baird and Hemphill being of the list. Men doing so are no better in that act than the accused. It is no small neighborhood offense, no mere orchard-robbing or fist-fight—this giving "aid and comfort" to the armed traitor or unarmed serpent. Our boys who are going to the eternal road for the cause at Vicksburg, crowding the graves by thousands daily—at least they are much mistaken if treason be so light a crime or loyalty so cheap a virtue.

Our affairs military seem prospering. Rosecrans is moving some way, but not backward. Grant is safe from all odds at Vicksburg. Hooker, a skillful and brave General, is smothered by that worst of our curses, Halleck.

As to that paper—I have been watching for it ever since. Jackson (our nigger) has searched till he was tired out. Last evening I spoke to one of the editors to watch for it.

I will probably visit you about the first week in July. Enclosed $10.00.
Ever yours,
Will. Tomlinson

Tomlinson to Eliza
Cincinnati, Ohio, June 17, 1863

Dearest Eliza,

As I will probably have an opportunity of sending this to you by J. Flora, who has promised to call for it, I have got up very early, having slept only about two hours. My general health is good, though since I wrote you I have been kept from work a great part of the time by rheumatism or pain in my right shoulder. It is now better. Crawford's all well. Yesterday saw John Evans. He is very much worn down. I am very sorry that I cannot send you any money, but so it is. Last week I had to buy some clothing to amt of $5.00, which exhausted me.

So what I warned your people of has thus soon become history. Raids of armed rebels are hovering around and doing their devilment when there is no immediate danger to their miserable carcasses. I would like to have been in the neighborhood when the cut-throats were in Maysville. I should have done my best to persuade a few shot and shell to seek their crowded company at the Lee House. As to what happens in Maysville, at best one thing is sure—Loyalty would not suffer if it were in ashes.

In the East things look squally. Our army seems to be strangely paralyzed. What was undertaken by Lee as a forlorn hope and dying struggle is terminating ruinously to us. Something's—wrong. No volunteering here. I want Byers, if again called out, if he can't raise a company of his own, not to go in the ranks of any company, but do as I used to—go as an independent scout, thus remaining master of his own movements. Write again. I will write fully Sunday. Belle—I can't come up as you want me. Will tell you when Sunday.

Flora didn't come, so I mail this. News a little better. I send you some papers.

Byers might not be master of his own volition yet, but, at sixteen years of age, he was on top of the latest news and ready to fight. He had also become a perceptive observer of human nature and an adept story-teller. As was often the case, Eliza filled the space that her son left in the following three letters to his father.

* * * * *

Byers (Son) to Tomlinson
Ripley, Ohio, June 21, 1863

Dear Pap,

I promised to let you know all I could about that Maysville raid, but I see that the papers tell about as much as I can. Instead of there being seven or eight hundred of them as we heard, there were only 250. They were led round to Union houses by people in Maysville. They came to the telegraph office and destroyed the machines, then left it, whereupon the telegraph operator went home and got another one and carried on a conversation with Burnside while the rebels were in the town. The tenth Kentucky cavalry gave these rebels a sound thrashing for their impudence and recaptured nearly all of their plunder. I have been looking to be called out every day since this last raid. It is reported that Morgan is this side of Lexington in great force. I think I can have my company ready for the fun by the time he comes. Our school is over now and we have a long vacation.

I was very glad to receive those bundles of papers and magazines which you sent up. It is quite a treat to me to read them. General Write or Wright, has caused a lot of certificates from Gov. Tod to be distributed among the squirrel hunters of the borders. I have got one together with a printed letter from David Tod, Governor. All this has been done for a reward to us for being so gallant and valiant last fall.

Goodbye,

W. B. Tomlinson

Eliza to Will

Ripley, Ohio, June 22, 1863

Dear Husband,

I have little to tell you, there is no news of importance that is reliable. Rumor says that Morgan is between this and Lexington with 15,000 of his cutthroats. We hear so many rumors that we do not know what to believe. It does look probable that starving thieves would now about harvest time make an effort to supply themselves from the abundant granary of the loyal states. I hope that Burnside will be equal to any emergency. I think that we ought to have soldiers stationed in camp at different points, say here, Cincinnati, etc., along the border, so as to be at all times ready for traitors and treachery. I anticipate one raid after another this summer and fall. It appears that the Lee House was not destroyed, but was compelled by our boys to hoist the stars and stripes.

This is the last week of school; examinations commenced on last Thursday, and end on next Friday. Belle's examination comes off on next Thursday. Byers has been so unwell that he has not attended school for the last week or two, so did not attend the examination. Belle has been quite unwell for a few days past but intends going to school this afternoon. Hope to see you about the fourth, as you promised.

Ever yours, etc.,

Eliza W. Tomlinson

Byers (Son) to Tomlinson

Ripley, Ohio, June 28, 1863

Dear Pap,

I would have written to you sooner but I had nothing to write about. There has not been any raid as I expected and there is little of interest going on here now days. Ripley seems to me like a very dull place. The people and especially the boys are hard to get to engage in anything new and useful; for instance, I have tried for several weeks to raise my company and have only got about 20 boys, and when I appointed a meeting to drill, only three or four came to it. Tomorrow the company is to meet to elect officers and to get some guns to celebrate the 4th. If no more come to this meeting than to the other, I will have to give up in despair. I intend to swear them all in the first time I get them together, if I ever can do that.

The richest men and those that own most property here are the last in most cases to turn out and defend it in case of a raid. In the last one I do not know of a rich man that fell in ranks at all; such men as Burner Car, A. Belchambers, and others slept on feather beds while we, the poor men and boys, defended them from destruction. The time of that great fire here, A. Belchambers never left his shop one minute to help put it out, while other men quit work and did all they could. But he has a shop there that may burn some day, and I hope if it does that not a man will help him quell the flames. He is the greatest miser in Ripley. I have no personal hatred to him, but I hate his conduct, and that of many other men of this place and hope they will get the reward they deserve.

It seems that the rebels are playing smash generally in Pennsylvania and Maryland, and I suppose would be in Ohio if it was not for the river, which is great protection to us, for they know that it will not be easy to cross it. But if they ever do get in this state, I think they will get peppered worse than the British did on their retreat from Lexington. The squirrel hunters will learn them a lesson that they won't forget soon.

Goodbye,

W. B. Tomlinson.

P.S. Little did I think while writing the above that a terrible scene was being enacted within a hundred yards of me, that in the same house where yesterday a joyful wedding took place, there was now wailing of a bereaved daughter mingled with the curses of a drunken man. But I must explain this to you. This scene took place in the house of old Mrs. Berry, which is next door to Mrs. Beuhel's, who was married. Mrs. Berry has a daughter married to a nephew of hers named Henry Sowers. This nephew has been drunk all day, perhaps from the effects of going to a jol-lification given by Mrs. Beuhel over her wedding last night. He had been quarreling with his wife all day. This evening they were near coming to blows—his (Sowers) wife is just passing our window now with heart-rending shrieks for her mother. Old Mrs. Berry, seeing her daughter as she thought about to be killed, was so badly frightened that she fainted or fell dead and cannot be revived. She is dead beyond any doubt. This calamity has shed a pall of gloom over the whole community. All this is caused by that powerful but cunning foe of mankind—Whiskey—it en-tices, but to ruin. When will it be conquered? The sooner the better for this world and the people in it. Thousands of horrible crimes have their origin in the still, and tens of thousands of torrents will the distiller suffer, before the devil gets his due. Even this horrible war has hardly lain as many victims in the grave in the same time as this subtle poison—whiskey—has. For my part I think it one of the worst curses to man that God has ever permitted to exist.

Goodbye again,

W. B. T.

<u>Monday morning</u>, June 29

Tis reported that there was fighting at Mount Sterling yesterday and there was a rumor that six thousand rebels are marching on Maysville. As to there being six thousand I do not believe it. Perhaps there is 600 or 60. One rebel could take Maysville as easy as 6000 could.

Eliza to Tomlinson

Ripley, Ohio, June 29, 1863

Dear Husband,

I have little to add in addition to what Byers has written other than we are in somewhat better health than what we were when I last wrote you. I think that the Governor ought to have detached bodies of soldiers stationed along the border at points most likely to be attacked. The truth is there is no knowing when, or where, the enemy may appear. There is nothing going on here on the Fourth that I hear of, but I think it probable that the good and loyal citizens will not suffer the day to pass off without some patriotic demonstration.

Well the 1st of August is again not far off; that insurance hangs over our heads. I know not what the amount will be for this year. I presume that after keeping it up for so many years, you do not intend to drop it now.

Please give my best respects to Mrs. Crawford and family. I have not seen John Evans since his return, but am told that he looks as if he had seen very hard times down in Dixie. I suppose that John's wife came up with him. I have not been able to take so long a walk or I would have gone out to see them.

Ever yours, etc.!

Eliza W. Tomlinson

Byers (Son) to Tomlinson
Ripley, Ohio, July 28, 1863

Dear Pap,

We are all very anxious to know where you are and how you are getting along. We do not know whether you have volunteered for the war or just for this emergency. We are glad to hear of Morgan's capture with the remnant of his forces. There is a man up here recruiting for the second regiment heavy artillery. He have a good many volunteered under him.

The citizens are not sticking up to their promises to uniform us (state militia) as they might, and it is very probable that if they don't, the company will disband and scarcely one in it will ever take a gun in his hand to defend the property of those who have lied to them and deceived them as the property holders of Ripley have.

If you are in Cincinnati, write to us soon and let us know all about your trip.

W. B. Tomlinson

Eliza to Tomlinson
Ripley, Ohio, July 28, 1863

Dear Husband,

It is now four weeks since we received a line from you. Why is this? We are and have been very uneasy about you! Do write or come up. It is now near about the time you promised to be here at any rate. I know of nothing of interest further than what you learn before we do from the papers. The war clouds appear to be breaking. Light shoots at last the horizon. There now appears to be a goodly prospect of this unholy rebellion being crushed out. God grant how soon!

I ever remain yours, etc.,

Eliza W. Tomlinson

* * * * *

Tomlinson must have already written the following letter before Eliza and Byers wrote of their concerns on July 28.

* * * * *

Tomlinson to Eliza
Cincinnati, Ohio, July 27, 1863

Dearest Eliza,

Yours and Byers' letters were indeed truly welcome. I would have answered last week but have been quite indisposed. This morning I feel better and have again gone to work. I expect to be up at Ripley next Friday or Saturday. Morgan is at last really taken and I suppose is in the city now.

As to that insurance, I will see about it when at Ripley.

Last week I sent bundle of papers, etc. Did you get them? Herewith I also send a parcel. Hope you will get them and that they will please you.

Byers writes excellent letters. He improves very fast, and I trust he will continue the practice. Must hurry to boat. In haste,

Yours ever,

Will Tomlinson

* * * * *

Tomlinson did not explain why he had been too indisposed to write earlier. No doubt Eliza would solicit an explanation when he came to Ripley, a place he seldom referred to as "home." But for the safety of his family, he must have been relieved to see Morgan finally brought under control. He may also have identified somewhat with the debonair outlaw. Both had served in the Mexican War and been a militia officer. Both preferred leading an independent company over enlistment in the regular military. And both enjoyed the excitement of guerrilla warfare. But the most striking similarity between the two may be that each of them could have been cast as a hero or a villain. By the summer of 1863 Morgan and his band of Lexington Rifles had already achieved legendary fame thanks to their own camp newspaper, the *Vidette,* and Sally Rochester Ford's popular novel, *Raids and Romance of Morgan and His Men.* Publications like these portrayed the raiders' exploits as the heroic feats of chivalrous leaders like Ivanhoe, the Knights of the Round Table, and Robin Hood. While Tomlinson never attained Morgan's visibility and status, he was a man of some renown and modest success in his own right. As a newspaper editor and publisher, he was known for his readiness to fight for causes he believed in, including the rights of the common man and the welfare of his adopted country. As captain of an independent company of Mountain Marksmen, he also made case after case for outfitting his men with better provisions and seeing that they were adequately compensated for their service.[4]

But Morgan and Tomlinson could also be characterized as villainous. Morgan was regarded by many as a vengeful thief intent on destroying anything associated with the Union cause, whether it was a bridge, railroad line, or someone's home. Tomlinson was remembered by former colleagues in Iowa for drunken, bellicose behavior and by his commanding officer in western Virginia for participation in the Jacksonville murders. He may also have left a trail of financial debt. Whatever his culpability was in any of those situations, he must have been aware of how challenging it could be to lead an honorable life. In his first newspaper, *Freedom's Casket*, he published the following aphorism: "The two most precious things this side of the grave are reputation and life, but it is to be lamented that the most contemptible whisper may deprive us of the one, and the weakest weapon deprive us of the other." Since Tomlinson's publication of that aphorism, numerous aspersions had been made on his character in the twenty years that had passed. But none would strike as close to the heart as the accusations he tried to address in the following letter fragment.[5]

The first eight pages of the following letter fragment are missing. The four extant pages are numbered and appear to be the last part of a thirteen-page letter. The four pages have no date, salutation, or signature. But in penmanship, style, and content, they give every indication of being written by Tomlinson to Eliza. They also appear to have been written in the late summer of 1863. With the exception of this fragment, there are no letters between Tomlinson and Eliza from July 27 until November 17 of that year, a period of almost four months. It is possible that Tomlinson, who was publishing a campaign newspaper in Ripley that fall, was there so often that he and Eliza did not feel the need to correspond. But Tomlinson did write to their son during that time, so it may be that he and Eliza were once again estranged. In the fragment below, Tomlinson was obviously writing to defend himself from accusations Eliza had made in a previous letter, which is missing from this collection. His embittered comment about Sarah Ann in the last paragraph probably referred to the wife of Eliza's brother, Dr. Thomas Byers Wylie. The letter fragment begins where Tomlinson was evidently addressing Eliza's most egregious allegations.[6]

* * * * *

After rampaging through southern Ohio in July of 1863, Confederate John Hunt Morgan was captured by the Union but escaped from the state penitentiary on November 27, 1863, the same day Will Tomlinson was shot by a Kentucky Copperhead. (Library of Congress Prints and Photographs Division)

Tomlinson to Eliza
Cincinnati, Late Summer, 1863

. . . the last, which comes from your brother. I will answer them separately. I utterly deny that I spend either time or money with strumpets or any other kind of woman, except money for boarding and washing. The only foundation I know of for any direct charge of the kind is, that a married man from <u>Ripley</u> called on me at the office one morning a year ago last fall, and asked me, first, to drink with him, and then take the street cars and accompany him to see some friend whom he had business with before the boat left. In ordinary friendship, and in utter ignorance and innocence of my destination, I found myself in a large, finely furnished house, where my companion seemed well acquainted, and two gaily-dressed women came into the parlor, with one of whom he retired, asking me to wait for him a few minutes. The other girl sat beside me a few minutes, at an open window overlooking the street and retired. After waiting for twenty minutes to half-an-hour, I gave expression to great impatience, and my companion returned, and I went with him to the boat, and that night he slept with his wife in Ripley. He is rich and respectable. Perhaps in his drunken moods, or boastings at Ripley, or on the boat, or here, he has thought it such a good joke on me as to speak of and magnify, till, lo, the mist which darkens and chills that warm heart and clear conscience of yours! So much—no more—for that rumor. This case covers the whole. About that room. I rented it for comfort and peace, of Mrs. Olcroft, against whom or her daughters I do not believe a slanderous imputation was ever before uttered. You have seen the lady and her family in her own house, and can judge. My room was next to that of Mr. Jones (our assistant foreman) and his family. There was a door in the partition between the two—and to reach my room I had to pass the doors in the halls of <u>four</u> families—including that of Mrs. Olcroft. Would you not consider that a rather dangerous gauntlet to run into or escape from, by a strumpet or any other evil person, especially when a full gaslight was burning in the hall every night until Mr. Jones and myself returned from work? And further, too, when Mr. Jones invariably first came through my room to have a smoke before retiring? I am thus particular, to satisfy you of what baseless fabrics so much misery is manufactured. "You gallanted a strumpet," &. Well might you exclaim—"Great God!" have you come so low?" My answer is very brief. I have never <u>gallanted</u> or accompanied a woman, or lady, or strumpet or otherwise, acquaintance or stranger, through Cincinnati, or in any part of Cincinnati, by day or night, excepting yourself, and a married lady of your acquaintance, but whose name I have forgotten. I told you about it at the time. She was the wife of a soldier, was hunting her husband, and is a daughter of John Walkington. Now, whether it be your brother, or a thousand brothers, or anybody else, who asserts such a thing, I say it is utterly, wholly, absolutely and entirely false, in every iota—in particular and in general! There it is, in black and white, and I stand ready to attest its truth to my dying breath!

Third—"Gambling and Debauchery."—As to gambling, it is a thing which I never did. I never played in a game of chance whatever for money. I do indulge in a game of euchre for beer, or billiards for recreation, frequently—but to gamble I never did, for great or small, and it is a vice for which I have no taste or toleration. "Debauchery." That I take it means drinking. I do drink. I drink a great deal. Lately in my gloom I have drank to such excess that I have been inebriated—intoxicated. Never so much so but I could walk erect and talk straight. I am in hopes this exposé may burst that cloud of gloom. Even now I feel greatly relieved. But you ask—What do I do with my money? Well—A few dollars go but a short way in treating such hangers-on as a liberal drinking man will everywhere fall in with. I know it was robbing you—but the devil has been in me. When you have refused to see me, or let my children do so, I have traced it back to some evil influence, and fought that influence with reckless riot in hopeless despair. As you quote—"Murder will out"—so is this mocking skeleton of our house. What next?

O, what a triumph it must be to that worse than whore, Sarah Ann, to gloat over the bleeding wounds sent by her words to your confiding heart. I am wicked, but she is baser though I were guilty as charged.

* * * * *

In language dripping with drama, Tomlinson and Eliza have inflicted deep wounds in each other. All the history they have built together—their trials and triumphs, their love and trust—come down to nothing more than a "mocking skeleton" of a house.

CHAPTER NINETEEN

~

Partisan Fever

To provide for yourself abundant matter for shame and repentance—act
under the influence of passion.
—*Freedom's Casket,* June 15, 1844

AS AUTUMN APPROACHED, the Union defeat at the Battle of Chickamauga
muted rounds of applause in the North for earlier victories at Vicksburg
and Gettysburg. Meanwhile, statewide elections in Ohio and other states
were gearing up, and Tomlinson was publishing the *Loyal Scout* in Ripley. The four-page tabloid promoted the Union ticket, with John Brough
for governor, and ran for seven issues, with the last issue dated October
10, 1863. Most of the articles in that issue focused on Union candidates
and their opponents. One opponent, the Copperhead Democrat Clement Vallandigham, was running for governor from Canada, where he had
eventually landed after leaving the Confederacy. His supporters in Ohio
thronged to rallies and sang out vehement denunciations of Lincoln:

> We are coming, Abraham Lincoln . . .
> With curses loud and deep,
> That will haunt you in your waking
> And disturb you in your sleep.[1]

Republicans and Unionists countered with their own chant: "Hurrah
for Brough and Abraham / And a rope to hang Vallandigham." Republican newspapers accused Vallandigham of being linked to antidraft riots

The last newspaper published by Will Tomlinson, the *Loyal Scout*, October 10, 1863, was found in 1970 in the attic of the home of the author's grandparents. (Wylie-Tomlinson Letter Collection)

in New York, Morgan's invasion of Ohio, and Lee's march into Pennsylvania. He was also thought to be working with the Knights of the Golden Circle to thwart Union success. His followers were often referred to as butternuts; they tended to be rural, relatively uneducated, resistant to the draft, and resentful of African American competition for jobs. They called Brough a "nigger lover" and a "fat Knight of the corps d'Afrique." In the final outcome, however, such epithets worked against them when Republicans used their opponents' racist propaganda to mount an offensive campaign. In linking emancipation to Union victory, Republicans managed to construe a vote for Copperhead Democrats as a vote against the Union.[2]

In Ripley, Tomlinson used the October 10 issue of the *Loyal Scout* to laud candidates on the Union ticket as good, true, and loyal men. He vilified their opponents as lying, cowardly, and traitorous vermin. The Union candidate running for clerk of court, for instance, was "honest, capable and loyal," while his opponent was "the dirty rebel, the coward dog, the drunken bully, the lazy thief; who would fight his grandmother for her gruel." Tomlinson's vituperation of anti-Union candidates was sometimes more than verbal. In a diatribe against one local politician, he issued the following challenge: "Chilton A. White can put this in his pipe and smoke it;—He, White, is a dirty liar, a contemptible coward, a traitor . . . whose greatness is like that of a pig following a cow—picking up what others drop. If this pot house loafer and liar and dog will meet me, Will Tomlinson, face to face, I will teach the whelp the merits of a good thrashing; and the world the value of a Congressman's carcass well skined [sic]." In another article, "Last Sunday in Ripley," Tomlinson described a flesh-and-blood encounter he had with "traitors" who broadcast "infamous and cowardly lies" about him. After giving one of the traitors "a profound settler on the mug," Tomlinson drew his pistol and drove the others back. Although the incident ended with the "original difficulty" being resolved between him and the other men, the editor of the *Loyal Scout* was clearly on the warpath. Any "humbugs and cowards" voting for Vallandigham, he wrote, deserved to be "kicked from one end of the corporation to the other."[3]

In "Patriot Then—Traitor Now," in the same issue, Tomlinson wrote that Brown County traitors like Pat McGroarty had "brains besotted by the meanest of Georgetown-doctored whisky" and had "forsaken the glorious cause of country." Debating causes of the war rather than fighting in it was pointless, he argued. "Let us put down rebellion, and then settle political questions about it." It made no difference, he wrote, "whether Joshua Giddings or Jeff. Davis got up the rebellion." No one, he said, should refuse to fight the Rebels even if he thought Lincoln violated the Constitution. "Who made you the judge?" Tomlinson asked. Lincoln was duly elected under the Constitution, Tomlinson noted, and even though he, himself, had not voted for him—nor would not at that time—he was still for "putting down the rebellion." Old-line Democrats like him, Tomlinson said, gave the South more than they were entitled to. But the rebellion had been fermenting for thirty years. So then, he asked, "Are twenty millions of people to be whipped by six? We must have troops. We can't let this war go on. . . . Men must come out to stop it."[4]

Ohio voters could not stop the war, but they could bring Vallandigham's current political career to an end. On October 13, Ohioans went to the polls in record numbers and unequivocally trampled Vallandigham and the Copperheads underfoot. Democrats won in only eighteen of the state's eighty-eight counties; Brown County was one of the eighteen. But in the Union Township section of Brown County, where Ripley was located, Vallandigham received only 197 votes to Brough's 719. The *Ripley Bee* and

Congressman Clement L. Vallandigham of Ohio was one of the leading Copperhead agitators lambasted by Will Tomlinson in his last newspaper, *Loyal Scout*. (Library of Congress Prints and Photographs Division)

Tomlinson's *Loyal Scout* probably played a role in that outcome. With the election over and the *Loyal Scout* discontinued, Tomlinson returned to work in Cincinnati and asked his son Byers to help him with a few loose ends back in Ripley. One of those, perhaps, was the strained communications between him and Eliza—as the closing of his letter may suggest. Byers, meanwhile, had recently had his own encounter with the butternuts.[5]

* * * * *

Tomlinson to (Son) Byers
Cincinnati, Ohio, October 22, 1863

My Dear Son,

I arrived here all safe yesterday morning, but had a hard trip of it. There was no sleeping place only on the bare floor, and the cabin was covered.

I am stopping at Crawford's. John is well, as are the rest of the family, except Lititia, who I understand is suffering dreadfully from the tooth-ache, without the courage to have the offending ivory extracted. She has lately had four pulled.

How did you get along in your Levanna trip? And I suppose today you are in Georgetown.

There is no news here. I will go to work again in the Gazette office as a sub. My business affairs I have explained to you as fully as I could, excepting a bill against Mr. J. J. Caldwell for advertising—$5.00.

Make the most of things, and if you want to sell all or any part, you have my sanction, the proceeds to go for the support of the family. The things are worth at least $100.00 in cash on a general sale. They cost me considerably over that.

That list of rebel voters in Union Township I will try and get printed next week. I suppose about 300 will be enough.

Remember me kindly to your mother and sister. Write soon.

Your affectionate father,

Will Tomlinson

Dear Pap,

I received your letter to me, last Saturday about dark.

I did what I could in Levanna. I went to Mr. Hines' house, and he said he had paid you, and on inquiring the whereabouts of the other men on the list, they were all in the country or at work in wine cellars miles away. I thought it was not of any use to hunt for them then, and Mr. Hines told me that he would collect it for me and bring it up. With this assurance, I gave him a copy of the list for Levanna and went home. But it is now over a week and he has not brought us the money yet, and I have concluded to go to Levanna today and see him about it.

I did not get to Georgetown last Friday, but went on Monday. When I got there, I found that Murray was on a spree and was so drunk that he could hardly walk, so I had to shift for myself. I went down to Lewis's new hotel and could not find any one and went back toward the square, and on inquiring, someone told me that Lewis did not take boarders because his house was not finished yet. When I was told this, I took my lodgings at Jenkins' house. I afterward found that he was a butternut and that Lewis *did* keep boarders, but it was too late then. I went round inquiring where this and that man lived 'till I had found nearly all on the list that lived in town and came to town, but some refused to pay because they had not given Murray any authority to put down their names in his list, and some "didn't have any change and would see me again." I collected about 12 dollars before I came home.

On Tuesday the Brough men had a great jollification over the election. They had a free supper in the fairgrounds and the finest fireworks in town that I ever saw. Wiley Young, Phil. Jolley, and others spoke to the people. Phil stood in the Court House yard in a voice that might be heard half a mile, gave particular thunder to the Court House rats, Chilton A. White, John G. Marshall, and E. Columbus. He said that he "had lived to help place those men in the Court House, and hoped to live to help kick them out." And turning his face toward old Dave Devore's house, he shamed him for his crying spells, etc. He said that Old Dave could not shed a tear over the thousands that have been slain in defense of our country, but could weep and lament because Vallandigham was sent to Canada. He went on in this way, giving the butternuts broadside after broadside. And the best of it was that he spoke so loud that all butternuts must hear him or leave the place.

A couple of butternuts got after Jim Mires, and he overheard them talking of him and rushed in front of them, saying, as near as I can recollect, "Here I am. You d—d traitors," and as they had great heavy rocks in their hands, he drew his revolver. At this I pulled my coat and stood by his side, alternately daring the rebels to throw and saying that I was a Ripleyite and thus all h—l shouldn't hurt Jim Mires, if I could help it. About this time I was pulled away, and Jim was caught and held, while some butternut grasped his revolver and all was commotion at length, although he was held by six or eight men. Jim succeeded in jerking his pistol from the hands of the rebel and cocked it. I had a single barreled self-cocker with me, and it was loaded with shot. I got it out and brought it to bear on the rebel's face, but there were several men between me and him, and I saw that I would hurt others, and tried to get closer, but it was a perfect jam, and I could scarcely move, seeing that I had no chance to get to him. I at last succeeded in getting out of the crowd and found "Alf" Loudon, who had taken my coat from my hands. He pointed me to the courtyard fence, and there I found it.

Jim Mires came out unhurt and so did I. But the rebel got a pretty black face.

I came home Wednesday morning, on foot.

Your son,

Byers

* * * * *

The Jim Mires whom Byers defended is probably the same James Myers that Tomlinson praised in the October 10 issue of the *Loyal Scout*. According to Tomlinson, Myers was a farmer who had been attacked by armed cowards, even though he had no pretensions to office. He had nevertheless taken up the cause of his country with "the whole of his big heart." His continuing work for the cause, Tomlinson maintained, constituted "as holy and pure a record as can be found on history's page." Counted among Myers's good deeds were many trips to Camp Dennison and western Virginia, where he provided much-needed goods for "the privates rather than officers." Myers knew nothing of the article being written about him, the *Loyal Scout* editor noted, adding that he could say nothing less than, "God bless Jim Myers." Tomlinson's magnanimity also seemed to permeate his mood after he returned to Cincinnati and wrote to Eliza, even though he had been ailing for some time.[6]

Well—I've taken a good
long rest, and will finish.
I am very sorry to hear of
Bro. Byers' serious illness.
I have noticed him failing
fast all summer. I fear
it is his last illness. Give
him my kindest wishes
and hopes.

Have you any money to
meet current wants for a
couple of weeks? If not
let me know and I will
borrow a few dollars, and
send you.

I will try do so, and you
try to help me keep up courage
for a few weeks, till things get
to working smoothly, and I trust
there is a brighter future for
us all after the immediate past.
Yours &c, Will Tomlinson

Cincinnati, Nov. 17, 1863.
Dearest Eliza:
A few minutes since
I received your so welcome
letter of yesterday. It has so
revived me that for the first
time since Saturday noon I
undertake to sit up to write
you an answer. It will be
rather slow work, but a
pleasant duty. I wrote you
on Sunday and yesterday,
so that you might know
from day to day how the
fight progressed between
the Doctor and the disease.

About an hour since the
gallant little Doc. dropped
in to see me, and hailed
"Hillo, old Soldier, what have
you done with that fever?"

He said it was all right
now, to keep on with the
medicines, and if to morrow
be a fair day, and I felt
able to walk, I might go
up as far as his office.
I don't think I'll get there
so soon.

That letter I sent on Saturday, expecting it to reach
you same evening.

As to taking care of myself,
I claim to have been exercising more than ordinary
prudence. (But I must not a little.)
The night I was taken I went
to bed, feeling all right, but in
the morning couldn't move.
A full suit of boarding house
bed clothes don't weigh much
just now, and when you get
tucked in on one side, out
comes the other. There's more warmth
in one of our blankets at home than half a dozen of the—

The Bee has come to me the
last two weeks all right. It
is very interesting. If I had
means I would buy out Old
Charley, as he wants to sell.
I will remember that hint
about Mrs. Cook. I have not
seen her lately. Dick was in
to see me yesterday.

Has there any arrival
yet at Ripley? As it is beginning to reach here. From
appearances there must certainly soon be a rise in
the river.

O, I have been so much
disappointed by this sickness.
I had just got a fat job,
and would have made about
$45 or $50 in the two weeks.
But my conscience is clear.
I've done all that I could
to hurry out of confinement

This was the last letter Will Tomlinson wrote to his wife, Eliza. William Byers
Tomlinson made the notation at the top of the first page: "Mother, just ten days
before father was killed." (Wylie-Tomlinson Letter Collection)

* * * * *

Tomlinson to Eliza
Cincinnati, Ohio, November 17, 1863

Dearest Eliza,

A few minutes since I received your <u>so</u> welcome letter of yesterday. It has so revived me that for the first time since Saturday noon I undertake to sit up to write you an answer. It will be rather slow work, but a pleasant duty. I wrote you on Sunday and yesterday, so that you might know from day to day how the fight progressed between the doctor and the disease.

About an hour since the gallant little doc. dropped in to see me, and hailed, "Halloo, old soldier, what have you done with that fever?" He said it was all right now, to keep on with the medicines, and if tomorrow be a fair day, and I felt able to walk, I might go up as far as his office. I don't think I'll get there so soon.

That letter I sent on Saturday, expecting it to reach you same evening.

As to taking care of myself, I claim to have been exercising more than ordinary prudence. (But I must rest a little.) The night I was taken I went to bed, feeling all right, but in the morning couldn't move. A full suit of boarding-house bedclothes don't weight much just now, and when you get tucked in on one side, out comes the other. There's more warmth in one of our blankets at home than half-a-dozen of the "spreads."

The Bee has come to me the last two weeks all right. It is very interesting. If I had means I would buy out Old Charley, as he wants to sell. I will remember that hint about Mrs. Cook. I have not seen her lately. Dick was in to see me yesterday.

Has there any coal arrived yet at Ripley? It is beginning to reach here. From appearances, there must certainly soon be a rise in the river.

O, I have been so much disappointed by this sickness. I had just got a fat job, and would have made about $45 or $50 in two weeks. But my conscience is clear. I've done all that I could to hurry out of confinement.

Well, I've taken a good long rest and will finish. I am very sorry to hear of Bro. Byers' serious illness. I have noticed him failing fast all summer. I fear it is his last illness. Give him my kindest wishes and hopes.

Have you any money to meet current wants for a couple of weeks? If not let me know and I will borrow a few dollars and send you.

I will try to do so, and you try to help me keep up courage for a few weeks, 'till things get to working smoothly, and I trust there is a brighter future for us all than the immediate past.

Yours affectionately,

Will Tomlinson

* * * * *

So ended the last letter he would ever write to Eliza.

CHAPTER TWENTY

~

Freedom's Casket

Our farewell must be brief. Readers will remember that we have never
misled them in our personal charges. What we have said and done has been
with the design of sustaining loyalty and crushing traitors.
So endeth "LOYAL SCOUT."
—*Loyal Scout,* October 10, 1863

THE ELECTIONS FOR OHIO'S GOVERNOR and state legislators were over,
and once again Tomlinson had no newspaper to publish or the means to
start one. He must have been at loose ends, wondering if he would ever
have another opportunity to influence the political landscape, especially
during a critical juncture in the nation's history. The trail ahead for him
probably looked less exciting than the one behind, and, as a man of passion and action, he would have needed a focus for his energy. On the
evening of Friday, November 27, he evidently found one. Six days later
the *Ripley Bee* published the following article:

> FATAL AFFRAY.—Last Friday night, WILL. TOMLINSON was shot in
> the side by Richard Mitchell of Kentucky. The wound was fatal. Mr.
> Tomlinson died Sunday night. We have heard various and conflicting
> accounts of this lamentable affair, and are unable to give a reliable
> account of it. In the rencontre, Mitchell was stabbed several times
> SEVERELY, but not dangerously, by a son of Mr. Tomlinson, about
> 16 years of age. For obituary notice of the deceased, the reader is
> referred to the appropriate column.[1]

* * * * *

The *Ripley Bee's* obituary notice included a typographical error for the date of Tomlinson's fatal injury; it was not December 28, as reported, but November 27. Tomlinson died two days later, on Sunday, November 29. The following obituary was published on December 3, 1863.

> WILL TOMLINSON, whose remains were on Tuesday last interred in the Ripley Cemetery by a great concourse of his friends, died from the effects of a pistol shot received on the night of the 28th of December 1863.
>
> Since 1844 he has been connected with the Newspaper business, and is well known as an able editor, having conducted several prominent journals in Ohio, and at one time the "Iowa State Journal." He has filled several civil offices, once one of the Clerks of the Iowa House of Representatives and Justice of the Peace at the City of Desmoines.
>
> At the breaking out of the rebellion, then at Cincinnati, he was among the first to go at his country's call and joined a company principally composed of printers, and was elected Lieutenant, which company camped at the first camp made in Ohio, CAMP HARRISON. After serving in that capacity and fighting the rebels in West Virginia, he raised a company there and was elected Captain. He was compelled to resign on account of a disease of the lungs contracted in the Virginia Mountains.
>
> His last editorial efforts were made in the publication of the "Loyal Scout" at this place which publication done much to change the political opinions of the voters of Brown county, a well known Democratic county. He himself, from the time he became a naturalized citizen (being of English birth) identified himself with the old Democratic party. But his adopted country being assailed, he at once knew on which side to stake his all and that was, "for his country first, last and all the time."[2]

Other newspapers that Tomlinson had been associated with also reported his death and the circumstances precipitating it. On Monday, November 30, the *Cincinnati Gazette* noted the following in "Melancholy Affray at Ripley, Ohio":

William Byers Tomlinson jotted notes on several of his parents' letters and accompanying envelopes. He also probably wrote the "Grandpa Tomlinson" on the above photo in reference to his father, Will Tomlinson. The photo would probably have been taken around 1863 when his father was about forty. (Wylie-Tomlinson Letter Collection)

We learn by private advices from Ripley, Ohio, that a difficulty occurred that place on Friday evening last, between Mr. Will Tomlinson, of Ripley, and a Mr. Mitchell of Charleston Bottom, Ky, in the course of which Mr. Mitchell drew a pistol and fired at Tomlinson, the ball taking effect in the left breast below the heart, and producing a wound which it thought would prove fatal. At this juncture, a son of Tomlinson, who was present, attacked Mitchell with a small pocket knife, and inflicted a number of very severe wounds in different parts of his body. Mitchell's condition is considered very critical. This sad occurrence will be a source of sorrow to the many friends of Mr. Tomlinson in this city and elsewhere, and also to his numerous editorial friends throughout the State, many of whom will remember him as the able editor some years since, of the Georgetown *Democratic Standard,* the Kenton *Nor'wester,* &c.

On Thursday, December 3, the *Gazette* reported Tomlinson's death and that his remains were interred with military honors on Tuesday.[3]

On December 12, the following note about his death appeared in the *Dubuque Herald:*

Everybody remembers Will Tomlinson, formerly of this State. He used to be a rip roaring democrat—but he went east, was offered a position in the army—accepted—became an abolitionist—got into a row with a Kentuckian—and was stabbed to death.

Tomlinson was not stabbed, of course, but shot, in the chest. Actually, it was his assailant who was stabbed—thirteen times, according to an account in a Maysville, Kentucky, newspaper. The same account stated that he and Mitchell were discussing current events "when high words ensued." According to a handwritten family history of the Mitchells, the Kentuckian had already started for home and was heading toward the river when Tomlinson and his son threw rocks at Mitchell, hitting him in the back of the head and knocking him down. When he stood up, rocks thrown by Tomlinson and his son struck him again, this time on the forehead. According to Mitchell, blood oozing from a gash on his forehead blinded him. Yet that did not prevent him from drawing his pistol and firing a shot. Nor did it prevent him from seeing that Tomlinson had not fallen. Mitchell then proceeded to knock him down and jump on him, only to be jumped on himself by Byers, who attacked him with a penknife.[4]

According to the *Dubuque* (Iowa) *Daily Times*, Tomlinson was shot through the body and lingered for a day or two in great agony. The *Daily Times* gave a brief summary of his career in Iowa before concluding with the following statement: "From the commencement of the war he was an ardent War Democrat, and during the recent campaign in Ohio, he published an able campaign paper in Ripley. He was a writer of considerable ability." None of the newspaper accounts at the time of his death, however, linked it with an occurrence that happened the same day Tomlinson was fatally wounded, November 27, 1863. That was also the day that Gen. John Hunt Morgan and six of his officers escaped from the Ohio State Penitentiary in Columbus.[5]

It is possible that Tomlinson knew of Morgan's escape before he encountered Mitchell and that his knowledge of the event triggered his attack upon the Kentucky Copperhead. After the intense backlash that arose late in 1863 against Copperheads like Clement L. Vallandigham, many Northern soldiers formerly opposed or lukewarm to Lincoln's Emancipation Proclamation became strong supporters of it. Like many Northern soldiers, especially those from the Border States, Tomlinson was irate at the Copperheads and itched to take them on—in print or in person—as the last issue of his

Union campaign paper, the *Loyal Scout,* clearly attests. Mitchell may have inadvertently been an unfortunate target for Tomlinson's vitriol. But it is also possible that Mitchell was involved in Copperhead intrigue and that he baited Tomlinson in retribution for attacking Copperheads in the *Loyal Scout.* With Morgan on the loose again, tension on both sides of the Ohio must have been running high, and Tomlinson, whose political vehemence had already erupted in violent outbursts, was probably more than ready to pounce on any Copperhead who crossed his path.[6]

One way or another Tomlinson's political views were apparently a primary cause of the affray. According to *History of the Republican Party in Ohio,* published in 1898, his publication of secret information in the *Loyal Scout* actually precipitated his death. He was not only "bitter against the Golden Circle and the 'copperheads,'" but had "by secret means gained a knowledge of the working of the Golden Circle." Moreover, the account maintains that he published that information in his paper, made many enemies in doing so, and, as a result, met his death at the hands of a "copperhead" whose enmity he incurred. Although the one extant issue of the *Loyal Scout,* dated Saturday, October 10, 1863, does not appear to include any exposé of the secret workings of the Golden Circle, earlier issues may have included innuendos, accusations, and details that some found threatening.[7]

How much of a threat secret Copperhead societies like the Knights of the Golden Circle, the Sons of Liberty, and the Order of the American Knights actually posed to the war effort and national security is debatable, but the fact is that many Northerners and some government officials, especially those in Border States, perceived them as dangerous and acted upon those assumptions. In Ohio in 1863 it was even rumored that tens of thousands of armed men stood ready to usher Vallandigham into Columbus, free Confederate soldiers from Ohio prisons, and join forces with Morgan near the border.[8]

If Tomlinson had infiltrated the Golden Circle and obtained secret information exposing Mitchell as treasonous, that in itself could have provoked a violent confrontation. It is possible that Mitchell even came gunning for Tomlinson. One family document notes that Tomlinson was "assassinated by Richard Mitchell, a Kentucky rebel, for political rancor." It is also possible that one or both men were acting under the influence of alcohol. Tomlinson's drunken behavior on the campaign trail in Iowa, his probable inebriation during the incident resulting in the Jacksonville murders, and his own confession to substantial consumption of alcohol would certainly lend credence to the occurrence of another situation in which his judgment was impaired by excessive drinking. In addition, from a twenty-first century perspective, some interesting speculations could be made on the role that Tomlinson's psychological state may have played in the situation. His susceptibility to alcoholism, for instance, may have exacerbated his difficulty with anger management and impulse control, and his recent history of failure and disappointment could have led him to project his own self-loathing onto someone else. Regardless of what triggered the unfortunate incident, however, the extent of Tomlinson's culpability in its outcome remains ambiguous. In the end, it is up to each reader to decide whether Tomlinson's role in the fatal affray was more closely aligned with that of a hero or a scoundrel.[9]

The account in the *History of the Republican Party* casts Tomlinson as "a fearless Union soldier" who "engaged in many a fight in Brown County during the war." Such a portrayal echoes two other brief encomiums. The last line of his obituary in the *Ripley Bee* states that he was "for his country first, last and all time," and the entry for him in "The Family History" states that he "was shot by Richard Mitchell (a Kentucky Copperhead) on November 27, 1863" and that "he sealed his devotion to his adopted country with his life's blood." The entry commends him to the hereafter with the epitaph, "Rest Patriot, thy warfare o'er." Nearly fifty years later, when Byers penned his own obituary prior to undergoing gall bladder surgery in 1914, he noted that his father had been "killed on account of his war service and earnest devotion to the Union cause."[10]

Hero or scoundrel—or, like most of us, a complex mixture of both— Tomlinson had finally come to the end of his battles. But Eliza's were far from ending. Despite the notices of her husband's death in Ohio, Kentucky, and Iowa, there were still people who needed to be informed, including Cousin Maggie Byers, who wrote to Eliza the day after Tomlinson died. Besides communicating line after line of news about various relatives, she wanted a photograph of Eliza and Tomlinson. Then there was the old Iowa colleague serving in Texas. It must have been a painful reminder for Eliza and the family when a letter addressed to their recently departed loved one arrived shortly after his death, especially a letter that sent warm sentiments from former cronies.[11]

* * * * *

J. Milt Walker to Tomlinson
Headquarters, Company B, 23rd Regiment, Iowa Volunteer Infantry
Fort Esperanza, Texas, December 24, 1863

My dear Will,

Open wide, in wonder and surprise, your eyes, and there with dear Will your heart, and after reading this write me immediately.

I have intended for a long time to write but not knowing where to address you and being constantly on the move up to the present time have overlooked it. Have been in the Service since August 1st, 1862. Am Capt., Co. B, 23rd Reg., Iowa Vol. Infantry; am the ranking captain of the regiment at present, and will probably advance the first opening. Our regiment has seen very hard service, we were all through the celebrated campaign under Gen. Grant, which resulted so gloriously to our armies in the Capture of Vicksburg. In that campaign alone we lost some three hundred men.

I heard once that you were in the army in the three months service and was compelled to leave the service on account of your health. I expect you to tell me all about this as well, as every thing relating to you Will, will be of great interest to me. I do not know where to reach you with this now but shall send it to Ripley, hoping if you are not there, that they will know where to find you. Dear Will, if I ever live to leave the army, I hope to visit you and once more spend many happy hours with you and your interesting family.

Our regiment left New Orleans on the 19th November, expecting to effect a landing at Brownsville, Texas. When we arrived near that point, we were ordered to Brazos Pass, where we safely landed on St. Joseph Island. From which point we started immediately by land (without tents, transportation, or any supplies) against this fort. We had quite an engagement here. The Rebs had some seven hundred troops here, we some fifteen hundred. We captured nine large guns, one being an one hundred and twenty-eight pounder. Several of the guns have the U.S. on them. It is said they were shipped here by Floyd. The larger one, which they called "The Rebel," was manufactured at Richmond. The loss of this fort will be severely felt by them, as it commands the entrance to the best bay (Matto Gordo Bay) on the coast. The works here are the best that I have ever seen and would have been impregnable against any naval force that could have been brought to [bear] against them. To contend against a land force they had made no calculations, on an attack from the rear, and were very badly <u>skeared</u> though not badly hurt, when they abandoned their works.

The weather here is delightful, as warm and pleasant now as is our May weather at home. Our boys go bathing in the bay every day. We have an abundance of fresh oysters, elegant fish, worlds of venison, and wild beef. I wish you were here with me for a month or so, am sure you would enjoy it hugely. You would find many warm Polk County friends here in our Reg. who would gladly grasp the hand of Will Tomlinson. Frank Weitman is sentinel in my company. Gus and John, my brothers, are also members of my company. They make good soldiers. Frank is one of the best officers in the Reg. Rev. A. J. Barton of Rising Sun is our chaplain. Four companies of the Reg. are from our county.

Who will be the next President? Tell me your choice. I am for Seymour, Grant, or Little Mc. Will, I have had some intimation that you have abandoned the democracy and gone in with the <u>Abolitionists</u>. This may be so, but I cannot believe it. Can it be possible that <u>Will,</u> is a <u>Linkum</u> man? I am still called a Radical, and if adhering strictly to the glorious Old Democracy—the Party that has made and preserved us as a nation—I am surely one. Every drop of blood in my vein is Democratic blood. And if there is any thing I <u>glory</u> in more than another it is that I am a <u>Democrat</u>. I love the name. I glory in the principles of that glorious old party. If I am killed in this war, it will be a democrat that dies. If I survive and get home, I shall devote my energies and what ability I may possess to the cause of the Democracy, for the reasons that I consider this the cause of my country.

Dear Will, how comical it would look to see you and <u>Sweet scented</u> Dixon walking arm in arm up to report to Hoxie, Dr. Davis, Witherorn, <u>et. al.,</u> ha, ha, ha, good sport.

Will, I must bring this to an end. I hope you will not feel angry towards me for anything herein contained, as you know I am <u>your Friend.</u>

Remember me kindly to Mrs. Tomlinson and the children, and believe me, dear Will,

Your True Friend,

J. Milt Walker

Do not fail to write me immediately.

* * * * *

There was also a letter from someone else who called Iowa home, Tomlinson's only sister, Anne. In 1852 she had sought a more salubrious environment for her fatherless son by sending him to live with Tomlinson and his family. Only eleven years had passed since she had counted on her brother to act as a kind and judicious father surrogate to Willie. Now, despite her grieving heart, she was relieved to hear that her only brother had had an opportunity to repent and had not taken his own life, however tragic the circumstances. She herself was no stranger to hard times, and, to add to her heartbreak, she had heard nothing from Willie.[12]

* * * * *

Anne to Eliza
Dubuque, Iowa, January 26, 1864

My Dear Sister,

Yesterday I received your letter of December 18th which was to me a very welcome messenger, notwithstanding the mournful intelligence which it contained, the death of my dear and only brother. I saw a notice of his death (but it was incorrect) in the Dubuque Herald about six weeks ago, and I longed to hear from you and his dear children, that we might share our mutual sorrow, and by this means dissipate part of the loneliness that we feel, on account of this sad and irreparable bereavement.

My mind is very much relieved since I received your letter. I now know that he had time for repentance, that he availed himself of that precious time, that he was at home, and died in the bosom of his family, that he did not bring about his own destruction, and now he occupies a much better place than his murderer. I have felt sure that he was at peace, on at least two occasions, even while my mind was tossed with uncertainty about the manner of his death. May God enable us to feel resigned to his will, and when our work is all done and our last tear shed, may we be so happy as to join him where war and murderers never come. Oh my Brother, it seems impossible that such a fate has befallen you. I sat down, thinking I could impart some little consolation on this occasion, but my own heart is ready to burst and I feel that God alone can send us consolation.

Mr. Skinner took your letter to the Herald office to have it published, but Mr. Hutchins is from home. Upon his return, if he does not publish it, we will send it to the Times office for publication, and I will forward as many copies to you as I can procure. I understood that there was quite a long complimentary article published in the Times but I could not obtain a copy.

You say the world seems dark to you, and it is surely so to me. I have quite as much cloudy as sunny weather here. I have peace, but we are very poor, having lost everything we owned; we are living in Dubuque and have been for the last fourteen months. Ann Jane is living in Cascade town; she married Wm. Skinner's son Harmon. She has a little girl eighteen months old. Issabella is married to a miner by the name of Wardle; she has a little boy nine months old. Willie is in the South, if alive. I have not seen him for seven years. Marion is with me. Eliza is with Ann Jane. I have four boys: the eldest is nine years; the youngest, seventeen months old. Mr. Skinner is collecting delinquent taxes now, and he has a fair prospect of obtaining an office in the spring.

I would like to hear how your mother is, likewise Byers and Sarah Bell, how old they are, and what business Byers intends to follow. I hope they will be good and try to make up, as far as possible, their loss of their father to you. Say to them that they are very dear to me although I have never seen them, and I would like to correspond with them. Please write soon and let me know what my brother said about me, or had he quite forgotten me. I do not know his reason for neglecting me so long. This in part makes me wish to know what he had to say, if anything, on his deathbed. Has any steps been taken for the arrest and punishment of his murderer or is he to run at large and kill all those who may happen to be sick and defenseless?

If you can spare me some of his hair, please send it as I have not anything that was his. Ann Jane has his likeness.

Ever your affectionate sister,
Anne T. Skinner

* * * * *

Anne's questions as to whether or not her brother remembered her and what he said on his deathbed remain unanswered. But eventually there was an answer to her question about what happened to the man who shot Tomlinson and left him bleeding on the ground. Richard Mitchell was not arrested for his role in the fatal affray and immediately afterward returned home to Kentucky, where he continued living in the way he had always lived—as a hardscrabble, hard-playing, and hard-nosed farmer. He died on August 3, 1885, of throat cancer. According to an account from the Mitchell family history, Mitchell said he always regretted his role in Tomlinson's death, which, he maintained, was unintentional and carried out in self-defense. Tomlinson, he said, had attacked him repeatedly to "to show his patriotism by whipping a rebel."[13]

Tomlinson was forty years old when he died. Eliza was forty-eight at the time. She remained in Ripley for the rest of her life as a single parent, caring for her two surviving children, Byers and Belle, and her ailing mother, Sarah, who died at the age of ninety-two in 1880. Byers and Belle each left home at the age of seventeen and continued to write to each other and their mother until she died at the age of seventy in 1885. The *Ripley Bee and Times* published the following obituary notice on July 8, 1885:

Another Landmark Disappears

Mrs. Eliza Tomlinson, widow of Capt. W. B. Tomlinson, died at the home of her brother, Dr. A. N. Wylie, in this city, on last Sunday afternoon at two o'clock.

Mrs. Eliza Wylie Tomlinson was a native of Washington county, Pennsylvania. She came to Ripley with her parents when a very small child. The place was then but a hamlet. She has been a resident ever since, with the exception of a few interims when her husband's business required their home elsewhere. The longest of these was in Des Moines, Iowa, where they lived from 1856 to 1860. From early years she had been a member of the Methodist Church—never demonstrative, but gentle, earnest and sincere. She was one of those sweet, bright, intelligent Christians, who could always give a reason for the faith that was in her. Her literary work, under various nom de plumes [sic], was always greeted with the highest appreciation. But few knew who the modest writer was. In disposition she was kind and pleasant, full of consideration for others, but when roused by conscience to oppose or condemn, there was a wonderful determination, and her words seemed fraught with resistless power. She has been sick for a year or more, not with any specific well defined disease. The fires of physical life have been gradually dying out. Since the last alarming change set in, less than a week ago, she suffered very little, and passed away gently, as a child would fall asleep.

The funeral took place yesterday afternoon from Dr. Wylie's residence, Rev. F. M. Clemans officiating. Her remains were deposited in Maplewood Cemetery beside those of her husband.[14]

Another notice of Eliza's death was published in the *Bulletin* in Maysville, Kentucky:

Mrs. Eliza Tomlinson

The many friends and relatives of this distinguished lady, among the readers of the BULLETIN, will with mournful interest, read the following extract from the Ripley Budget:

Mrs. Tomlinson was born near Washington, Pa., and came with her parents to Ripley, when very small. She has been a resident of this place most of the time since. She was the daughter of Dr. Adam Wylie and wife Sarah Byers Wylie, and came of a talented and distinguished ancestry, inheriting wonderful mental power coupled with a remarkably loveable disposition. She was a member of the Methodist Church, and no one could doubt the purity and sincerity of her religion. She was modest and quiet in all the walks of life and sensitively honorable.

In the fall of '63 she was widowed by the tragic death of her husband, Capt. Will Tomlinson, well known for his journalistic genius and gallant patriotism. Since then her sole care seemed for the two surviving children from her family of five. She gave them a good education and all the moral influences one of the best mothers could exert.

In her early days she devoted some attention to literary work, and as a writer ranked among the best.

For several years her home has been with her brother, Dr. A. N. Wylie. It was there she passed quietly away Sunday afternoon. Her sickness had lasted almost a year. Death came from a gradual exhaustion of her delicate physical powers. Trouble and sorrow wore upon her sensitive nature. The deaths of children, brothers, sisters, and husband and mother were terrible afflictions and it was her way to bear the burden in her heart, saying nothing. In her death this community loses one of its brightest and purest minds. The funeral services at the Doctor's residence, Tuesday afternoon, called together a remarkably large attendance of the oldest residents of the city and country surrounding. The discourse by Rev. F. M. Clemens was very touching and appropriate. Her mortal remains were laid at rest beside those of her husband, in Maplewood Cemetery.[15]

Eliza lived twenty-two years after her husband died. During their eighteen years together as husband and wife, they gave birth to ten newspapers and five children. None of their newspapers survived, and three of their children died at an early age. But what they lost does not begin to tell the story of what they left behind. As a couple and as individuals, they influenced political orientations and civic development in Iowa and Ohio. Throughout an era of vast change, unprecedented turmoil, and deadly divisiveness, they never vacillated in their loyalty to the Union. They were loved, hated, and respected by family, friends, and acquaintances. But utlimately their most enduring legacy may be the hundreds of letters they wrote and saved. Besides providing an intimate portrait of who they were, their letters show how one thoughtful and articulate family refused to give up hope through the disruption and tragedy of the Civil War in the Ohio River borderlands.

Epilogue
The Journey of the Letters

There are a lot of war-time letters between my father and mother.
These are mostly in a cigar box, now located, I think,
in the middle-room closet.
—William Byers Tomlinson to his children, December 1917

IN A LETTER TO ELIZA in July of 1862, Will Tomlinson wrote that he would like his letters on the war as published to be preserved. Given the context of that comment, he was presumably referring to his letters to the editor published in the *Ripley Bee*. But if actions are any indications of intent, he and Eliza were also committed to the preservation of their personal letters, even when long-distance relocation and wartime upheaval made doing so inconvenient. The Tomlinsons, in fact, must have been quite resourceful when it came to keeping their letters safe. Tomlinson himself would have encountered formidable challenges in saving, protecting, and carrying letters from his wife, children, and friends as he moved from job to job, from one boarding house to another, and from one military outpost to the next. Evidently, the Tomlinson children also placed a high value on their family's letters. The epigraph to this epilogue is from a letter that Byers wrote to his children in his final days. In it he gave explicit instructions for his funeral and earthly possessions, including the letters he had saved. Apparently he and his sister each ended up with approximately half of the Wylie-Tomlinson Letter Collection of about 300 letters.[1]

After the siblings went their separate ways as young adults, Belle taught in small-town schools in central and southern Ohio. During that time she met Alonzo Frescoln Smith, another schoolteacher, and they conducted a

The family portraits sketched in this letter around 1869 by William Byers Tomlinson probably include his mother, Eliza Wylie Tomlinson (left), and his grandmother, Sarah Byers Wylie (middle). The sketch of the other woman may depict his first wife, Alice, or his sister, Belle. The sketch of the male may be Eliza's brother, Dr. Adam Newton Wylie, or Byers himself. (Wylie-Tomlinson Letter Collection)

courtship through a voluminous and occasionally coded correspondence. They married in 1880, moved to his hometown area in Pennsylvania, and eventually settled in Corning, New York, where they raised five children. Belle corresponded with her mother and brother until Eliza's death in 1885 and died in Corning in 1925.[2]

Byers joined the Second Independent Battery of the Ohio National Guard in 1864. Like his father, he is listed in his official muster-in roll as being a printer who was five feet and eight inches tall with blue eyes, dark hair, and a dark complexion. While serving at Johnson's Island, near Sandusky, Ohio, he contracted a chronic case of catarrh (sinus and bronchial congestion) from standing guard for hours on end in the cold, damp winds coming off Lake Erie. He was afflicted with that for the rest of his life, but his many applications to procure disability compensation from the federal government were unsuccessful.[3]

After the war he continued his studies in Cincinnati and began a career there in the newspaper business, despite his mother's pleas to return to Ripley. He spent most of his life editing and publishing newspapers in southern Ohio and in 1875 returned home to edit and publish the *Ripley Bee*. He sold it in 1880, marking the end of an era of journalistic contributions that two generations of Tomlinsons had made to Ripley and Brown County. In his farewell column in the April 29, 1880, issue of the *Bee*, Byers wished his successors well and acknowledged the difficulty of leaving people he had known and loved since childhood. He also used the opportunity to justify himself to those who had "mistaken and misinterpreted his motives." In less than five years, he wrote, they would endorse everything he had said. For it was a "business fact," he added, "that the most dangerous rock the editor can strike is the TRUTH." In severing his ties to Ripley, he closed with the following lines:

> For telling the truth, when the safety of public interests demanded it, we have been maligned by saint and sinner, and our only reward is a conscience void of offence. But eventually they will see the facts for themselves, and the vindication will come. But that is no matter of ours. We don't care now and never did, whether the populace were unanimously in our favor. Right is our aim, and we have tried to hit the bull's eye. "Farewell to friends, farewell to foes—Our peace with these, our love with those."[4]

Byers then moved upriver to Ironton, Ohio, where he started another newspaper, the *Ironton Busy Bee*. Besides the newspapers mentioned, he was, over the course of his career, associated with the *Hillsboro News Herald*, *Huntington Daily Herald*, and *Portsmouth Blade*. In 1885 he was elected as a representative to the Ohio State Legislature from Lawrence County. He was, according to *History of the Republican Party in Ohio*, "a prominent factor in politics" and "one of the best known men in Ohio." A staunch Republican, he gained a reputation for strong writing on political topics and pungent prose that adhered to the facts. He was also known for writing poetry imbued with heartfelt sentiment.[5]

In Ironton, his first wife, the former Alice Killin of Catlettsburg, Kentucky, died in 1884, leaving him with four young children. In 1885, he

This photo of William Byers Tomlinson
was probably taken in 1914 when he was
about sixty-seven. It was pasted inside
the cover of a chapbook of his poetry.
(Wylie-Tomlinson Letter Collection)

married Caroline Thomas of Ironton, and they had three daughters. Their
second daughter, Florence Adele Tomlinson, married Roscoe (Ross) Noel
Donohoe in 1913 in Portsmouth, Ohio. Byers died on December 31, 1917,
and the letters he saved ended up in a cracker tin in the Donohoe home on
Baird Avenue. Florence served as regent of a local chapter of the Daughters of the American Revolution and enjoyed researching family history.
But after her death in 1952, many family mementos were packed away in
an attic closet. The cracker tin full of letters was relegated to a high shelf
in a hallway alcove in the back of the house. There it sat, unnoticed, for
decades. But it was not entirely forgotten. Florence and Ross had three
children, and the oldest, William Ross Donohoe, was my father. Two
younger sisters followed. The youngest sister, Betsy, lived in the family
home on Baird Avenue for most of her life. Thanks to her generosity and
foresight in responding to a question posed by my sister Betsy, the letters
were passed on to the next generation of family historians.[6]

Research involving the letters has taken me further afield than I ever
dreamed it would. With every new lead I have come across, dozens more
have begged for my attention. My husband, Dave, and I have made several
trips to Ripley and visited a number of other places, including Ogdens-

burg, New York; Cincinnati, Ohio; the Wylie House Museum in Bloomington, Indiana; Quebec, Canada; Northern Ireland; and the province of Cumberland in England. So many people along the way have been so helpful with this project that it would be impossible to mention them all, but I have tried to mention as many as possible in the Acknowledgments. Thanks to all who have had a hand in this project, many fortuitous convergences have contributed to its fruition.

I will always be grateful for the commitment that went into preserving the letters from one generation to the next, for the opportunity I have had to work with them, and for the illumination brought to one small slice of history by the story of Will and Eliza Wylie Tomlinson. Their story may not be about the famous or extraordinary, but time after time they showed exceptional courage in continuing to hope. Regardless of the news of the day, they believed that things could change for the better.

Appendix

NEWSPAPERS EDITED AND PUBLISHED BY WILL TOMLINSON

Freedom's Casket, May/June 1844, Ripley, Ohio. Weekly paper of record and general interest; included articles and anecdotes reprinted from other publications, antislavery sentiment, commentary on local politics, and advertisements. Slogan: "Principles—not prejudice."

Hickory Sprout, August 1844–45, Piketon, Ohio. Weekly paper of record and general interest; included articles and anecdotes reprinted from other publications, promoted national and local Democratic nominees, and sold advertising at the rate of one dollar per inch for three insertions. Slogan: "As little government as possible; that little emanating from and controlled by the People, and uniform in its application."

Western Wreath, 1845, Georgetown, Ohio.

Democratic Standard, 1845–47 and 1849–50, Georgetown, Ohio. Weekly paper of record and general interest; included articles and anecdotes reprinted from other publications, political commentary, and advertisements. Slogan same as *The Hickory Sprout* until 1850, then became "An intelligent people—faithful officers—a simple and energetic government."

Democratic Union, 1851–54, Georgetown, Ohio. Weekly paper formed by merger of the *Democratic Standard* and the *Democrat and Journal.*

Granite Rock, 1852, Ripley, Ohio. A Democratic campaign paper for Franklin A. Pierce for U.S. President.

Ripley Herald, 1852, Ripley, Ohio. A local paper published by Tomlinson and a company of spiritualists. Included articles advocating spiritualism, items of general interest, and advertising. Promoted the "free communication of thoughts" as "one of the invaluable rights of man." After nineteen issues, Tomlinson sold his interest in the paper.

Nor'wester, April 19, 1853–August 1854, Kenton, Ohio. A twenty-four column sheet published to bolster the Democratic Party in Hardin County.

Iowa Statesman, 1855–56 and 1858, Des Moines, Iowa. Weekly paper with Democratic orientation.

Loyal Scout, 1863, Ripley, Ohio. A Union campaign paper.

Newspapers that Employed Will Tomlinson

St. Lawrence Republican, 1840, Ogdensburg, New York. Weekly paper of record and general interest; promoted Democratic policies and candidates.

Dubuque Express and Herald, 1854, Dubuque, Iowa. Daily paper with Democratic orientation.

Iowa State Journal, 1859–60, Des Moines, Iowa

Cincinnati Daily Gazette, 1860–63, Cincinnati, Ohio. Daily paper promoting Republican policies and candidates.

Athens Messenger, 1863. Republican orientation.

Other Publications

Letters to the Editor by Will Tomlinson, the *Ripley (Ohio) Bee,* July 4, 1861; also January 23, April 3, April 10, June 12, July 31, November 6, and November 20, 1862.

"The Poison Cup," a short story by Will Tomlinson, published in the *Columbian Magazine,* October 1844, 184–86.

Notes

INTRODUCTION

1. J. M. Dixon, *The Valley and the Shadow: Experiences of a Blind Ex-Editor* (New York: Russell Brothers, 1868), 57; Will Porter, *Annals of Polk County, Iowa, and the City of Des Moines* (Des Moines, Iowa: George A. Miller Printing Company, 1898), 602; "Fatal Affray," *Ripley (Ohio) Bee*, Dec. 3, 1863; Gerald Fowke, "The Mitchells of Charleston Bottoms, Mason County, Kentucky," Mason County Museum Center, Maysville, Ky., 126.

2. A composite portrait of the small-town newspaper editor and printer in nineteenth-century America has been synthesized from the following sources listed in alphabetical order: Gerald J. Baldasty, *The Commercialism of News in the Nineteenth Century* (Madison: Univ. of Wisconsin Press, 1992); David W. Bulla and Gregory A. Borchard, *Journalism in the Civil War Era* (New York: Peter Lang, 2010); David Dary, *Red Blood and Black Ink: Journalism in the Old West* (New York: Alfred A. Knopf, 1998); George H. Douglas, *The Golden Age of the Newspaper* (Westport, Conn.: Greenwood Press, 1999); Robert S. Harper, *The Ohio Press in the Civil War* (Columbus: Ohio State Univ. Press, n.d.); Robert F. Karolevitz, *Newspapering in the Old West: A Pictorial History of Journalism and Printing on the Frontier* (New York: Bonanza Books, 1965), and *From Quill to Computer: The Story of America's Community Newspapers* (National Newspaper Foundation, 1985); Frank Luther Mott, *American Journalism* (New York: MacMillan Company, 1962); David Paul Nord, *Communities of Journalism: A History of Newspapers and Their*

Readers (Urbana: Univ. of Illinois Press, 2001); Jeffrey L. Pasley, *The Tyranny of Printers: Newspaper Politics in the Early American Republic* (Charlottesville: Univ. of Virginia Press, 2001); Michael Schudson, *Discovering the News: A Social History of American Newspapers* (New York: Basic Books, 1978); Rollo G. Silver, *The American Printer 1787–1825* (Charlottesville: Univ. of Virginia Press, 1967).

3. Ross MacDonald of Brightwork Press in Connecticut says "the most admired impression" from an old letterpress was "the one that was the richest and the lightest, called 'the printer's kiss.'" Quoted in Micheal Neault, "Wood Type Rising," *City: Rochester's Alternative Newsweekly* (June 29, 2005), www.rochestercitynewspaper.com/archives/2005/06/Wood-type-rising/.

4. Dary, *Red Blood and Black Ink*, 21–27, 195–96, and 258–59.

5. See List of Newspapers Edited and Published by Will Tomlinson, Appendix; Porter, *Annals*, 602.

6. See Tomlinson's naturalization record, Brown County Genealogy Society, Naturalizations, Georgetown, Ohio, Journal 13, 1844–45, 388. In the *Hickory Sprout* (Piketon, Ohio), Aug. 29, 1844, Tomlinson noted that the *St. Lawrence Republican* editors praised his former employment with them in Ogdensburg, N.Y. See *St. Lawrence Republican* (Ogdensburg, N.Y.), Aug. 13, 1844, Northern New York Library Network, Northern New York Historical Papers, http://news.nnyln.org; Porter, *Annals*, 602.

7. *Hickory Sprout*, Aug. 29, 1844; *Loyal Scout* (Ripley, Ohio), Oct. 10, 1863; *Freedom's Casket* (Ripley, Ohio), June 15, 1844; Will Tomlinson, letters to the editor, *Ripley Bee*, Jan. 14, 1862, and Apr. 10, 1862; Will Tomlinson to Eliza Tomlinson, Feb. 13, 1863, and Apr. 9, 1863, Wylie-Tomlinson Letter Collection.

8. *Loyal Scout*, Oct. 10, 1863.

9. "William Tomlinson," Q. M. Sgt., Regimental Descriptive Book, N. C. S. [Noncommissioned Service] and Band, Company I, 5th Reg't. Ohio Infantry, Apr. 20, 1861, Cincinnati, Ohio, U.S. National Archives and Records Administration, Washington, D.C.; West Virginia Union Militia Rosters: Upshur County, West Virginia State Archives, West Virginia Division of Culture and History, www.wvculture.org/history/wvmemory/militia/rostersupshur.html; Harper, *Ohio Press in the Civil War*, 6; James G. Smart, ed., introduction to *A Radical View: The "Agate" Dispatches of Whitelaw Reid, 1861–1865*, (Memphis, Tenn.: Memphis State Univ. Press, 1976), 1:4; *Loyal Scout*, Oct. 10, 1863.

10. Stanley Harrold, *Border War: Fighting over Slavery before the Civil War* (Chapel Hill: Univ. of North Carolina Press, 2010), 15–16, 72, 94–95, and 101–4.

11. *The History of Brown County, Ohio* (Chicago: W. H. Beers & Co., 1883), 423–24. For an explanation of Ripley's suspicious attitudes toward strangers professing to support abolitionists and the origins of the town's nickname as an "abolitionist hellhole," see Fergus M. Bordewich, *Bound for Canaan: The Epic Story of the Underground Railroad, American's First Civil Rights Movement* (New York: HarperCollins, 2005), 189–90 and 208–9; also, Ann Hagedorn, *Beyond the*

River: The Untold Story of the Heroes of the Underground Railroad (New York: Simon and Schuster, 2002), 43 and corresponding note on 292. Hagedorn's thorough account of Ripley's role in the Underground Railroad details the contributions of the Reverend John Rankin and others.

12. For a history of Utopia, a Clermont County village based on the principles of the Fourierite and utopian movements, see Henry Howe, *Historical Collections of Ohio: An Encyclopedia of the State,* The Ohio Centennial Edition, (Cincinnati: The State of Ohio, 1888; reprint 1907), 1:420. For an informative overview of utopian experiments in Ohio, see George W. Knepper, *Ohio and Its People,* 3rd ed. (Kent, Ohio: Kent State Univ. Press, 2003), 170-71. For a detailed description of spiritualist groups in Cincinnati, see William T. Coggeshall, *The Signs of the Times: A History of the Spirit-Rappings, in Cincinnati and Other Places* (Cincinnati: William T. Coggeshall, 1851). For information on Cincinnati as a publishing center, see Knepper, *Ohio and Its People,* 189-90. For more details about Ripley's business enterprises in the mid-1800s, see *The History of Brown County, Ohio,* 429-30 and 441-42; Howe, *Historical Collections of Ohio,* 1:336-38; and Hagedorn, *Beyond the River,* 201.

13. Marriage record for Will and Eliza Wylie Tomlinson: Book G-7, #4314, 72-73, Brown County Annex, Georgetown, Ohio. For Eliza's feelings about her marriage, see Eliza Wylie Tomlinson to Sarah and Margaret Wylie, Nov. 5, 1844, Wylie-Tomlinson Letter Collection.

14. "The Family History," a genealogical document from the Wylie-Tomlinson Letter Collection, lists the Tomlinson's five children as George Wylie Tomlinson (born in Georgetown, Ohio, July 23, 1845; died in Ripley, Ohio, June 23, 1851); William Byers Tomlinson (born in Ripley, Ohio, Mar. 23, 1847; died in Cincinnati, Ohio, Dec. 31, 1917); Margaret Eliza Tomlinson (born in Ripley, Ohio, July 26, 1848; died in Ripley, Ohio, Aug. 2, 1853); Adam Newton Tomlinson (born in Georgetown, Ohio, Dec., 3, 1850; died in Georgetown, Ohio, Jan. 2, 1851); and Sarah Isabella Tomlinson (born in Ripley, Ohio, Mar. 14, 1853; died in Corning, N.Y., Oct. 6, 1923). The disputed accounts of Tomlinson's fatal encounter are mentioned in "Fatal Affray," *Ripley Bee,* Dec. 3, 1863. For more details regarding the circumstances of his death, see chapter 20 and accompanying notes.

15. Robert Glossop, "A Place in Time: Families, Family Matters, and Why They Matter," The Glossop Lawson Lecture Series, The Vanier Institute of the Family, The Lawson Foundation (Oct. 18, 2007), 12, www.vifamily.ca/media/node/345/attachments/Glossop_Lawson_public_lecture.pdf.

EDITING NOTES

1. For information on the Scotch-Irish and English border cultures, especially naming practices, see David Hackett Fischer, *Albion's Seed: Four British Folkways in America* (New York: Oxford Univ. Press, 1989), 683-86.

1. Tomlinson's Origins

1. "The Family History" lists Tomlinson's birthplace as Seaton, in the county of Northumberland, in England. However, in his sworn statement for his naturalization record, Tomlinson says that he was a native of Cumberland County in the Kingdom of Great Britain. See Naturalizations, Brown County (Ohio) Genealogy Society, Journal 13, 1844–45, 388. Extensive research regarding Tomlinson's ancestors is inconclusive. Some information regarding Tomlinson's christening and parents can be accessed at the *Bishop's Transcripts for Camerton, 1663–1870,* International Genealogical Index for Great Britain, vol. 5, www.familysearch. org. See Anne T. Hunter to Will Tomlinson, July 21, 1852, and Aug. 2, 1852; also, Anne T. Skinner to Eliza Wylie Tomlinson, Jan. 26, 1864, Wylie-Tomlinson Letter Collection.

2. Fischer, *Albion's Seed,* 794, 676–79, and 687–90.

3. Fischer, *Albion's Seed,* 638–39; James Webb, *Born Fighting* (New York: Broadway Books, 2004), 12–13; Knepper, *Ohio and Its People,* 56; Naturalizations, Brown County Genealogy Society, Journal 13, 1844–45, 388.

4. Helen I. Cowan, *British Emigration to British North America: The First Hundred Years,* rev. ed. (Toronto: Univ. of Toronto Press, 1961), 27–30.

5. John Bartlet Brebner, *North Atlantic Triangle: The Interplay of Canada, the United States and Great Britain,* The Relations of Canada and the United States Series, Carnegie Endowment for International Peace, Division of Economics and History, James T. Shotwell, Director (New Haven, Conn.: Yale Univ. Press, 1945), 139–40; Allan Greer, "Rebellion of 1837–1838," in *The Oxford Companion to Canadian History,* ed. Gerald Hallowell (Don Mills, Ontario: Oxford Univ. Press Canada, 2004), 530–31; W. R. Wilson, "Van Dieman's Land," *Historical Narratives of Early Canada,* www.uppercanadahistory.ca/tt/tt11.html.

6. "The Life of a Prisoner," *Freedom's Casket,* June 15, 1844.

7. *Freedom's Casket,* June 8, 1844.

2. Eliza's Heritage

1. I have chosen to use the term "Scotch-Irish," rather than "Scots-Irish" or "Scottish Irish," because that is what I grew up hearing my relatives use in reference to our ancestors. For a detailed account of the origins and usage of "Scotch-Irish," see James G. Leyburn, "The Name 'Scotch-Irish,'" *The Scotch Irish: A Social History* (Chapel Hill: Univ. of North Carolina Press, 1962), Appendix 1, 326–34. Leyburn states that the term "Scotch-Irish" is more historically correct and has no accurate substitute. For a more succinct history of the term, see Patrick Griffin, *The People with No Name: Ireland's Ulster Scots, America's Scots Irish, and the Creation of a British Atlantic World, 1689–1764* (Princeton, N.J.: Princeton Univ. Press, 2001), note 5, 175–76. Griffin notes that "Scotch-Irish" had a negative connotation

in the eighteenth century but was assimilated into everyday parlance in the late nineteenth century to distinguish later-arriving Irish Catholics from earlier Protestant immigrants. According to Griffin, the term "Scots Irish" was a "sanitized name" subsequently created by some historians. Fischer, *Albion's Seed,* 676–79, 687, 794; "Samuel Brown Wylie," Wiley Genealogy, www.wiley.com/library/bios/SBWylie/index.phtml; Steve St. Martin, "Descendants of Adam Wylie," June 16, 2010; Boyd Crumrine, *History of Washington County, Pennsylvania* (Philadelphia: L. H. Everts, 1882), 687 and 980; *Commemorative Biographical Record of Washington County, Pennsylvania* (Chicago: J. H. Beers, 1893), 233; Byron Williams, *History of Clermont and Brown Counties, Ohio,* reprint of the 1913 edition with a new index, Clermont County Genealogical Society (Baltimore: Gateway Press, 1987), 389. Eliza's maternal grandfather, Thomas Byers, is listed in Captain George Sharp's Company, in the Third Battalion of Pennsylvania's Washington County Militia in 1782; Eliza's paternal grandfather, Adam Wylie, is listed in Captain Swearingen's Company in the Third Battalion of Pennsylvania's Washington County Militia, also in 1782. See Thomas Lynch Montgomery, ed., *Pennsylvania Archives,* 6th series, vol. 2 (Harrisburg: Harrisburg Publishing Co., 1906), 106–7.

2. Rocking the cradle to the tune of *"Nooo* bishops!" was something I heard from my Presbyterian relatives in southern Ohio. It probably comes from a statement made by King James I of England, who when challenged by Puritans seeking reform of the Church of England in 1604, said, "If you aim at a Scots Presbytery, it agreeth as well with monarchy as God and the devil!" The King then declared, "No Bishops, no King!" "The King James Bible," *ICONS: A Portrait of England,* www.icons.org.uk/theicons/collection/king-james-bible/features/iconarticle. The term "cradle Presbyterian" has commonly been used by American Presbyterians to describe someone who was born of Presbyterian parents and reared in the Presbyterian denomination. For basic tenets of the Presbyterian faith, see John H. Leith, *An Introduction to the Reformed Tradition,* rev. ed. (Atlanta: John Knox, 1981), 100; Donald K. McKim, *Introducing the Reformed Faith* (Louisville, Ky.: Westminster John Knox, 2001), 178; "The Historic Principles of Church Order," *The Book of Order: The Constitution of the Presbyterian Church (U.S.A.), Part II, 2005/2007* (Louisville, Ky.: Office of the General Assembly, 2005), G1.0300; "The Westminster Confession of Faith," *Book of Confessions: Study Edition, The Constitution of the Presbyterian Church (U.S.A.), Part I* (Louisville, Ky.: Office of the General Assembly, 1996), G6.109–6.111.

3. "Byers," *Raymond M. Bell Anthology,* http://chartiers.com/raybell/1995-byers.html; Crumrine, *History of Washington County,* 687 and 980.

4. "Fallen Asleep," obituary for Sarah Byers Wylie, *Ripley Bee,* Mar. 18, 1880; Charles Henry Ambler, *A History of Transportation in the Ohio Valley* (Westport, Conn.: Greenwood, 1931), 38–49.

5. Ambler, *History of Transportation in the Ohio Valley,* 47–48; Robert E. Chaddock, *Ohio Before 1850: A Study of the Early Influence of Pennsylvania and Southern*

Populations in Ohio, Studies in History, Economics, and Public Law, vol. 41, no. 2 (New York: AMS Press, 1967), 151–52; Howe, *Historical Collections of Ohio,* 1:336; Hagedorn, 9–10.

6. "The Family History," Wylie-Tomlinson Letter Collection; *History of Brown County,* 420; Eliese Bambach Stivers, *Ripley, Ohio: Its History and Families* (Ripley, Ohio: Sesquicentennial Historical Committee, 1965), 50; *Ripley Bee,* Aug. 10, 1870. See tax receipts for lots 3, 8, 13, 14, 61, and 82 in Ripley to Adam and Sarah Wylie, Estate of Adam Wylie, Brown County (Ohio) Probate Court Records, 1839, #6565.

7. Hagedorn, *Beyond the River,* 52–55 and 43–44.

8. "Fallen Asleep," *Ripley Bee,* Mar. 18, 1880; Hagedorn, *Beyond the River,* 65–66; Ambler, *History of Transportation in the Ohio Valley,* 373. Of all the town lots owned by Adam and Sarah Wylie, only lot 82, assessed at $549 in 1839, the year of Dr. Adam Wylie's death, appears to be valued enough to have had a significant structure on it. Lot 82, on the corner of Locust and Second Streets, was on a ridge parallel to the river and may have been the site of Adam and Sarah Wylie's home. See tax receipts for lots 3, 8, 13, 14, 61, and 82 in Ripley to Adam and Sarah Wylie, Estate of Adam Wylie, Brown County Probate Court Records, 1839, #6565; and 1850 Map of Ripley, Ohio, by W. F. Wylie, private collection of Thomas F. and Jane Zachman, Ripley, Ohio. (The W. F. Wylie credited on the map was probably Eliza's younger brother.) "Panic of 1837," *Ohio History Central,* Ohio Historical Society, www.ohiohistorycentral.org/entry.php?rec=536.

9. A. N. Wylie to A. Wylie, Sept. 16, 1839, in Bonnie Williams and Elaine Herold, eds., *Affectionately Yours: The Andrew Wylie Family Letters,* 1828–1859, 2nd ed., 2 vols. (Bloomington: Wylie House Museum, Indiana Univ., 1994) 1:7; A. N. Wylie to Eliza Wylie, Dec. 20, 1840, Wylie-Tomlinson Letter Collection.

10. Brown County (Ohio) Common Pleas, *Democratic Standard,* May 8–June 5, 1845; Estate of Dr. Adam Wylie, Brown County Probate Court Records, 1839, #6565; Crumrine, *History of Washington, County, Pennsylvania,* 687; "Andrew Wylie," *Wiley Genealogy,* www.wileygenealogy.com/library/bios/AndrewWylie1789PA/index.phtml; Williams and Herold, *Affectionately Yours,* 1:229–31; Faye Mark and Bonnie Williams, eds., *The Life and Diaries of Theophilus A. Wylie, 1810–1895* (Bloomington: Indiana Univ. Office of Publications, n.d.), 2.

11. Obituary for "Mrs. Eliza Tomlinson," *Maysville (Ky.) Bulletin,* July 16, 1885; "Another Landmark Disappears," obituary for Eliza Tomlinson, *Ripley Bee,* July 8, 1885; A. N. Wylie to Eliza Wylie, Dec. 20, 1840, Wylie-Tomlinson Letter Collection; Barbara Weisberg, *Talking to the Dead: Kate and Maggie Fox and the Rise of Spiritualism* (New York: HarperCollins, 2004), 24–25; "Another Landmark Disappears," *Ripley Bee,* July 8, 1885; "Fallen Asleep," *Ripley Bee,* Mar. 18, 1880; Bordewich, *Bound for Canaan,* 192; Hagedorn, *Beyond the River,* 225.

12. Obituary for Elizabeth [Pangburn] Wylie, *Ripley Bee,* Jan. 8, 1863; "Notes," Hagedorn, *Beyond the River,* 286. An obituary notice for Dr. A. N. Wylie includes

a commendation that sounds suspiciously like an oblique reference to his support of the Underground Railroad: "Though his left hand knew not what the right hand did, and the doctor never whispered his good works to the nearest friend, there are many who have reason to bless his memory for substantial aid in their hour of need. No cry of an anguished heart failed of response from this sensitive soul." See "Dr. A. N. Wylie," *Transactions of the Forty-Eighth Annual Meeting of the Ohio State Medical Society* (Cincinnati: Earhart & Richardson, 1893), 381–83. "Notes," Hagedorn, *Beyond the River,* 286; Eliza Wylie Tomlinson to Will Tomlinson, Sept. 2 and 16 and Oct. 22, 1861; Will Tomlinson to Eliza Wylie Tomlinson, Apr. 19 and June 17, 1863; Will Tomlinson to Byers Tomlinson, Apr. 28, 1863, Wylie-Tomlinson Letter Collection. See also Andrew Evans to Sam Evans, Dec. 6, 1863, and Ann Evans to Samuel Evans, Dec. 6, 1863, in Robert F. Engs and Corey M. Brooks, eds., *Their Patriotic Duty: The Civil War Letters of the Evans Family of Brown County, Ohio* (New York: Fordham Univ. Press, 2007), 220–22. For allusions to the Underground Railroad, see Eliza Wylie Tomlinson to Will Tomlinson, Sept. 2, 1861; and William Byers Tomlinson to Will Tomlinson, Oct. 29, 1863, Wylie-Tomlinson Letter Collection.

13. Bordewich, *Bound for Canaan,* xvi, 206, and 190.

3. Bringing Forth

1. Marriage record of Will Tomlinson to Eliza Wylie Tomlinson: Book G-7, #4314, 72–73, Brown County Annex, Georgetown, Ohio; *Hickory Sprout,* Oct. 3, 1844; *Hickory Sprout,* Aug. 29, 1844.

2. "Resistance to Tyrants is Obedience to God!", Whig protest, Ripley, Ohio, June 10, 1848, Wylie-Tomlinson Letter Collection; "Dr. Thomas Byers Wylie, M.D.," Marshall Family, Rootsweb, http://wc.rootsweb.ancestry.com/cgibin/igm.cgi?op=REG&db=wtm&id=I3818; Thomas A. Baily, *Democrats vs. Republicans: The Continuing Clash* (New York: Meredith Press, 1968), 54; James M. McPherson, *Battle Cry of Freedom: The Civil War Era* (New York: Ballantine Books, 1988), 27–31.

3. Obituary for William F. Wylie, Esq., *Ripley Bee,* Apr. 19, 1860; "Gospel Plow," also known as "Hold on," www.negrospirituals.com/news-song/hold_on.htm; Knepper, *Ohio and Its People,* 170; "Millerites," *Ohio History Central,* www.ohiohistorycentral.org/entry.php?rec=607.

4. "Prominent Physician Passed Away," obituary for Dr. A. N. Wylie, *West Union (Ohio) People's Defender,* Dec. 17, 1891; "Dr. A. N. Wylie," *Transactions of the Forty-Eighth Annual Meeting of the Ohio State Medical Society,* 381–83; "J. L. Wylie," *History of Brown County,* 90–91; "Died," obituary for Dr. T. B. Wylie, *Ripley Bee,* Feb. 4, 1864.

5. Daniel Walker Howe, *What Hath God Wrought: The Transformation of America, 1815–1848* (Oxford: Oxford Univ. Press, 2007), 564–65, 538–39, and 556; Knepper, *Ohio and Its People,* 171–72, 309; Andrew R. L. Cayton, *Ohio: The*

History of a People (Columbus: Ohio State Univ. Press, 2002), 22–24; *History of Cincinnati and Hamilton County, Ohio: Their Past and Present* (Cincinnati: S. B. Nelson & Company, 1894), 4, 10, 19, and 21, www.heritagepursuit.com/HamiltonIndex.htm.

6. *History of Brown County*, 423; Hagedorn, *Beyond the River*, 58; Howe, *Historical Collections of Ohio*, 2:427–28.

7. *Hickory Sprout*, Oct. 3, 1844; Will Tomlinson, "The Poison Cup," *Columbian Magazine*, Oct. 1844, 184–86; C. Hugh Holman, "Gothic Novel," *A Handbook to Literature*, 4th ed. (Indianapolis: Bobbs-Merrill Educational Publishing, 1981), 204–5.

8. *History of Brown County*, 396. There is no official record of Tomlinson's service in the Mexican War, but it is mentioned in a letter that his son Byers wrote to his children on his deathbed. The letter is undated, but since Byers died on December 31, 1917, it must have been written shortly before that. In the letter, Byers refers to his children's "grandfather Tomlinson," who fought in the Mexican war, Indian war, and the Civil War, bearing captain's commission in the last two. See William Byers Tomlinson to His Children, Deathbed Wishes, Wylie-Tomlinson Letter Collection. For information on Gen. Thomas Hamer and the Mexican War, see *History of Brown County*, 335; Howe, *Historical Collections of Ohio*, 1:331. The birth and death dates of the Tomlinson children are listed in "The Family History" and cited in note 14 for the Introduction.

4. Looking for Relief

1. *History of Brown County*, 396; for birth and death dates of the Tomlinson children, see "The Family History," Wylie-Tomlinson Letter Collection, and note 14 for Introduction.

2. "The Family History."

3. *History of Brown County*, 396 and 424; Jean H. Baker, *Affairs of Party: The Political Culture of Northern Democrats in the Mid-Nineteenth Century* (Ithaca: Cornell Univ. Press, 1983), 323; McPherson, *Battle Cry of Freedom*, 119.

4. McPherson, *Battle Cry*, 75; Hagedorn, *Beyond the River*, 251–54.

5. *Ripley (Ohio) Herald*, May 27, 1852; Harrold, *Border War*, 7; *History of Brown County*, 424.

6. *Ripley Herald*, May 27, 1852; Adam Clarke, *Memoirs of the Wesley Family*, 2nd rev. ed., George Peck, ed. (New York: Lane and Tippett, 1848), 217–22.

7. Weisberg, *Talking to the Dead*, 3, 138, and 135; Coggeshall, *The Signs of the Times*, 11, 15, and 26; *Ripley Herald*, May 27, 1852.

8. John B. Buescher, *The Other Side of Salvation: Spiritualism and Nineteenth-Century Religious Experience* (Boston: Skinner House Books, 2004), 85.

9. *Ripley Herald*, May 27, 1852; "Another Landmark Disappears," obituary for Eliza Wylie Tomlinson, *Ripley Bee and Times*, July 8, 1885; *History of Brown County*, 424.

10. Nevin Otton Winter, *A History of Northwest Ohio: A Narrative Account of Its Historical Progress and Development* (Chicago: Lewis Pub. Co., 1917), 1:452; *Portrait and Biographical Record of Marion and Hardin Counties, Ohio* (Chicago: Chapman Pub. Co., 1895), 556; "The Family History," Wylie-Tomlinson Letter Collection.

11. Eugene H. Roseboom, *The History of the Civil War Era, 1850–1873*, vol. 5 of *The History of the State of Ohio*, ed. Carl Wittke, (Columbus: Ohio State Archaeological and Historical Society, 1944; reprt. Columbus: Ohio Historical Society, 1968), 9; David L. Lendt, *The Demise of the Democracy: The Copperhead Press in Iowa, 1856–1870* (Ames: Iowa State Univ. Press, 1973), 4.

12. *History of Brown County*, 396 and 424; "Will Tomlinson," *Dubuque (Iowa) Times*, Dec. 16, 1863; Lendt, *Demise of the Democracy*, 38–41; Bulla and Borchard, *Journalism in the Civil War Era*, 169; "Will Tomlinson," *Dubuque Times*, Dec. 16, 1863.

13. Porter, *Annals of Polk County*, 175 and 573; J. M. Dixon, *Centennial History of Polk County, Iowa* (Des Moines: State Register, 1876), 111; Porter, *Annals of Polk County*, 603; Dixon, *The Valley and the Shadow*, 53 and 90–91; "Iowa Rail History," Office of Rail Transportation, www.iowadot.gov/iowarail/history/history.htm; Anne T. Skinner to Eliza Tomlinson, Jan. 26, 1864, Wylie-Tomlinson Letter Collection.

14. Lendt, *Demise of the Democracy*, 4, 13, and 19–25; Porter, *Annals of Polk County*, 603; obituary for Will Tomlinson, *Ripley Bee*, Dec. 3, 1863; Dixon, *Centennial History of Polk County*, 226; Porter, *Annals of Polk County*, 175 and 573.

15. Lendt, *Demise of the Democracy*, 42; McPherson, *Battle Cry of Freedom*, 188–91; Porter, *Annals of Polk County*, 579 and 603; Dixon, *Valley and the Shadow*, 57.

16. Lendt, *Demise of the Democracy*, 50; McPherson, *Battle Cry*, 152–53, 205, and 208; Harrold, *Border War*, 190–93; *Iowa State Journal*, Sept. 10, 1859, quoted in Louis Pelzer, *Augustus Caesar Dodge: A Study in American Politics*, Ph.D. diss., University of Iowa, 1909.

17. Rick L. Woten, "Dodge, Augustus Caesar," *The Biographical Dictionary of Iowa* (Iowa City: Univ. of Iowa, 2009), http://uipress.lib.uiowa.edu; *Burlington (Iowa) Weekly Hawk Eye and Telegraph*, Sept. 17, 1859; *Davenport (Iowa) Daily Gazette*, July 2, 1858; Oct. 6, 1859; and May 7, 1860.

5. TOGETHER AND APART

1. Porter, *Annals of Polk County*, 573 and 575; Lendt, *Demise of the Democracy*, 7–8; "The Iowa Legislature," www.legis.iowa.gov/Legislators/legislator.aspx?GA=12&PID=5189.

2. Porter, *Annals of Polk County*, 1063–64 and 602.

3. Letters written on Iowa Senate Chamber letterhead include Will Tomlinson to Eliza Wylie Tomlinson, June 9, 1860; and F. I. Yokauer to Mrs. E. W. Tomlinson, June 24, 1860, Wylie-Tomlinson Letter Collection.

4. Roseboom, *Civil War Era*, 147–48; Silver, *American Printer*, 124.

5. I am indebted to Brian P. Lawler, Shakepeare Press Museum, California Polytechnic State University, for a detailed explanation of the typesetting process that a compositor would have used in the 1860s. See Brian P. Lawler, email to author, Sept. 15, 2013.

6. Pasley, *Tyranny of Printers*, 24–28; Dary, *Red Blood and Black Ink*, 33; Silver, *American Printer*, 8–9.

7. Roseboom, *Civil War Era*, 57–58; 1860 Census for Ripley, Ohio; "Obituary for Wm. F. Wylie, Esq.," *Ripley Bee*, Apr. 19, 1860.

8. Obituary for Dr. T. B. Wylie, *Ripley Bee*, Feb. 4, 1864; *Ripley Bee*, Apr. 2, 23, and 30, 1859; "Prominent Physician Passed Away," obituary for Dr. A. N. Wylie, *West Union People's Defender*, Dec. 17, 1891; "Dr. A. N. Wylie," *Transactions of the Forty-Eighth Annual Meeting of the Ohio State Medical Society*, 381–83; Deed from William F. Wylie to Adam N. Wylie for purchase of one-fourth of lot 61, Apr. 15, 1859, Brown County (Ohio) Recorder Office, Deed Book K-36; Deed for William Tomlinson and wife Eliza to sell one half of lot 61 to Adam N. Wylie, Dec. 9, 1859, Brown County Recorder Office, Deed Book L-37; Deed from A. N. Wylie and wife to Milo I. Chase, Nov. 20, 1862, Brown County Recorder Office, Deed Book N-39; "Chase Brothers Piano," www.muskegonmuseum.org/_documents/Essays/CHASE.doc.

9. McPherson, *Battle Cry*, 220 and 215–16.

10. *History of Polk County, Iowa* (Des Moines: Union Historical Society, 1880), 802; Porter, *Annals of Polk County*, 602; Baker, *Affairs of the Party*, 52 and 125; Roseboom, *Civil War Era*, 202.

11. Roseboom, *Civil War Era*, 366; Baker, *Affairs of the Party*, 125; McPherson, *Battle Cry*, 232; Will Wylie identified as Eliza's distant relative: see Eliza Tomlinson to Will Tomlinson, Nov. 27, 1860, note on last page written by William Byers Tomlinson, Wylie-Tomlinson Letter Collection.

12. George H. Porter, *Ohio Politics during the Civil War Period*, Ph.D. diss. (New York: Columbia University, 1911; rprt. Kessinger Publishing, n.d.), 13–14.

13. "Croton oil," *Webster's New Twentieth Century Dictionary*, 2nd ed. (New York: Simon and Schuster, 1979); McPherson, *Battle Cry*, 215.

14. For the other essay by William Byers Tomlinson, see "Morgan's Raid by W. B. Tomlinson: A Former Resident of Ripley," in Eliese Bambach Stivers, *Ripley, Ohio*, 33.

15. Cayton, *Ohio*, 148; Roseboom, *Civil War Era*, 226 and 60.

16. Undated letter fragment signed by Eliza Wylie Tomlinson, Wylie-Tomlinson Letter Collection.

17. For a detailed description of the Wide Awakes and the designation of them by Southerners as "Black Republicans," see Scott Reynolds Nelson and Carol Sheriff, *A People at War: Civilians and Soldiers in America's Civil War, 1854–1877* (Oxford: Oxford Univ. Press, 2007), 42–44.

18. McPherson, *Battle Cry*, 232; Roseboom, *Civil War Era*, 371; *History of Brown County*, 440; E. B. Long with Barbara Long, *The Civil War Day by Day: An Almanac 1861–1865* (New York: Da Capo, 1971), 2, 8–9, 12–13, and 15.

6. COLLISION COURSES

1. Long, *Civil War Day by Day*, 20, 22, and 31; McPherson, *Battle Cry*, 260.

2. "The Presidential Progress: Mr. Lincoln at Cincinnati," *New York Times* Archive, www.nytimes.com/1861/02/18/news/presidential-progress; "The Lincoln Log for February 12, 1861," www.thelincolnlog.org/view/1861/2/12; Long, *Civil War Day by Day*, 36.

3. McPherson, *Battle Cry*, 262; Howe, *Historical Collections of Ohio*, 1: 286; Roseboom, *Civil War Era*, 191.

4. Henry Howe, *Historical Collections of Ohio*, 1:331 and 287; Long, *Civil War Day by Day*, 45–47.

5. Long, *Civil War Day by Day*, 50–51; Bruce M. Metzger and Roland E. Murphy, eds., *The New Oxford Annotated Bible, with the Apocryphal/Deuterocanonical Books,* New Revised Standard Version (New York: Oxford Univ. Press, 1991), Genesis 34:1–29.

6. "The Family History," Wylie-Tomlinson Letter Collection.

7. VOLUNTEER FRENZY

1. James Bissland, *Blood, Tears, and Glory: How Ohioans Won the Civil War* (Wilmington, Ohio: Orange Frazer Press, 2007), 27; McPherson, *Battle Cry*, 274; Roseboom, *Civil War Era*, 380; *Ripley Bee*, Apr. 18, 1861.

2. Robert S. Harper, *Ohio Handbook of the Civil War,* Ohio Civil War Centennial Commission (Columbus: Ohio Historical Society, 1961), 10; John M. Paver, *What I Saw from 1861 to 1864: Personal Recollections,* facsimile (Kessinger Publications, n.d.), 14 and 20.

3. "William Tomlinson," Q. M. Sgt., Regimental Descriptive Book, N.C.S. [Noncommissioned Service] and Band, Company I, 5th Reg't. Ohio Infantry, Apr. 20, 1861, Cincinnati, National Archives and Records Administration, Washington, D.C.; James M. McPherson, preface to *For Cause and Comrades: Why Men Fought in the Civil War* (New York: Oxford Univ. Press, 1997), viii–ix; "Will Tomlinson," Prvt. [Private], Company Descriptive Book, Company I, 5th Reg't Ohio Infantry, n.d., National Archives. An interesting footnote to Tomlinson's enlistment history is that eighty years later during World War II, a direct descendant of Tomlinson's, William Ross Donohoe (my father), subtracted two years from his age and lied about being married in order to enlist in officer's training and flight school in the U.S. Navy. He successfully completed both and became a pilot instructor at the U.S. Naval Airbase, Corpus Christi, Texas.

4. Will Tomlinson to Eliza Wylie Tomlinson, June 22, 1861, Wylie-Tomlinson Letter Collection; McPherson, *For Cause and Comrades*, 5-6.

5. Eliza Wylie Tomlinson to Will Tomlinson, Aug. 26 and Oct. 7, 1861; Eliza Wylie Tomlinson to Will Tomlinson, July 3, 1861, Wylie-Tomlinson Letter Collection; *Ripley Bee*, Apr. 25, 1861.

6. Christine Dee, ed., *Ohio's War: The Civil War in Documents*, The Civil War in the Great Interior (Athens: Ohio Univ. Press, 2006), 67; "Shoddy," Whitelaw Reid, June 6, 1861, in James G. Smart, ed., *A Radical View*, 1:14; Dee, *Ohio's War*, 67-68.

7. Long, *The Civil War Day by Day*, 74; Paver, *What I Saw*, 14-15; Howe, *Historical Collections*, 1:767; Bissland, *Blood, Tears, and Glory*, 73-74 and 99.

8. Rushed Waiting

1. Mark M. Boatner III, *The Civil War Dictionary* (1959; rprt., New York: Random House, 1991), 12; Hagedorn, *Beyond the River*, 43-50; *History of Brown County*, 423; Greg and Lisa Haitz, *Images of America: Brown County* (Charleston, S.C.: Arcadia Publishing, 2006), 47; Boatner, *The Civil War Dictionary*, 352-53.

2. Long, *Civil War Day by Day*, 84.

3. Paver, *What I Saw*, 15; Dee, ed., *Ohio's War*, 54; "Imperfect Pay-rolls," newspaper clipping enclosed with letter, Eliza Wylie Tomlinson to Will Tomlinson, Sept. 2, 1861, Wylie-Tomlinson Letter Collection.

4. *Ripley Bee*, July 4, 1861.

5. *Ripley Bee*, July 4, 1861; "The Hunters of Kentucky," *History Matters*, http://historymatters.gmu.edu/d/6522.

6. For details about the war in western Virginia in 1861, see Bissland, *Blood, Tears, and Glory*, 95-102; McPherson, *Battle Cry*, 297-304; Stan Cohen, *The Civil War in West Virginia: A Pictorial History*, rev. ed. (Charleston, W.V.: Pictorial Histories, 1999), 13-75; Long, *Civil War Day by Day*, 70-153; and Paver, *What I Saw*, 21-25. For a brief account of McClellan's military career, see Boatner, *The Civil War Dictionary*, 524-25.

7. McPherson, *Battle Cry*, 347; Long, *Civil War Day by Day*, 92; Paver, *What I Saw*, 22.

9. Into the Hills

1. H. E. Matheny, *Wood County, West Virginia in Civil War Times, with an Account of the Guerrilla Warfare in the Little Kanawha Valley* (Parkersburg, W.V.: Trans-Allegheny Books, Inc., 1987), 112-15; McPherson, *Battle Cry*, 301-2; Cohen, *Civil War in West Virginia*, 43.

2. Cohen, *Civil War in West Virginia*, 43; Bissland, *Blood, Tears, and Glory*, 96.

3. Hagedorn, *Beyond the River*, 7; *History of Brown County*, 339; "Lee in the Mountains," Whitelaw Reid, Aug. 19, 1861, in James G. Smart, ed., *A Radical*

View, 1:40–41; McPherson, *Battle Cry*, 294–95; for newspapers that Eliza sent to Tomlinson, see her letters to Tomlinson dated Sept. 9, Oct. 7 and 28, Nov. 4 and 28, 1861, Wylie-Tomlinson Letter Collection. The *Cincinnati Gazette* is specifically mentioned in the last two and would likely have been read first by Eliza since Tomlinson had worked there as a compositor.

4. Paver, *What I Saw*, 22–24; Betty Hornbeck, *Upshur Brothers of the Blue and the Gray* (Parsons, W.V.: McClain Printing Co., 1967), 3.

5. Cohen, *Civil War in West Virginia*, 39; "Carrick's Ford," Whitelaw Reid, July 14, 1861, in Smart, ed., *A Radical View*, 1:28–31; McPherson, *Battle Cry*, 302; Ambler, *Transportation in the Ohio Valley*, 371 and 373.

6. Lenette S. Taylor, *The Supply for Tomorrow Must Not Fail: The Civil War of Captain Simon Perkins, Jr., A Union Quartermaster* (Kent, Ohio: Kent State Univ. Press, 2004), 12–14.

7. "Preston King," *Biographical Directory of the United States Congress*, http://bioguide.congress.gov/scripts/biodisplay.pl?index=K000211; "Preston King," *Mr. Lincoln and New York*, www.mrlincolnandnewyork.org/inside.asp?ID=61&subjectID=3; "James W. Grimes," *Biographical Directory of the United States Congress*, http://bioguide.congress.gov/scripts/biodisplay.pl?index=G000475.

8. Richard O. Curry and F. Gerald Ham, eds., "The Bushwhackers' War: Insurgency and Counter-Insurgency in West Virginia," *Civil War History* 10 (Dec. 1964), 417–18; H. E. Matheny, *Wood County*, 46; Curry and Ham, "Bushwhackers' War," 418–19.

9. Matheny, *Wood County*, 47–49, 50–51, and 101.

10. Randall Osborne and Jeffrey C. Weaver, *Virginia State Rangers and State Line*, Virginia Regimental Historic Series (Lynchburg, Va.: H. W. Howard, Inc., 1994).

11. Charles Leib, *Nine Months in the Quartermaster's Department; or The Chances for Making a Million* (Cincinnati: Moore, Wilstach, Keys and Co., 1862), 88.

12. Curry and Ham, "Bushwhackers' War," 421; Leib, *Nine Months*, 85; Curry and Ham, "Bushwhackers' War," 421 and 428; Matheny, *Wood County*, 311.

13. For a list of some Ripley-area residents involved in the Underground Railroad, see Hagedorn, "Notes," *Beyond the River*, 286. An account of the mutilated Union corpse can be found in an excerpt from the diary of Captain James Stanley of the 36th Ohio, in Curry and Ham, "Bushwhackers' War," 423. The loneliness and dangers of being a scout or spy in the Civil War are explained in Darl L. Stephenson, *Headquarters in the Brush: Blazer's Independent Union Scouts* (Athens: Ohio Univ. Press, 2001), 12–14. For an incredible story of a conspiracy for good in World War II, see Philip Hallie, *Lest Innocent Blood Be Shed: The Story of the Village of Le Chambon and How Good Happened There* (1979; rprt., New York: HarperCollins, 1994). I believe that a similar conspiracy existed in mid-nineteenth-century Ripley. According to Hallie, "In an ethic of life and death, there is an ethic of refusal and there is an ethic of positive action." The ethic for positive action characterized many residents of Ripley.

10. Curse This Idleness

1. H. E. Matheny, *Major General Thomas Maley Harris and Roster of the 10th West Virginia Volunteer Infantry Regiment, 1861–1865* (Parsons, W.V.: McClain Printing, 1963), 16, 24, and 26; D. D. T. Farnsworth to Francis H. Pierpont, Sept. 28, 1861, West Virginia Archives and History, West Virginia Division of Culture and History, www.wvculture.org/history/wvmemory/militia/upshur04-06.html.

2. For insight into stereotypes common to Ohio humor, see Andrew R. L. Cayton, *Ohio: The History of a People*, 107–8 and 292.

3. McPherson, *Battle Cry*, 333–35; Hagedorn, *Beyond the River*, 268–69; Paver, *What I Saw*, 24.

4. Michael J. Varhola, *Everyday Life during the Civil War: A Guide for Writers, Students, and Historians* (Cincinnati: Writer's Digest Books, 1999), 107; Hagedorn, *Beyond the River*, 201; Eugene H. Roseboom, *Civil War Era*, 4:288–89; George W. Knepper, *Ohio and Its People*, 168.

5. McPherson, *Battle Cry*, 131; Roseboom, *Civil War Era*, 4:216; Cayton, *Ohio*, 69 and 148.

6. McPherson, *Battle Cry*, 132–34.

7. Roseboom, *Civil War Era*, 4:288–89; Cayton, *Ohio*, 145–46.

8. Bell Irvin Wiley, *The Life of Billy Yank: The Common Soldier of the Union*, updated ed., with foreword by James L. Robertson Jr. (Baton Rouge: Louisiana State Univ. Press, 1952; rprt. 2008), 249–50, 252, and 261.

9. Long, *Civil War Day by Day*, 116–17 and 122; Cohen, *Civil War in West Virginia*, 39 and 43; McPherson, *Battle Cry*, 321 and 361.

11. Mustering Men and Courage

1. Capt. Will Tomlinson's "Farnsworth Blues"—Muster Rolls/Rosters, West Virginia Adjutant Generals' Papers, Union Militia 1861–1865, Upshur County; D. D. T. Farnsworth to Governor Francis Pierpont, Sept. 28, 1861, West Virginia Adjutant Generals' Papers, Union Militia 1861–1865, Upshur County, www.wvculture.org/history/wvmemory/militia/upshur04-06.html; Matheny, *Thomas Maley Harris*, 25.

2. D. D. T. Farnsworth to Governor Francis Pierpont, Oct. 15, 1861, West Virginia Adjutant Generals' Papers, Union Militia 1861–1865, Upshur County; Will Tomlinson to Governor Francis Pierpont, Oct. 15, 1861, Capt. Will Tomlinson's "Farnsworth Blues," West Virginia Adjutant Generals' Papers, Union Militia 1861–1865, Upshur County, www.wv-culture.org/history/wvmemory/militia/upshur04-06.html.

3. Matheny, *Thomas Maley Harris*, 27. Details about Camp Pickens were taken from "Old Fort Pickens at Duffy, West Va.," a newspaper article written by J. Troy Pickens, June 15, 1963, from the collection of Shirley Boggs Webster of

Ireland, W.V. Pickens and Webster are both descendants of men in Tomlinson's company, the Farnsworth's Blues, 133rd Militia of the West Virginia State Troops, 1861. Webster and her husband also gave my husband and me a tour of the camp site and monument in June 2012.

4. Long, *Civil War Day by Day*, 120, 122, 124, and 133; "The Civil War Archive: Union Regimental Histories," Ohio, 59th Infantry, www.civilwararchive.com/Unreghst/unohinf4.htm#59th.

5. Dee, ed., *Ohio's War*, 67–68; McPherson, *Battle Cry*, 303.

6. Roy Bird Cook, *Lewis County in the Civil War, 1861–1865* (Charleston, W.V.: Jarret Printing, 1924), 81; Proclamation by Governor Francis H. Pierpont, Nov. 19, 1861, Virginia Governor Executive Papers: Francis Harrison Pierpont, Library of Virginia; Matheny, *Thomas Maley Harris*, 27–28; Anne T. Hunter to Will Tomlinson, July 21, 1852, Wylie-Tomlinson Letter Collection.

7. "Wendell Phillips," Bartleby.com, www.bartleby.com/73/1073.html.

12. MOUNTAIN DESPERADOES

1. Will Tomlinson to Thomas M. Harris, Nov. 3, 1861, Virginia Governor Executive Papers: Francis Harrison Pierpont, Library of Virginia.

2. Thomas M. Harris to Governor Francis H. Pierpont, Nov. 5, 1861, Virginia Governor Executive Papers: Francis Harrison Pierpont, Library of Virginia.

3. Harris to Pierpont, Nov. 5, 1861, Virginia Governor Executive Papers: Francis Harrison Pierpont, Library of Virginia.

4. Matheny, *Thomas Maley Harris*, 13–17 and 24.

5. Cohen, *Civil War in West Virginia*, 53; Joe Geiger Jr., "The Tragic Fate of Guyandotte," *West Virginia History*, 54 (1995), West Virginia Division of Culture and History, www.wvculture.org/history/journal_wvh/wvh54-2.

6. McPherson, *Battle Cry*, 362; Long, *Civil War Day by Day*, 129–32.

7. Matheny, *Thomas Maley Harris*, 224; Unsigned letter in the handwriting of Thomas M. Harris to Governor Francis H. Pierpont, Nov. 15, 1861, West Virginia Adjutant Generals' Papers, Union Militia 1861–1865, Upshur County, West Virginia State Archives, West Virginia Division of Culture and History.

8. Matheny, *Thomas Maley Harris*, 32–33; Betty Hornbeck, *Upshur Brothers*, 182; Matheny, *Thomas Maley Harris*, 34 and 227.

9. U.S. Service records, Discharge for William Tomlinson, Fifth Ohio, Nov. 1., 1861, signed by General Rosecrans, U.S. Archives; Unsigned letter in the handwriting of Thomas M. Harris to Governor Francis H. Pierpont, Nov. 15, 1861, West Virginia Adjutant Generals' Papers, Union Militia 1861–1865, Upshur County.

10. A synopsis of the incident has been drawn from the following: J. Holt to Governor Francis H. Pierpont, Nov. 18, 1861, Virginia Governor Executive Papers: Francis Harrison Pierpont, Library of Virginia; Thomas M. Harris to Francis H.

Pierpont, Nov. 22, 1861, Virginia Governor Executive Papers: Francis Harrison Pierpont, Library of Virginia; Cook, *Lewis County in the Civil War,* 81-83; and Matheny, *Thomas Maley Harris,* 28.

11. Proclamation by Governor F. H. Pierpont, Nov. 19, 1861, Virginia Governor Executive Papers: Francis Harrison Pierpont, Library of Virginia; Harris to Pierpont, Nov. 22, 1861, Virginia Governor Executive Papers: Francis Harrison Pierpont, Library of Virginia.

12. S. B. Phillips to Governor F. H. Pierpont, Nov. 29, 1861, Virginia Governor Executive Papers: Francis Harrison Pierpont, Library of Virginia; J. Holt to Governor Francis Pierpont, Nov. 18, 1861, Virginia Governor Executive Papers: Francis Harrison Pierpont, Library of Virginia; Allen Simpson to Governor F. H. Pierpont, Dec. 2, 1861, Virginia Governor Executive Papers: Francis Harrison Pierpont, Library of Virginia; Cook, *Lewis County in the Civil War,* 83; Holt to Pierpont, Nov. 18, 1861, Virginia Governor Executive Papers: Francis Harrison Pierpont, Library of Virginia.

13. Daniel E. Sutherland, *A Savage Conflict: The Decisive Role of Guerillas in the American Civil War* (Chapel Hill: Univ. of North Carolina Press, 2009), 86; Cook, *Lewis County in the Civil War,* 81; Holt to Pierpont, Nov. 18, 1861, Virginia Governor Executive Papers: Francis Harrison Pierpont, Library of Virginia; Harris to Pierpont, Nov. 22, 1861, Virginia Governor Executive Papers: Francis Harrison Pierpont, Library of Virginia; Cook, *Lewis County in the Civil War,* 81.

14. Matheny, *Thomas Maley Harris,* 29; Cook, *Lewis County in the Civil War,* 85-86.

15. Matheny, *Thomas Maley Harris,* 204 and 190-99.

16. Williams and Herold, *Affectionately Yours,* 2:150-51.

17. Will Tomlinson to Governor Francis Pierpont, Nov. 18, 1861, Virginia Governor Executive Papers: Francis Harrison Pierpont, Library of Virginia.

13. Disarmed

1. Obituary for Will Tomlinson, *Ripley Bee,* Dec. 3, 1863.

2. Gary W. Gallagher, *The Union War* (Cambridge, Mass.: Harvard Univ. Press, 2011), 2, and 44-47; Porter, *Ohio Politics,* 18-19; Engs and Brooks, introduction, *Their Patriotic Duty,* xvii-xx; W. Sherman Jackson, "Emancipation, Negrophobia and Civil War Politics in Ohio, 1863-1865," *The Journal of Negro History,* 65: 3 (Summer 1980), 250, www.jstor.org/stable/2717098; Porter, *Ohio Politics,* 14.

3. See entries for "Cupping and Blistering" and "Pneumonia," Glenna R. Schroeder-Lein, *The Encyclopedia of Civil War Medicine* (Armonk, N.Y.: M. E. Sharpe, 2008), 75-76 and 247-48; Thomas J. Marrie, *Community Acquired Pneumonia* (New York: Kluwer Academic/Plenum Publishers, 2001), 5; Janet King, "Civil War Medicine," *Vermont in the Civil War,* http://vermontcivilwar.org/medic/medicine2.php.

4. *Ripley Bee,* Apr. 3, 1862; Charles R. Wilson, "Cincinnati's Reputation During the Civil War," *The Journal Southern History,* 2:4 (Nov. 1936), 468 and 475, www.jstor.org/stable/2192033.

5. "Fifth Ohio Infantry, Hamilton County, Ohio," http://files.uswarchives.net/oh/hamilton/history/ford/pg85.txt; Long, *Civil War Day by Day,* 188; McPherson, *Battle Cry,* 425 and 304–5; "The Tom Thumb Archive," The Lost Museum, http://chnm.gmu.edu/lostmuseum/searchlm.php?function=find&exhibit=thumb&browse=thumb.

6. Long, *Civil War Day by Day,* 183; McPherson, *Battle Cry,* 324 and 348–49; Boatner, *Civil War Dictionary,* 792.

7. Nikki Taylor, *Frontiers of Freedom: Cincinnati's Black Community, 1802–1868* (Athens: Ohio Univ. Press, 2005), note 82, 287, and 50, 111, 117, and 197–98.

14. Hatching New Hope

1. Frederick H. Dyer, *A Compendium of the War of the Rebellion,* Part 3, "The Civil War Archive: Regimental Index," www.civilwararchive.com/Unreghst/unohinf1.htm#5th3yr; "Fifth Ohio Volunteer Infantry," Cincinnati Civil War Round Table, www.cincinnaticwrt.org/data/ohio%20in%20the%20war/units/5th_OVI.html; Long, *Civil War Day by Day,* 187–88; Paver, *What I Saw,* 14; Matheny, *Thomas Maley Harris,* 26.

2. Long, *Civil War Day by Day,* 195–97; Dee, ed., *Ohio's War,* 76–77; Frank L. Klement, *The Limits of Dissent: Clement L. Vallandigham and The Civil War,* with a preface by Steven K. Rogstad (Lexington: Univ. Press of Kentucky, 1970; rprt., New York: Fordham Univ. Press, 1998), 2, 69, and 106.

3. Long, *Civil War Day by Day,* 219–20; McPherson, *Battle Cry,* 462–71; Long, *Civil War Day by Day,* 236.

4. Long, *Civil War Day by Day,* 178 and 182; McPherson, *Battle Cry,* 377–78.

5. Boatner, *Civil War Dictionary,* 497–98; Long, *Civil War Day by Day,* 220.

6. Andrew S. Coopersmith, *Fighting Words: An Illustrated History of Newspaper Accounts of the Civil War* (New York: New Press, 2004), 95–97.

7. Long, *Civil War Day By Day,* 235–36; *New York Times Archive,* July 4, 1862, www.nytimes.com/1862/07/04/news/gen-m-clellan-great-battle-continued-through-seven-days-immense-losses-both.html.

15. Attacks from Within and Without

1. Bulla and Borchard, *Journalism in the Civil War Era,* 159 and 167; McPherson, *Battle Cry,* 464–71.

2. Nikki Taylor, *Frontiers of Freedom,* 197–98; Long, *Civil War Day by Day,* 237–240; Roseboom, *Civil War Era,* 397.

3. Long, *Civil War Day by Day,* 242.

4. Stivers, *Ripley, Ohio,* 33; Long, *Civil War Day by Day,* 243; *Ripley Bee,* July 31, 1862.

5. *Dubuque (Iowa) Herald,* Dec. 22, 1863.

6. Dee, ed., *Ohio's War,* 94–95; McPherson, *Battle Cry,* 515–18; Long, *Civil War Day by Day,* 261.

1. Roseboom, *Civil War Era*, 398–99; Taylor, *Frontiers of Freedom*, 181–83; Dee, ed., *Ohio's War*, 85–87; Howe, *Historical Collections of Ohio*, 1:772–77.

2. Greg and Lisa Haitz, *Brown County*, 43; Harper, *Ohio Handbook of the Civil War*, 24–26; Ohio Adjutant General's Department, Roll of Ohio Army of Squirrel Hunters in Service September 1862, Ohio Historical Society, GR3986, 455; Bissland, *Blood, Tears, and Glory*, 239–40.

3. James M. McPherson, *Crossroads of Freedom: Antietam*, Pivotal Moments in American History (Oxford: Oxford Univ. Press, 2002), 3; John W. Schildt, *Union Regiments at Antietam*, 2nd ed. (Sharpsburg, Md.: Antietam Publications, 2010), 98 and 142.

4. McPherson, *Crossroads of Freedom*, 155 and 139; Long, *Civil War Day by Day*, 270; McPherson, *Crossroads of Freedom*, 141; Porter, *Ohio Politics*, 143.

5. Roseboom, *Civil War Era*, 401–3; Long, *Civil War Day by Day*, 270–71; Dee, ed., *Ohio's War*, 129–30.

6. Roseboom, *Civil War Era*, 399–402.

7. Long, *Civil War Day by Day*, 305 and 285; Bissland, *Blood, Tears, and Glory*, 236 and 258.

17. NURSING THE WOUNDED

1. McPherson, *Battle Cry*, 580 and 582; Long, *Civil War Day by Day*, 311.

2. Joseph Glatthaar, *The Civil War's Black Soldiers*, National Park Civil War Series (No place given: Eastern National Park and Monument Association, 2007), 7 and 12–14; Eric Foner, *Reconstruction: America's Unfinished Revolution, 1863–1877*, The New American Series, edited by Henry Steele Commager and Richard B. Morris (1988; New York: HarperCollins, 2002), First Perennial Classics edition, 7–8.

3. For a discussion of the historical significance of the Emancipation Proclamation, see "Historians' Forum: The Emancipation Proclamation," *Civil War History*, 59:1 (Mar. 2013), 7–29.

4. Roseboom, *Civil War Era*, 408–10; Harper, *Ohio Press in the Civil War*, 13.

5. Harper, *Ohio Press in the Civil War*, 4–6; Roseboom, *Civil War Era*, 411; Porter, *Ohio Politics*, 160–61.

6. Porter, *Ohio Politics*, 160–65.

7. Porter, *Ohio Politics*, 165; Harper, *Ohio Press in the Civil War*, 20–22.

8. Will Tomlinson to S. I. Tomlinson, May 21, 1863, sold on eBay, Mar. 4, 2013, and transcribed by Patricia A. Donohoe from copy posted on eBay; *Ripley Bee*, May 14, 1863; Will Tomlinson to S. I. Tomlinson, May 21, 1863.

9. Will Tomlinson to S. I. Tomlinson, May 21, 1863; Long, *Civil War Day by Day*, 348; McPherson, *Battle Cry*, 645.

10. Will Tomlinson to S. I. Tomlinson, May 21, 1863.

11. Versalle F. Washington, *Eagles on Their Buttons: A Black Infantry Regiment in the Civil War* (Columbia: Univ. of Missouri Press, 1999), 9, 12-13, and 81.

12. Washington, *Eagles on Their Buttons,* 17-18; Engs and Brooks, *Patriotic Duty,* 138-43.

13. Washington, *Eagles on Their Buttons,* 15 and 17-20.

18. CLOSE TO HOME

1. Long, *Civil War Day by Day,* 373-74, 361, 369, and 378-79; *Ripley Bee,* May 28, 1863; Obituary for Selina Kendall Norris, widow of William Norris, *Ripley Bee,* Apr. 4, 1888.

2. Long, *Civil War Day by Day,* 367 and 381-83; Harper, *Ohio Handbook,* 27; *Ripley Bee,* Dec. 25, 1862, and Jan. 1, 1863; Greg and Lisa Haitz, *Brown County,* 42.

3. Harper, *Ohio Handbook,* 27-30; Dee Alexander Brown, *Morgan's Raiders* (New York: Konecky and Konecky, 1959), 210.

4. Sutherland, *Savage Conflict,* 76-79; Brown, *Morgan's Raiders,* 69, 109, 174, 31, and 34; Porter, *Annals of Polk County,* 175, 573, and 602-3; Obituary for Will Tomlinson, *Ripley Bee,* Dec. 3, 1863; Obituary for Eliza Tomlinson, *Maysville Bulletin,* July 16, 1885; Joseph Patterson Smith, ed., *History of the Republican Party in Ohio,* 2 vols. (Chicago: Lewis Publishing Co., 1898), 1:796; B. Collin to Capt. Tomlinson, Mountain Marksmen, Oct. 16, 1861, Wylie-Tomlinson Letter Collection.

5. Sutherland, *Savage Conflict,* 76-79; *Burlington Weekly Hawkeye and Telegraph,* Sept. 17, 1859; *Davenport Daily Gazette,* May 7, 1860; Dixon, *Valley and the Shadow,* 3; Porter, *Annals of Polk County,* 603; Unsigned letter in the handwriting of Thomas M. Harris to Governor Francis H. Pierpont, Nov. 15, 1861, West Virginia Adjutant Generals' Papers, Union Militia 1861-1865, Upshur County, West Virgina State Archives, West Virginia Division of Culture and History; Eliza Tomlinson to Will Tomlinson, Sept. 9, 1861, Wylie-Tomlinson Letter Collection; *Freedom's Casket,* June 15, 1844.

6. Undated letter fragment attributed to Will Tomlinson in the late summer of 1863, Wylie-Tomlinson Letter Collection.

19. PARTISAN FEVER

1. Long, *Civil War Day by Day,* 412; McPherson, *Battle Cry,* 684-88; *History of Brown County,* 424; *Loyal Scout,* Oct. 10, 1963; Roseboom, *Civil War Era,* 414 and 420.

2. Klement, *Limits of Dissent,* 242-44; Roseboom, *Civil War Era,* 420; McPherson, *Battle Cry,* 684-88.

3. *Loyal Scout,* Oct. 10, 1863.

4. *Loyal Scout,* Oct. 10, 1863.

5. Bissland, *Blood, Tears, and Glory,* 319; Roseboom, *Civil War Era,* 421–22; Porter, *Ohio Politics,* 183; *History of Brown County,* 440; Obituary for Will Tomlinson, *Ripley Bee,* Dec. 3, 1863. See the *Loyal Scout,* Oct. 10, 1863, for articles berating Copperhead Democrats, including some reprinted from the *Ripley Bee.*

6. *Loyal Scout,* Oct. 10, 1863.

20. FREEDOM'S CASKET

1. *Ripley Bee,* Dec. 3, 1863.

2. *Ripley Bee,* Dec. 3, 1863.

3. *Cincinnati Gazette,* Nov. 30 and Dec. 3, 1863.

4. *Dubuque Herald,* Dec. 12, 1863; *Maysville (Ky.) Dollar Weekly Bulletin,* Dec. 10, 1863; Gerard Fowke, "The Mitchells of Charleston Bottom, Kentucky," a handwritten family history, Maysville Museum Center.

5. *Dubuque Daily Times,* Dec. 16, 1863; "Mitchell's of Kentucky," reprinted from the *Maysville (Ky.) Eagle,* Mar. 26, 1879, Maysville Museum Center; Nelson Wiley Evans and Emmons B. Stivers, *A History of Adams County, Ohio* (E. B. Stivers, 1900), 370.

6. McPherson, *For Cause and Comrades,* 120–26 and 144–45; *Loyal Scout,* Oct. 10, 1863.

7. Smith, ed., *History of the Republican Party in Ohio,* 1:796.

8. Frank L. Klement, *Dark Lanterns: Secret Political Societies, Conspiracies, and Treason Trials in the Civil War* (Baton Rouge: Louisiana State Univ. Press, 1984), 1–6 and 33; Harper, *The Ohio Press during the Civil* War, 17–18; Porter, *Ohio Politics,* 182 and 186–87.

9. Handwritten notation by R. Eva Byers beside entry for "Eliza Wylie" in Andrew S. Eagleson, "Byers Family Record," Washington, Pa., 1908, Doc. #4778781/ A017975/M563918, Daughters of the American Revolution.

10. Smith, ed., *History of the Republican Party in Ohio,* 1:796; *Ripley Bee,* Dec. 3, 1863; "The Family History," Wylie-Tomlinson Letter Collection; William Byers Tomlinson, "Old Newspaper Man," self-penned obituary for *Ripely Bee,* June 17, 1914, Wylie-Tomlinson Letter Collection.

11. Maggie Byers to Eliza Tomlinson, Nov. 30, 1863, Wylie-Tomlinson Letter Collection.

12. Anne T. Hunter to Will Tomlinson, July 21, 1852; Anne T. Hunter to Will Tomlinson, Aug. 2, 1852, Wylie-Tomlinson Letter Collection.

13. Fowke, "The Mitchells of Charleston Bottom, Kentucky," Maysville Museum Center.

14. "The Family History," Wylie-Tomlinson Letter Collection; *Ripley Bee and Times,* July 8, 1885.

15. *Maysville Bulletin,* July 16, 1885.

1. Will Tomlinson to Eliza Wylie Tomlinson, July 15, 1862, Wylie-Tomlinson Letter Collection. William Byers Tomlinson died on December 31, 1917, so his deathbed letter to his children was probably written in December 1917.

2. See correspondence between Sarah Isabella (Belle) Tomlinson and Alonzo Frescoln (Fritz) Smith, 1879–1870, and "The Family History," Wylie-Tomlinson Letter Collection.

3. "William Byers Tomlinson," Battery Muster-in and Descriptive Roll, Second Independent Battery, Ohio National Guard, Ohio (Light) Artillery (60 Days, 1864), Dec. 19, 1864, U.S. Archives.

4. See letters by William Byers Tomlinson from 1864 through 1872, Wylie-Tomlinson Letter Collection; Smith, ed., *Republican Party in Ohio,* 1:796; *History of Brown County,* 424–25; *Ripley (Ohio) Bee,* Apr. 29, 1880.

5. Smith, ed., *Republican Party in Ohio,* 1:796; Obituary for W. B. Tomlinson, *Ironton (Ohio) Register,* Jan. 2, 1918.

6. Obituary for Alice Tomlinson, *Ironton (Ohio) Register,* Dec. 11, 1884; "The Family History," Wylie-Tomlinson Letter Collection; Marriage Record for Will B. Tomlinson and Carrie Thomas, Dec. 22, 1885, Lawrence County, Ohio, Probate Court, #204; Marriage Record for Roscoe N. Donohoe and Florence A. Tomlinson, Aug. 27, 1913, Scioto County, Ohio, Probate Court, #141; Obituary for Mrs. Ross Donohoe, *Ironton (Ohio) Tribune,* Aug. 20, 1952.

Selected References

PRIMARY SOURCE MATERIALS

Biograpical Directory of the United States Congress, http://bioguide.congress.gov.

Bishop's Transcripts for Camerton, 1663–1870. International Genealogical Index for Great Britain. Vol. 3, www.familysearch.org.

Book of Confessions: The Constitution of the Presbyterian Church (U.S.A.). Study edition. Louisville, Ky.: Office of the General Assembly, 1996.

Book of Order: The Constitution of the Presbyterian Church (U.S.A.). Louisville, Ky.: Office of the General Assembly, 2005.

Brown County Genealogy Society, Georgetown, Ohio

Brown County Probate Court Records, Georgetown, Ohio

Coggeshall, William T. *The Signs of the Times: A History of the Spirit-Rappings, in Cincinnati and Other Places.* Cincinnati: William T. Coggeshall: 1851.

Eagleson, Andrew S. "Byers Family Record." Washington, Pa., 1908. Doc. #4778781/A017975/M563918, Daughters of the American Revolution Archives, Washington, D.C.

Fowke, Gerard. "The Mitchells of Charleston Bottom, Mason County, Kentucky." On file at the Mason County Museum Center, Maysville, Ky.

"The Family History." A genealogy of the Tomlinson, Wylie, and Byers families. Author's private collection.

Lawrence County Probate Court Records, Ironton, Ohio.

Map of Ripley, Ohio. W. F. Wylie, 1850. Thomas F. and Jane Zachman Collection, Ripley, Ohio.

National Archives and Records Administration, Washington, D.C.

Ohio Adjutant General's Department, Roll of Ohio Army of Squirrel Hunters in Service September 1862, Ohio Historical Society, GR3986, 455.

Tomlinson, Will. "The Poison Cup," in *Columbian Magazine* (Oct. 1844), 184–86.

Virginia Governor Executive Papers: Francis Harrison Pierpont, Library of Virginia, Richmond.

West Virginia Adjutant Generals' Papers: Union Militia 1861–1865, West Virginia State Archives, West Virginia Division of Culture and History, Charleston, W.V.

Wylie-Tomlinson Family Letters and Documents. Author's private collection.

NEWSPAPERS

Burlington (Iowa) Weekly Hawk Eye and Telegraph
Cincinnati (Ohio) Gazette
Davenport (Iowa) Daily Gazette
Democratic Standard, Georgetown, Ohio
Dubuque (Iowa) Herald
Dubuque (Iowa) Times
Freedom's Casket, Ripley, Ohio
Hickory Sprout, Piketon, Ohio
Iowa State Journal, Des Moines, Iowa
Ironton (Ohio) Register
Ironton (Ohio) Tribune
Loyal Scout, Ripley, Ohio
Maysville (Ky.) Bulletin
Maysville (Ky.) Eagle
New York Times Archive
Ripley (Ohio) Bee
Ripley (Ohio) Herald
St. Lawrence Republican, Ogdensburg, N.Y.
West Union (Ohio) People's Defender

SECONDARY SOURCE MATERIALS

Ambler, Charles Henry. A History of Transportation in the Ohio Valley. Westport, Conn.: Greenwood Press, 1970. First printing by Arthur H. Clark Company, 1931.

Baily, Thomas A. *Democrats vs. Republicans: The Continuing Clash.* New York: Meredith Press, 1968.

Baker, Alan. *The Civil War in America.* Garden City, N.Y.: Doubleday and Company, Inc., 1961.

Baker, Jean H. *Affairs of Party: The Political Culture of Northern Democrats in the Mid-Nineteenth Century.* Ithaca, N.Y.: Cornell Univ. Press, 1983.

Baldasty, Gerald J. *The Commercialism of News in the Nineteenth Century.* Madison: Univ. of Wisconsin Press, 1992.

Bissland, James. *Blood, Tears, and Glory: How Ohioans Won the Civil War.* Wilmington, Ohio: Orange Frazer Press, 2007.

Boatner, Mark M., III. *The Civil War Dictionary.* New York: Random House, 1959.

Boggs, John Andrew. "Boggs: The Greenbrier Line Since 1754," http://zert.info/Documents/Greenbrier_Line.pdf.

Borchard, Gregory A. "From Pink Lemonade to Salt River: Horace Greeley's Utopia and the Death of the Whig Party," in *Journalism History,* 32:1 (Spring 2006), 22–33.

Bordewich, Fergus M. *Bound for Canaan: The Epic Story of the Underground Railroad, America's First Civil Rights Movement.* New York: HarperCollins, 2005.

Brebner, John Bartlet. *North Atlantic Triangle: The Interplay of Canada, the United States and Great Britain.* The Relations of Canada and the United States Series prepared under the direction of the Carnegie Endowment for International Peace, Division of Economics and History. James T. Shotwell, director. New Haven, Conn.: Yale Univ. Press, 1945.

Brown, Dee Alexander. *Morgan's Raiders.* New York: Konecky and Konecky, 1959.

Brown, Jeffrey P., and Andrew R. L. Cayton. *The Pursuit of Public Power: Political Culture in Ohio, 1787–1861.* Kent, Ohio: Kent State Univ. Press, 1994.

Buescher, John B. *The Other Side of Salvation: Spiritualism and the Nineteenth-Century Religious Experience.* Boston: Skinner House Books, 2004.

Bulla, David W., and Gregory A. Borchard. *Journalism in the Civil War Era.* New York: Peter Lang, 2010.

Caton, Bruce. *The Civil War.* New York: Houghton Mifflin, 2004.

Cayton, Andrew R. L. *Ohio: The History of a People.* Columbus: Ohio State Univ. Press, 2002.

Chaddock, Robert E. *Ohio Before 1850: A Study of the Early Influence of Pennsylvania and Southern Populations in Ohio.* Studies in History, Economics and Public Law. Vol. 31, no. 2. New York: AMS Press, Inc., 1967.

"Chase Brothers Piano," *www.muskegonmuseum.org;_documents/Essays/CHASE.doc.*

"The Civil War Archive: Union Regimental Histories." Ohio 59th Infantry, www.civilwararchive.com/Unreghst/unohnf4.htm#59th.

Clark, Peter H. *The Black Brigade of Cincinnati: Report of Its Labors and a Muster Roll of Its Members; Together with Various Orders, Speeches, Etc., Relating to It.* Cincinnati: Joseph H. Boyd, 1864. Reprint, New York: Arno Press and The New York Times, 1969.

Clarke, Adam. *Memoirs of the Wesley Family.* 2nd rev. ed. Edited by George Peck. New York: Lane and Tippett, 1848.

Cohen, Stan. *The Civil War in West Virginia: A Pictorial History.* Rev. ed. Charleston, W.V.: Pictorial Histories Publishing, 1999.

Commemorative Biographical Record of Washington County, Pennsylvania. Chicago: J. H. Beers, 1893.

Cook, Roy Bird. *Lewis County in the Civil War, 1861–1865*. Originally published in 1924. Transcribed and indexed by Cindy E. Etheir-Kostka for the Hacker's Creek Pioneer Descendants, Horner, W.V., 2000.

Coopersmith, Andrew S. *Fighting Words: An Illustrated History of Newspaper Accounts of the Civil War*. New York: The New Press, 2004.

Cowan, Helen I. *British Emigration to British North America: The First Hundred Years*. Rev. ed. Toronto: Univ. of Toronto Press, 1961.

Crumrine, Boyd. *History of Washington County, Pennsylvania, with Biographical Sketches of Many of Its Pioneers and Prominent Men*. Philadelphia: L. H. Everts & Co., 1882.

Curry, Richard O., and F. Gerald Ham, eds. "The Bushwhackers' War: Insurgency and Counter-Insurgency in West Virginia." *Civil War History* 10 (Dec. 1964), 417–18.

Dary, David. *Red Blood and Black Ink: Journalism in the Old West*. New York: Alfred A. Knopf, 1998.

Davis, William C. *Fighting Men of the Civil War: Rebels and Yankees*. London: Chrysalis Books, 1989. Reprint, 2004.

Dee, Christine, ed. *Ohio's War: The Civil War in Documents*. The Civil War in the Great Interior. Athens: Ohio Univ. Press, 2006.

Dixon, J. M. *Centennial History of Polk County, Iowa*. Des Moines, Iowa: State Register, 1876.

———. *The Valley and the Shadow: Experiences of a Blind Ex-Editor*. New York: Russell Brothers, 1868.

Douglas, George H. *The Golden Age of the Newspaper*. Westport, Conn.: Greenwood Press, 1999.

Dyer, Frederick H. Dyer. *A Compendium of the War of the Rebellion*. Part 3. "The Civil War Archive: Regimental Index," www.civilwararchive.com/Unreghst/unohinf1.htm#5th3yr.

Engs, Robert F., and Corey M. Brooks, eds. *Their Patriotic Duty: The Civil War Letters of the Evans Family of Brown County, Ohio*. New York: Fordham Univ. Press, 2007.

Evans, Nelson W., and Emmons B. Stivers. *A History of Adams County, Ohio, from Its Earliest Settlement to the Present Time*. West Union, Ohio: E. B. Stivers, 1900.

Faust, Drew Gilpin. *This Republic of Suffering: Death and the American Civil War*. New York: Alfred A. Knopf, 2008.

"Fifth Ohio Infantry, Hamilton County, Ohio," http://files.uswarchives.ent/oh/hamilton/history/ford/pg85.txt.

"Fifth Ohio Volunteer Infantry." Cincinnati Civil War Round Table, www.cincinnaticwrt.org/data/ohio%20in%20th%20war/units/5th_OVI.html.

Fischer, David Hackett. *Albion's Seed: Four British Folkways in America*. New York: Oxford Univ. Press, 1989.

Foner, Eric. *Reconstruction: America's Unfinished Revolution, 1863–1877*. The New American Series, edited by Henry Steele Commager and Richard B. Morris. Reprint, New York: HarperCollins, 2002. Page references are to First Perennial Classics edition.

Frohman, Charles. E. *Rebels on Lake Erie*. Columbus: Ohio Historical Society, 1965.

Gallagher, Gary W. *The Union War*. Cambridge, Mass.: Harvard University Press, 2011.

Gara, Larry. *The Liberty Line: The Legend of the Underground Railroad*. Lexington: Univ. of Kentucky Press, 1961.

Geiger, Joe, Jr. "The Tragic Fate of Guyandotte." *West Virginia History* 54 (1995), West Virginia Division of Culture and History, www.wvculture.org/history/journal_wvh/wvh54-2.

Glatthaar, Joseph. *The Civil War's Black Soldiers*. National Park Civil War Series. Eastern National, 2007.

Glossop, Robert. "A Place in Time: Families, Family Matters, and Why They Matter," The Glossop Lawson Lecture Series, The Vanier Institute of the Family, The Lawson Foundation (Oct. 18, 2007), www.vifamily.ca/media/node/345/attachments/GlossopLawsonpubliclecture.pdf.

Greene, Wilson A., and Gary W. Gallagher. *Civil War: National Geographic Guide to the National Battlefield Parks*. Washington, D.C.: National Geographic Society, 1992.

Greer, Allan. "Rebellion of 1837-38." In *The Oxford Companion to Canadian History*, edited by Gerald Hallowell, 530-31. Don Mills, Ontario: Oxford Univ. Press Canada, 2004.

Griffin, Patrick. *The People with No Name: Ireland's Ulster Scots, America's Scots Irish, and the Creation of a British Atlantic World, 1689-1764*. Princeton: Princeton Univ. Press, 2001.

Hagedorn, Ann. *Beyond the River: The Untold Story of the Heroes of the Underground Railroad*. New York: Simon & Schuster, 2002.

Haitz, Greg and Lisa. *Images of America: Brown County*. Charleston, S.C.: Arcadia Publishing, 2006.

Hallie, Phillip. *Lest Innocent Blood Be Shed: The Story of the Village of Le Chambon and How Good Happened There*. New York: HarperCollins, 1994.

Harper, Robert S. *Ohio Handbook of the Civil War*. Ohio Civil War Centennial Commission. Columbus: Ohio Historical Society, 1961.

———. *The Ohio Press in the Civil War*. Ohio Civil War Centennial Commission. Columbus: Ohio State Univ. Press for the Ohio Historical Society, n.d.

Harrold, Stanley. *Border War: Fighting over Slavery before the Civil War*. Chapel Hill: Univ. of North Carolina Press, 2010.

Hendrick, George and Willene, eds. *Fleeing for Freedom: Stories of the Underground Railroad, as Told by Levi Coffin and William Still*. Chicago: Ivan R. Dee, 2004.

"Historians' Forum: The Emancipation Proclamation." *Civil War History* 59:1 (Mar. 2013), 7-29.

History of Brown County, Ohio. Chicago: W. H. Beers Company, 1883.

History of Cincinnati and Hamilton County, Ohio: Their Past and Present. Cincinnati: S. B. Nelson and Company, 1894.

History of Polk County, Iowa. Des Moines: Union Historical Society, 1880.

"Hold on," www.negrospirituals.com/news-song/hold_on.htm.

Holman, C. Hugh. *A Handbook to Literature*. 4th edition. Indianapolis: Bobbs-Merrill Educational Publishing, 1981.

Hooper, Osman Castle. *History of Ohio Journalism, 1793-1933*. Series in American Studies. Ed. Joseph J. Kwiat. Columbus, Ohio: Spahr and Glenn Company, 1933. First reprinting, New York: Johnson Reprint Corporation, 1969.

Hornbeck, Betty. *Upshur Brothers of the Blue and the Gray*. Parsons, W.V.: McClain Printing, 1967.

Howe, David Walker. *What Hath God Wrought: The Transformation of America, 1815-1848*. The Oxford History of the United States. David M. Kennedy, ed. New York: Oxford Univ. Press, 2007.

Howe, Henry. *Historical Collections of Ohio: An Encyclopedia of the State*. The Ohio Centennial Edition. 2 vols. Cincinnati: The State of Ohio, 1907.

Hughes, Mark. *The New Civil War Handbook: Facts and Photos for Readers of All Ages*. New York: Savas Beatie, 2009.

"The Hunters of Kentucky." *History Matters*, http://historymatters.gmu.edu/d.6522.

"Iowa Legislature," www.legis.iowa.gov/Legislators/legislator.aspx?GA=12&PID=5189.

"Iowa Rail History." Office of Rail Transportation, www.iowadot.gov/iowarail/history/history/htm.

Jackson, W. Sherman. "Emancipation, Negrophobia and Civil War Politics in Ohio, 1863-1865." *Journal of Negro History* 65:3 (Summer 1980), www.jstor.org/stable/2717098.

Josyph, Peter, ed. *The Wounded River: The Civil War Letters of John Vance Lauderdale, M.D.* East Lansing: Michigan State Univ. Press, 1993.

Karolevitz, Robert F. *From Quill to Computer: The Story of American's Community Newspaper*. National Newspaper Foundation, 1985.

———. *Newspapering in the Old West: A Pictorial History of Journalism and Printing on the Frontier*. New York: Bonanza Books, 1965.

"The King James Bible." In *ICONS: A Portrait of England*, www.icons.org.uk/theicons/collection/king-james-bible/features/iconarticle.2005-12-26.6328188026.

King, Janet. "Civil War Medicine." In *Vermont in the Civil War*, http://vermontcivilwar.org/medic/medicine2.php.

Klement, Frank L. *Dark Lanterns: Secret Political Societies, Conspiracies, and Treason in the Civil War*. Baton Rouge: Louisiana State Univ. Press, 1984.

———. *The Limits of Dissent: Clement L. Vallandigham and The Civil War*. New York: Fordham Univ. Press, 1998.

Knepper, George W. *Ohio and Its People*. 3rd ed. Kent, Ohio: Kent State Univ. Press, 2003.

Leib, Charles. *Nine Months in the Quartermaster's Department; or The Chances for Making a Million*. Cincinnati: Moore, Wilstach, Keys, and Company, 1862.

Leith, John H. *An Introduction to the Reformed Tradition: A Way of Being the Christian Community*. Revised edition. Atlanta: John Knox Press, 1981.

Lendt, David L. *Demise of the Democracy: The Copperhead Press in Iowa, 1856-1870*. Ames: Iowa State Univ. Press, 1973.

Leyburn, James G. *The Scotch Irish: A Social History*. Chapel Hill: Univ. of North Carolina Press, 1962.

"The Lincoln Log for February 12, 1861," www.thelincolnlog.org/view/1861/2/12.

Long, E. B., with Barbara Long. *The Civil War Day by Day: An Almanac 1861–1865*. Foreword by Bruce Catton. New York: Da Capo, 1971.

Lystra, Karen. *Searching the Heart: Women, Men, and Romantic Love in Nineteenth-Century America*. New York: Oxford Univ. Press, 1989.

Mark, Faye, and Bonnie Williams, eds. *The Life and Diaries of Theophilus A. Wylie, 1810–1895*. Bloomington: Indiana Univ. Office of Publications, n.d.

Marrie, Thomas J. *Community Acquired Pneumonia*. New York: Kluwer Academic/Plenum Publishers, 2001.

Matheny, H. E. *Major General Thomas Maley Harris and Roster of the 10th West Virginia Volunteer Infantry Regiment, 1861–1865*. Parsons, W.V.: McClain Printing, 1963. Second printing, 1996.

———. *Wood County, West Virginia, in Civil War Times, with an Account of the Guerrilla Warfare in the Little Kanawha Valley*. Parkersburg, W.V.: Trans-Allegheny Books, 1987.

McKim, Donald K. *Introducing the Reformed Faith: Biblical Revelation, Christian Tradition, Contemporary Significance*. Louisville, Ky.: Westminster John Knox Press, 2001.

McKivigan, John R. *The War Against Proslavery Religion: Abolitionism and the Northern Churches, 1830–1865*. Ithaca, N.Y.: Cornell Univ. Press, 1984.

McPherson, James M. *Battle Cry for Freedom: The Civil War Era*. New York: Ballantine, 1989. First published 1988, Oxford University Press.

———. *Crossroads of Freedom: Antietam*. Pivotal Moments in American History. Oxford: Oxford Univ. Press, 2002.

———. *For Cause and Comrades: Why Men Fought in the Civil War*. New York: Oxford Univ. Press, 1997.

———. *This Mighty Scourge: Perspectives on the Civil War*. New York: Oxford Univ. Press, 2007.

Montgomery, Thomas Lynch, ed. *Pennsylvania Archives*. 6th series. Vol. 2. Harrisburg: Harrisburg Publishing Company, 1906.

Mott, Frank Luther. *American Journalism: A History: 1690–1960*. New York: MacMillan Company, 1962.

Neault, Michael. "Wood Type Rising." In *City: Rochester's Alternative Newsweekly* (June 29, 2005), www.rochestercitynewspaper.com/archives/2005/06/Wood-type-rising/.

Nelson, Scott Reynolds, and Carol Sheriff. *A People at War: Civilians and Soldiers in America's Civil War, 1854–1877*. Oxford: Oxford Univ. Press, 2007.

Noll, Mark A. *The Civil War as a Theological Crisis*. Chapel Hill: Univ. of North Carolina Press, 2006.

Nord, David Paul. *Communities of Journalism: A History of American Newspapers and Their Readers*. Urbana: Univ. of Illinois Press, 2001.

Osborne, Randall, and Jeffrey C. Weaver. *Virginia State Rangers and State Line.* Virginia Regimental Historic Series. Lynchburg, Va.: H. W. Howard, Inc., 1994.

"Panic of 1837." *Ohio History Central.* Ohio Historical Society, www.ohiohistory-central.org/entry.php?rec=536.

Pasley, Jeffrey L. *The Tyranny of Printers: Newspaper Politics in the Early American Republic.* Charlottesville: Univ. of Virginia Press, 2001.

Paver, John M. *What I Saw from 1861 to 1864: Personal Recollections.* Facsimile. Kessinger Publishing Rare Reprints, n.d.

Pelzer, Louis. "Augustus Caesar Dodge: A Study in American Politics." PhD diss., University of Iowa, 1909.

Phillips, David L., ed., and Rebecca L. Hill, researcher. *War Stories: Civil War in West Virginia.* Leesburg, Va.: Gauley Mount Press, 1991.

Pickens, J. Troy. "Old Fort Pickens at Duffy, West Va." Article from unspecified W.V. newspaper, June 15, 1963. Collection of Shirley Boggs Webster, Ireland, W.V.

Pinkerton, Allan. *The Spy of the Rebellion; Being a True History of the Spy System of the United States Army during the Late Rebellion.* Introduction by Patrick Bass. Lincoln: Univ. of Nebraska Press, 1989.

Porter, George H. "Ohio Politics During the Civil War Period." New York: PhD diss., Graduate School in Political Science, Columbia University, 1911.

Porter, Will. *Annals of Polk County, Iowa, and the City of Des Moines.* Des Moines, Ia.: George A. Miller Printing Company, 1898.

Portrait and Biographical Record of Marion and Hardin Counties, Ohio. Chicago: Chapman Publishing Company, 1895.

"Preston King." *Mr. Lincoln and New York,* www.mrlincolnandnewyork.org.

Raymond M. Bell Anthology, http://chartiers.com/raybell/1995.

Roseboom, Eugene H. *The Civil War Era: 1850–1873.* The History of the State of Ohio. Edited by Carl Witke. Vol. 4 of 5. Columbus: Ohio State Archaeological and Historical Society, 1944. Reprint, Columbus, Ohio Historical Society, 1968.

Saxe, Stephen O. *American Iron Hand Presses: The Story of the Iron Hand Press in America.* With Wood Engravings by John DePol. New Castle, Del.: Oak Knoll Books, 1991.

Schildt, John W. *Union Regiments at Antietam.* 2nd edition, 2nd printing. Sharpsburg, Md.: Antietam Publications, 2010.

Schudson, Michael. *Discovering the News: A Social History of American Newspapers.* New York: Basic Books, 1978.

Shaffer, John W. *Clash of Loyalties: A Border County in the Civil War.* Morgantown: West Virginia Univ. Press, 2003.

Schroeder-Lein, Glenna R. *The Encyclopedia of Civil War Medicine.* Armonk, N.Y.: M. E. Sharpe, 2008.

Siebert, Wilbur H. *The Underground Railroad from Slavery to Freedom: A Comprehensive History.* Introduction by Albert Bushnell Hart. New York: Macmillan Company, 1898. Republished, Mineola, N.Y.: Dover Publications, 2006.

Silver, Rollo G. *The American Printer 1787–1825.* Published for the Bibliographical Society of the University of Virginia. Charlottesville: Univ. of Virginia Press, 1967.

Smart, James. G., ed. *A Radical View: The "Agate" Dispatches of Whitelaw Reid, 1861–1865.* 2 vols. Memphis: Memphis State Univ. Press, 1976.

Smith, Joseph Patterson, ed. *History of the Republican Party in Ohio.* 2 vols. Chicago: Lewis Publishing Company, 1898.

Snell, Mark A. *West Virginia and the Civil War: Mountaineers Are Always Free.* Charleston, S.C.: The History Press, 2011.

Sprague, Stuart Seely, ed. *His Promised Land: The Autobiography of John P. Parker, Former Slave and Conductor on the Underground Railroad.* New York: W. W. Norton, 1996.

Spaulding, Lily May and John, eds. *Civil War Recipes: Receipts from the Pages of Godey's Lady's Book.* Lexington: Univ. of Kentucky Press, 1999.

Stevenson, Darl L. *Headquarters in the Brush: Blazer's Independent Union Scouts.* Foreword by Brian C. Pohanka. Athens: Ohio Univ. Press, 2001.

St. Martin, Steve. "Descendants of Adam Wylie." Unpublished manuscript received via email, June 16, 2010.

Stivers, Eliese Bambach. *Ripley, Ohio: Its History and Families.* Ripley, Ohio: Sesquicentennial Historical Committee, 1965.

Still, William. *The Underground Railroad: Authentic Narratives and First-Hand Accounts.* Edited and with Introduction by Ian Frederick Finseth. Mineola, N.Y.: Dover Publications, 2007.

Sutherland, Daniel E. *A Savage Conflict: The Decisive Role of Guerillas in the American Civil War.* Civil War America. Chapel Hill: Univ. of North Carolina Press, 2009.

Taylor, Lenette. S. *The Supply for Tomorrow Must Not Fail: The Civil War of Captain Simon Perkins, Jr., a Union Quartermaster.* Kent, Ohio: Kent State Univ. Press, 2004.

Taylor, Nikki M. *Frontiers of Freedom: Cincinnati's Black Community, 1802–1868.* Athens: Ohio Univ. Press, 2005.

"Dr. Thomas Byers Wylie." Marshall Family. Rootsweb, http://wc.rootsweb.ancestry.com.

"The Tom Thumb Archive." The Lost Museum, *http://chnm.gmu.edu/lostmuseum/searchlm.php?function=find&exhibit-thumb&browse=browse=thumb.*

Transactions of the Forty-Eighth Annual Meeting of the Ohio State Medical Society. Cincinnati: Earhart and Richardson, 1893.

Varhola, Michael J. *Everyday Life during the Civil War: A Guide for Students and Historians.* Cincinnati: Writer's Digest Books, 1999.

Washington, Versalle F. *Eagles on Their Buttons: A Black Infantry Regiment in the Civil War.* Columbia, Mo.: Univ. of Missouri Press, 1999.

Webb, James. *Born Fighting: How the Scots-Irish Shaped America.* New York: Random House, 2004.

Weisberg, Barbara. *Talking to the Dead: Kate and Maggie Fox and the Rise of Spiritualism*. New York: HarperCollins, 2004.

"Wendell Phillips." Bartleby.com, www.bartleby.com/73/1073.html.

Wiley, Bell Irvin. *The Life of Billy Yank: The Common Soldier of the Union*. Updated edition, with foreword by James I. Robertson Jr. Baton Rouge: Louisiana State Univ. Press, 2008. First printing, 1952.

Wiley Genealogy, www.wiley.com/library.

Williams, Bonnie, and Elaine Herolds, eds. *Affectionately Yours: The Andrew Wylie Family Letters*. 2nd edition. 2 volumes. Bloomington: Wylie House Museum, Indiana Univ., 1994.

Williams, Byron. *History of Clermont and Brown Counties, Ohio*. Reprint of 1913 edition with new index. Clermont County Genealogical Society. Baltimore: Gateway Press, 1987.

Wilson, Charles R. "Cincinnati's Reputation during the Civil War." *Journal of Southern History* 2:4 (Nov. 1936), www.jstor.org/stable/2192033.

Wilson, W. R. "Van Dieman's Land." In *Historical Narratives of Early Canada*, www.uppercanadahistory.ca/tt/tt11.html.

Winter, Nevin Otton. *A History of Northwest Ohio: A Narrative Account of Its Historical Progress and Development*. Lewis Publishing Company, 1917.

Wooten, Rick L. "Dodge, Augustus Caesar." *Biographical Dictionary of Iowa*. Iowa City: Univer. of Iowa, 2009.

Index

Ada (New Orleans widow), 165–66
African Americans, enlistment of, 184–85, 186, 201, 202, 214–15. *See also* slavery
Allen, B. T., 75, 159–60, 177
Allen, Mrs., 208
Allen, William, 189
Ammen, David, 19, 83
Ammen, Jacob, 82–84, 92, 98, 117, 124, 191
Ammen, Mrs., 76
Anderson, Robert, 53, 122
"Answer to the composition of Miss E. Denison on Temperance and Intemperance" (Byers Tomlinson), 47–48
Armstrong, "Bill," 191
Armstrong, Capt., 77
Arnold, Porter J., 133
Arnold, Porter M., 138–40

Baggs, John P., 102
Baird, Chambers, 76, 89, 125, 183, 188, 218
Banks, Nathaniel P., 156
Barton, A. J., 247
Beach, Dr., 75
Beauregard, Pierre Gustave Toutant, 115, 116
Bedini, Gaetano (Archibishop), 112
Belchambers, Alfred, 55, 195, 222
Bell, John, 53
Bell, Mr., 205

Bennington, Mrs., 88, 208
Berry, Mrs., 222–23
Beuhel, Mrs., 222
Blackberry Cordial (recipe), 48
Black Brigade (Cincinnati), 186
Blair, George, 138–40
Borchard, David C., 256
"borderers," 2
Bostona (steamship), 82, *171*, 174, 196
Bradford, Dr., 210
Bragg, Braxton, 185
Brake, William, 138–40
Breckinridge, John C., 40, 45, 53
Brough, John, 230, 232–34
Brown, John, 32, 40
Brown County, Ohio. *See also* Ripley, Ohio; Court of Common Pleas, 9; 1860 election results, 53; ethnic composition of, 2
Brownlow, Parson, 151
Brown's Hotel (Athens, Ohio), 67
Buchanan, James, 53
Buell, Don Carlos, 192
Buell, Geo. P., 144
Burnside, Ambrose E., 206, 211
Bushnell, G. B., 28
bushwhackers, 99, 101–2, 103–15, *132*
Butler, Benjamin, 165–66
"butternuts," 231, 235

Byers, Maggie, 245
Byers, Thomas (Eliza's maternal grandfather), 6

Caldwell, J. J., 234
Campbell, Net, 117
Campbell, Shelby, 18
Camp Dennison, 77, 81–92, *84*
Camp Harrison, 70, 77
Camp Pickens, 120–21
Canadian Patriot Movement, 3–4
Car, Burner, 222
Carondelet (gunboat), 157
Cary, Capt., 79
Castigator (Ripley, Ohio), 7, 84
Catholicism, prejudice against, 111–12
Cattell, Jonathan, 35
Chase, Milo, 38
Cincinnati Enquirer, 190, 206
Cincinnati Gazette: Reid on Civil War events and, 73, 96; Republican leanings of, 41; on Tomlinson's death, 241–42; Tomlinson's work at, 143–53, 234; on Vallandigham, 155
Cincinnati Times, 101, 110
Civil War: Antietam (battle), 189; bushwhackers, 99, 101–2, 103–15, *132*; Chancellorsville (battle), 214; early secession by Southern states, 57–58, 59; effects on Ripley, Ohio, 92–95; events leading to, 45, 46, 52–53; events of spring of 1862, 154–55, 156–58, 160–61, 163–64; Fifth Regiment, Ohio Volunteer Infantry, 70–72, 81–93, *84*, 96, 189, 212–13; Fort Sumter (battle), 54, 60, 70; Gauley bridge events and, 95–96; Great Bethel, Virginia (battle), 84, 85; Jacksonville murders incident (October 30, 1861), 130–42, 143; Kentucky secession and threats to Ohio, 92–95, 116, 122, 174, 175–76, 184–85, 186–87, *187*; Manassas (battle), 84; Maysville raid, 220; racial tension in Ohio during, 152–53, 173–74, 207, 231 (*see also* Copperheads); *Revised Regulations for the Army of the United States, 1861*, 100; Seven Days Campaign, 155, 171–72, 173, 174–75; Stone's River (battle), 200; telegraph control during, 173; Union Army, camp life, 109–10, *112*, 115; Union Army, formation, 70–80;

Union Army, recruitment literature, *119*; Union Army, uniforms, 77, 85
Clay, Henry, 14
Clemans, Rev. F. M., 251–52
Clyde, Kitty, 35
Coggeshall, William T., 28, 37
Collin, B., 121–22
Collins, Lieut., 77
Collins, Tom, 44
Columbian Magazine, 20
Columbus, E., 235
compositing, defined, 37–38
Compromise of 1850, 26–27
Cook, Mrs., 238
Cook, S. H., 199
Coon, Mr. (teacher), 196
Copperheads: *Crisis* office destruction and, 204; *Harper's Weekly* depiction of, *204*; in Indiana, 214; in Iowa, 32; Mahony and, 29; Tomlinson's death and, 230–34, 243–45; Vallandigham and, 155, 204, 206, 211–12, 230
Copple, Mrs., 207–8
Cornell, P., 203–4
Cother, Mr., 88
Cox, Jacob, 96
Cox, Samuel S., 152
Crawford, David, 22
Crawford family (Cincinnati): Jennie, 182, 195; John, 205, 207; Lititia, 234
Tomlinson as boarder of, 156
Crisis (Columbus, Ohio), 204, 206
Crocker, M. M., 75
croton oil, 45
Cumberland, Ireland, 1–2
Cunningham, Enoch, 138–39
"cupping," 148
Curtis, Gen., 188

Daily Gazette (Davenport, Iowa), 33
Darcy, Dr., 210
Davis, Jefferson, 60, 96
Dawson, Mrs., 88
Dayton Daily Journal, 211
DeBolt, William, 126
Decline of Protestantism and Its Causes, The (Hughes), 111
Democrat and Journal (Georgetown), 22
Democratic Party. See also *individual names of politicians;* 1860 election and, 40, 51, 53; in Iowa, 31–32; Pierce campaign and, 26

Democratic Standard (Georgetown, Ohio), 20, 22

Democratic Union (Georgetown, Ohio), 22, 26, 29

Dennison, William, 70, 73, 126

Descriptive Book for Company I (Fifth Regiment, Ohio Volunteer Infantry), 71

Devore, Dave, 235

Dick, Mrs., 176

Dodge, A. C., 32–33

Donohoe, Betsy, 256

Donohoe, Patricia, 256–57

Donohoe, Roscoe ("Ross") Noel, 256

Donohoe, William Ross, 256

Douglas, Stephen A., 40, 53

Dubuque Daily Times, 243

Dubuque Express and Herald, 29

Dubuque Herald, 181, 242–43, 248

Dunning, Samuel H., 71, 131

Easton, Bob, 78

Eddy (pet bird in Iowa), 35, 65, 68, 75

Eddy (pet bird in Ohio), 149

Emancipation Proclamation, 189–90

Evans, Ally, 117

Evans, Capt., 107, 117, 124, 209

Evans, Eliza, 170

Evans, James, 119

Evans, John, 223

Evans, Mrs., 168, 205, 207

Evans, Oliver, 104

Evans, Sam, 215

Evans family, 10

Farnsworth, D. D. T., 118, 120, 121

Farnsworth Blues, 117

Fifth Regiment, Ohio Volunteer Infantry, 70–72, 81–93, *84*, 96, 189, 212–13

Finch, Daniel O., 40, 42, 122–23

Flora, J., 219

Floyd, John B., 96

Ford, Sally Rochester, 225

Fosters, J. D., 217

Fox, Kate, 27

Fox, Maggie, 27

Fox, Mr., 73

Francis, William, 138–39

Freedom's Casket, 3–4, 19, 84, 226

Frick, D. U., 75

Fuller, Margaret, 10, 27

Garnett, Robert S., 92

Garrison, William Lloyd, 19

Gates, Uncle and Aunt, 44

Gillespie, John, 13

"Gospel Plow" (folk song), 16

Granite Rock, The, 26

Grant, Ulysses S., 84, 192

Greg, Mr., 117

Grimes, James W., 31, 99, 100

"Guthrie Greys," 85–86

Guy, Jim, 180

Guyandotte incident, 135–37

Haman, Ben., 164

Hamer, Thomas L., 20, 63, 64

Hamlin, Dr., 44

Hamor (biblical character), 66, 67

Hannows (widow Penn's husband), 50

Harper's Weekly, 132, 204

Harris, Thomas Maley: on Jacksonville murders incident, 132–34, 137–41, 143; in Kentucky, 128; Lincoln assassination and, 141; Moccasin Rangers and, 102; photo, *134*; regiments formed by, 105, 118–20, 121

Hawthorne, Nathaniel, 26

Haymond, Ben, 102, 133

Haymond's Rangers, 126

Hays, Mrs., 110

Heath, Gen., 191

Hendrix, Mrs., 117

Hickory Sprout, 14, 19, 84

Higginson, Thomas Wentworth, 202

Highland Guards, 114

Hill, Charles W., 92

Hillsboro News Herald, 255

Himble, Lizzie, 104

Hindman, Mr., 55

Hines, Mr., 235

History of the Republican Party in Ohio, 244, 245, 255

"Hold On, Hold On" (folk song), 16

Holt, J., 140

Home Guard units, 105, 179, 180

Hooker, "Fighting Joe," 212

Hosie, H., 75

Howard, Jim, 208

Hughes, John (Archbishop), 111

Hull, Albert, 188

Hunter, Willey (Tomlinson's nephew), 24–26, 29, 31, 249

Huntington Daily Herald, 255
Hutchins, Mr., 248
Hyde, John, 168

Independent Order of Odd Fellows, 31, 34
Inegary, Mrs., 41
Iowa State Journal, 32
Iowa Statesman, 31, 32, 35, 40
Irish Regiment, 85–86
Ironton Busy Bee, 255

Jackson, Andrew, 8, 14
Jackson, Stonewall, 155, 156, 171, 214
Jackson (*Cincinnati Gazette* employee), 219
Jacksonville murders incident (October 30, 1861), 130–42, 143
Jeff (horse), 105, 114, 115
John (soldier), 98
Johnson, Andrew, 141
Johnson, Sergeant, 156
Johnston, Albert Sidney, 137
Johnston, DeWitt, 22
Johnston, Joseph E., 155
Johnston, S. W., 195
Joice, M. E., 110
Jolley, Mr., 183
Jolley, Phil, 188, 235
Jones, J. W., 75
Jones, Mr., 228

Kason, Mr., 68
Kerr, Mrs., 149
Killin, Alice, 255
Kilpatrick, R. L., 118–20, 121
King, Michael, 177
King, Preston, 99, 100
Kinsey, L., 75
Knights of the Golden Circle, 155, 231, 244

Lafabre, John, 209
Lambis, Mr., 41
Langston, John Mercer, 214
Lee, Robert E., 96, 99, 155
Leggitt, Sid, 197
Liberator, 19
Ligget, Lieutenant, 158
Lincoln, Abraham: African American soldiers and, 205, 206; assassination of, 141; assassination plot against (1861), 61; in Cincinnati (1861), 59–60; Copperheads and, 243; 1860 election of,

40–41, 46, 53, 54, 68; emancipation of slaves by, 154; Emancipation Proclamation, 189–90; events of spring 1862 and, 155; *Loyal Scout* (Tomlinson) editorial on, 232; McClellan demoted by, 146, 151–52; McClellan dismissed by, 192; Militia Act, 202; Order No. 38, 206, 211; views of McClellan, 92
Lindsay, Oliver, 107
Lindsey, Bony, 168, 180, 181, 208
Long, Maj., 77
Low, Col., 117
Lowry, Mary, 76, 95, 104
Lowry, William: early acquaintance with Tomlinson, 34–35; Iowa news from, 61, 122–23, 177
Iowa property management and, 42, 65, 74, 76, 95, 131, 159–60; as tenant, 67–68
Loyal Scout, 230–34, *231,* 236, 244
Lyon, Nathaniel, 161, *161*

Maggy (bird), 149, 170, 182
Magnolia, 162, 175
Magruder, Gen., 171–72
Maguire, Belle, 213
Mahony, Dennis A., 29
Marcus the Miller, 209
Marsh, A. N., 177
Marshall, John G., 235
McClellan, George B.: as commander, Department of the Ohio, 77; demotion of, 146, 151–52; dismissal of, 192; on drunkenness, 115; Ohio troops deployed by, 81, 92; Seven Days Campaign, 155, 171–72, 173, 174–75
McDowell, Irwin, 192
McGroarty, Pat, 232
McMillan, George, 12–13
McMillan, Jane, 13
McMillan, Sarah, 22, 23
McMillin, "Jim," 191
Medary, Sam, 204, 206
Meigs, Montgomery C., 100
Memoirs of the Wesley Family (Fuller), 10, 27
Mercer, Thomas, 68
Messenger (Athens, Ohio), 62, 64
Methodism: Methodist church (Ripley, Ohio), 10; Methodist Episcopal Sabbath School Library (Ripley, Ohio), 27; Wesley and, 10, 27
Mexican War, Tomlinson's service in, 20

Militia Act, 184–85, 202
Miller, Jas. W., 13
Miller, William, 16
Milroy, R. H., 138
Mitchell, Gen., 164
Mitchell, Miss (teacher), 170
Mitchell, Mr., 104
Mitchell, Mr. (teacher), 106, 124
Mitchell, Richard, 240–45, 249–50
Moccasin Rangers, 101, 102, 164
Morgan, John Hunt: capture of, 217, 221, 227; Morgan's Raiders, 174, 176–77, 178, 179, 186–87; prison escape by, 243, 244
Murphey (family), 18
Murphy, Ad, 66
Myers, James (Jim Mires), *231*, *236*

newspaper vendor carts, *112*
New York Times, 60, 171
New York Tribune, 3–4
Norris, Bent., 124
Norris, Wm., 216, 218
Northumberland, Ireland, 1–2
Nor'wester, The (Kenton, Ohio), 28, 29

Ohio National Guard, 254
oil wells, 63, 68
Olcroft, Mrs., 45, 228

Pangburn, Lyons, 59
Pangburn, Sam, 76, 95, 196, 197
Panic of 1837, 8, 16
Panic of 1857, 32
Parker, John, 27
Parker, Mr. (teacher), 124
Patrick, John H., 71
Pearce, Mr., 23
Peters, Bob, 205
Phillips, Wendell, 129
Pickens, William, 118
Pierce, Franklin A., 26
Pierpont, Francis H., 105, 118, 120, 133–34, 137–41
Pierson, William G., 126–27, 137–41
Piketon, Ohio, Tomlinsons in, 14–20
Pittsburg (gunboat), 157
Poe, Edgar A., 20
"Poison Cup, The" (Tomlinson), 20
Pope, Gen., 157, 164
Pope, John, 154

Porter, Jane, 208
Porter, Will, 35, 36, 49
Portsmouth Blade, 255
Presbyterian church (Ripley, Ohio), 7
Presbyterian church (Scotland), 5–6
Printing: compositing, 37–38; definitions, 35, 39–40, 181
"Progressive Wonder" (*Ripley Herald*), 28

"quire," 35

Raids and Romance of Morgan and His Men (Ford), 225
Rankin, Col., 86
Rankin, Miss (teacher), 106
Rankin, Reverend John, 7, 19, 84
"rapping," 28
Rebellions of 1837/1838, 3–4
Reid, Whitelaw, 73, 96
Republican Party, advent of, 32, 64. *See also* Lincoln, Abraham
Restored Government of Virginia, 105
Revised Regulations for the Army of the United States, 1861, 100
Rhett, Barnwell, 171–72
Ridgway, Clain, 92, 128, 158
Ripley, Ohio: businesses of, 109; cannon of, 217, *218*; Civil War threat to, 92–95, 116, 122, 174, 175–76, 184–85, 186–87, *187*; 1840s illustration of, *8*; Eliza, Byers, Belle in, 34–53; fire (1861), 106; Underground Railroad and, 10–11; Wide Awakes in, *49*, 51
Ripley Bee: Byers Tomlinson as editor/publisher of, 255; Eliza's publication in, 72–73; on fire in Ripley (May 1863), 213–14; news items, 149–52, 216–17, 232–34; Porter and, 35; Tomlinson's correspondence, preservation of, 253; Tomlinson's correspondence to, 90, 91–92, 144–46, 156–58, 163–65, 175, 178, 190–91, 192–94; on Tomlinson's death, 240–41; Tomlinson's desire to resume ownership, 238; Tomlinson's first enlistment, 70
Ripley Herald, 26, 27, 28, 29
Robinson, Capt., 191
Roman Catholicism, prejudice against, 110, 111–12
Rosecrans, William S., 92, 96, 113, 114, 115, 121, 139

Ross, "Doc," 191
Rudolph, Lieut., 77

St. Lawrence Republican, 100
Scott, Mrs., 75
Scott, Winfield, 67, 108
"Scotty," defined, 109
Seven Days Campaign, 173, 174-75
Shaw, Billy, 191
Shaw, Frank, 104
Shaw, Mr., 43, 44
Shaw, Mrs., 45
Shaw, Will, 50, 180
Shepherd, Mr., 21
Sherman, Hoyt, 131
Signs of the Time, The (Coggeshall), 28
Simons, Christian, 139
Skinner, Anne Tomlinson Hunter: broth-
    er's death and, 248-49; brother's move
    to Iowa and, 29; letters from, 1, 24-26;
    son of, 24-26, 31
Skinner, Ann Jane, 249
Skinner, Eliza, 249
Skinner, Harmon, 249
Skinner, Marion, 249
Skinner, Mr., 248
slavery: Compromise of 1850, 26-27;
    emancipation of Border States, 154;
    Emancipation Proclamation, 189-90;
    Tomlinson's anti-slavery writings, 14,
    19-20; Tomlinson's letter to *Bee* about
    (1/23/62), 144-46; Underground Rail-
    road, 10-11; Wylie family on, 7; Yancey
    and, 45
Smith, Alonzo Frescoln, 253
Smith, E. Kirby, 185, 186-87
Smith, Lot, 63
Snake Hunters, 101-2, 106
Sniffens, Mr., 170
Sowers, Henry, 222-23
spiritualist movement, 27-28
Squirrel Hunters, 186-87, *187,* 217, 220
Stanton, Edwin M., 141, 152, 164, 192,
    214-15
Star (Des Moines), 40
Star of the West, 54
State Journal (Iowa), 35
steamboat, *83*
Straw, Frank, 68
Surratt, Mary, 141

"tater hole," 121
Teesdale, John, 35
Thomas, Caroline, 256
Thompson, Gen. John W., 107, 206, 209
Thompson, Mrs., 123
Thompson, W., 191
Thompson, Will, 123
Thumb, Tom, 150, 151
tobacco, 110, 111
Tod, David, 174, 210, 214, 217, 220
Todhunter, Jane, 1
Todhunter, Sir William, 1
Tomlinson, Adam Newton (son), 20, 22, 74
Tomlinson, Eliza Wylie: Athens (Ohio)
    relocation plans and, 54, 62-69; birth
    of children of, 29; Blackberry Cordial
    (recipe), 48; in Cincinnati, 158, 163;
    on Civil War threat to Ripley, Ohio,
    92-95; death of, 250-52; death of chil-
    dren of, 22, 23-24, 29; in Georgetown,
    Ohio, 21-29; health of, 79, 82; heri-
    tage of, 5-11, 72; husband's death and,
    240-50; on insurance matters, 178, 183;
    Iowa home of, 29-33, 34-37, 41-42,
    43, 49-52, 55-56, 59, 61, 64, 65, 66,
    67-68, 73-76, 95, 117, 131, 144, 159-60,
    162-63, 177, 188; Jacksonville murders
    incident, knowledge of, 143; marital
    friction, 48-53, 226, 228-29; newspa-
    pers/magazines sent to husband by,
    135; sewing by, 66, 76-77; spiritualist
    movement and, 27-28; Union cause
    supported by, 72-80; warnings to
    husband by, 130-31, 134-35, *136,* 177,
    178; wedding of, 12-20; writing by,
    28; Wylie-Tomlinson Letter Collection
    preservation and, 253-57, *254*
Tomlinson, Florence Adele (granddaugh-
    ter), 256
Tomlinson, George (father), 1
Tomlinson, George Wylie (son), 20, 21,
    23-24
Tomlinson, Margaret Eliza (daughter),
    20, 22, 29
Tomlinson, Sarah Isabella "Belle" (daugh-
    ter): adult life of, 253-54; birthday of
    (1861), 68; birth of, 29; croton oil inci-
    dent, 45, 46; education of, 50, 60, 83,
    106, 124, 144, 168; gift of birds, from
    father, 146-47, 168, 170; health of, 51,

66, 202; letters to/from, *169*, 170, 182, 195, 208; mother's death and, 250; sketch of, *254*

Tomlinson, Will: as Army captain, 118; Army quartermaster duties of, 84, 85, 86, 97–99, 100–101, 105, 109–10; in Athens, Ohio, 54, 61–69; birth of children, 29; characterization/alcoholism of, 2, 32, 33, 46, 48, 101–2, 137–38, 225–26, 244–45; death of, 240–52; death of children of, 22, 23–24, 29; early enlistment by, 70–80; education of, 198; Farnsworth Blues company, 117–18; in Georgetown, Ohio, 21–29; heritage of, 1–4; income of, 39–40, 108, 128; Iowa home of, 29–33, 34–37, 41–42, 43, 49–52, 55–56, 59, 61, 64, 65, 66, 67–68, 73–76, 95, 117, 131, 144, 159–60, 162–63, 177, 188; Jacksonville murders incident and, 130–42, 143; loans of, 113; marital friction, 48–53, 226, 228–29; military commission sought by, 200–215; mother-in-law and, 56, 57, 58–59; move to Cincinnati, 34–53; newspapers sent to wife by, 149–50; non-newspaper jobs of, 31, 32; photo, *242*; physical description and age at time of enlistment, 71; religious beliefs of, 4, 71; spiritualist movement and, 27–28; Squirrel Brigade joined by, 186–87, *187*; U.S. Service commission controversy/demotion, 120, 125–26, 137–41; wedding of, 12–20; Wylie-Tomlinson Letter Collection preservation and, 253–57, *254*

Tomlinson, William Byers (son): adult life of, 254–56; on alcohol, 222–23; attempt to raise militia by, 216, 219, 220, 221; birth of, 20, 21; drilling by, 188; education of, 50, 106, 124, 166, 184; father's death and, 240–45; health of, 51, 143, 146–48, 149, 158, 159; inventions of, 195–96, 198, 209–10; letters to/from, 88, *89*, 125, 131, 160–61, *161*, 198, *198*, 220, 222–23, 224, 235–36; on Morgan's Raiders, 179; mother's death and, 250; photo, *256*; sketches by, *254*; Squirrel Brigade joined by, 187; Underground Railroad and, 10; visits to father, 81–83, 91, 184, 201; writing by, 46–48

Tri-Weekly Citizen, 35

Typographical Union, 71

Underground Railroad, 10–11
Union Township Library (Ohio), *218*
U.S.S. *Monitor,* 156

Vallandigham, Clement L.: Copperheads and, 155, 204, 206, 211–12, 230; gubernatorial race of, 230–31, 232–34, *233;* as Ohio congressman, 93, 190; rejected by South, 216
Van Dieman's Land (Tasmania), 3–4
Vidette, 225
Vohres, Mary, 208
Vorhees, Ike, 191

Walker, Gus, 247
Walker, J. M., 123, 188, 245, 246–47
Walker, John, 247
Walker, Milton, 188
Walkington, John, 229
Wallace, Lewis, 186
Wardle, Issabella, 249
Washington press, 30
Weitman, Frank, 247
Wesley, John, 10, 27
"Western Fair" (*Ripley Herald*), 27
Western Wreath, 20
West Virginia, statehood of, 216
Wheeling Intelligencer, 101
Whig Party, 14, *15*
Whitcom, George, 150–51
White, Chilton A., 232, 235
Whitson, Caleb C., 71, 86, 98, 114, 121, 154, 156
Wide Awakes, 49, *51*
Wilkes, Mr., 206, 208, 209
Wilkinson, Nathan, 140
Williamson, James A., 34, 41, 50, 51, 56, 68, 75, 95, 123, 124, 131, 188, 196
Williamson, T. A., 75
Wise, Henry A., 95–96
Woodward, Dr., 113
Write (Wright), Gen., 220
Wylie, Adam (Eliza's father), 7–8
Wylie, Adam (Eliza's grandfather), 6
Wylie, Adam Newton "Newt" (Eliza's brother): Byers (nephew) and, 184; at Camp Dennison, 83; contribution for cannon by, 217; early life of, 6, 9, 10,

Wylie, Adam Newton "Newt" (Cont.)
16; Eliza's death and, 250-52, 251; family
of, 38; health of, 60; loans to Tomlinson, 113, 167; sketch of, *254;* soldiers
treated by, 159
Wylie, Andrew ("Andy") Jr. (Eliza's cousin), 141
Wylie, Andrew, Sr. (Eliza's uncle), 9, 141
Wylie, Henry Clay (Eliza's nephew), 14
Wylie, Jeff (Eliza's nephew), 127, 183, 184
Wylie, Lizzie Pangburn (Eliza's sister-in-
law), 10, 38, 44, 83, 86, 95, 159, 183, 196
Wylie, Margaret Shannon (Eliza's sister),
8, 17-19, 20
Wylie, Mrs. (Eliza's distant relative),
166-68
Wylie, Nellie (Eliza's distant relative), 55,
166-68
Wylie, Samuel Brown (Eliza's relative), 9
Wylie, Sarah Ann Elizabeth Cook (Eliza's
mother): death of, 240; Eliza and
children living in Ripley with, 38, 51;
Eliza's heritage and, 6-9; Eliza's wedding and, 14, 17-19; health of, 56, 60,
64, 66, 127; sketch of, *254;* Tomlinson
and, 56, 57, 58-59; travel by, 79

Wylie, Sarah Ann (Eliza's sister-in-law),
226, 229
Wylie, Theophilus Adam (Eliza's relative), 9
Wylie, Thomas Byers (Eliza's brother): early life of, 6, *11,* 14, 16; family of, 38, 226;
health of, 238; travel by, 79, 163, 166
Wylie, Will (Eliza's distant relative), 41,
51, 55, 166-68
Wylie, William B. F. (Eliza's brother), 8,
14-16
Wylie, William (Eliza's uncle), 9
Wylie-Tomlinson Letter Collection, preservation of, 253-57, *254*

Yancey, William, 45, 46
Yokauer, Frank: Army enlistment by,
104; as caretaker of Tomlinsons' Iowa
home, 34-37, 43, 49-52, 55, 61, 64, 65,
66, 67-68, 188; death of, 123, 124; Eliza's mistrust of, 76-77, 95
Young, Wiley, 235